Subdivision Valuation

Readers of this text may be interested in the following publications from the Appraisal Institute:

- *The Appraisal of Real Estate*
- *The Dictionary of Real Estate Appraisal*
- *Market Analysis for Real Estate*
- *Scope of Work*

Subdivision Valuation
Second Edition

by Don M. Emerson, Jr., MAI, SRA

Appraisal Institute • 200 W. Madison • Suite 1500 • Chicago, IL 60606 • www.appraisalinstitute.org

The Appraisal Institute advances global standards, methodologies, and practices through the professional development of property economics worldwide.

Reviewers: Stephanie Coleman, MAI, SRA, AI-GRS, AI-RRS
Stephen F. Fanning, MAI, AI-GRS
Michael S. MaRous, MAI, SRA
John A. Schwartz, MAI

Director of Professional Services and Resources: Evan R. Williams, CAE, IOM
Senior Manager, Publications: Stephanie Shea-Joyce
Senior Technical Book Editor: Emily Ruzich
Manager, Book Design/Production: Michael Landis

For Educational Purposes Only

The materials presented in this text represent the opinions and views of the developers. Although these materials may have been reviewed by members of the Appraisal Institute, the views and opinions expressed herein are not endorsed or approved by the Appraisal Institute as policy unless adopted by the Board of Directors pursuant to the Bylaws of the Appraisal Institute. While substantial care has been taken to provide accurate and current data and information, the Appraisal Institute does not warrant the accuracy or timeliness of the data and information contained herein. Further, any principles and conclusions presented in this publication are subject to court decisions and to local, state and federal laws and regulations and any revisions of such laws and regulations.

This book is sold for educational and informational purposes only with the understanding that the Appraisal Institute is not engaged in rendering legal, accounting or other professional advice or services. Nothing in these materials is to be construed as the offering of such advice or services. If expert advice or services are required, readers are responsible for obtaining such advice or services from appropriate professionals.

Nondiscrimination Policy

The Appraisal Institute advocates equal opportunity and nondiscrimination in the appraisal profession and conducts its activities in accordance with applicable federal, state, and local laws.

© 2017 by the Appraisal Institute, an Illinois not for profit corporation. All rights reserved. No part of this publication may be reproduced, modified, rewritten, or distributed, either electronically or by any other means, without the express written permission of the Appraisal Institute.

Library of Congress Cataloging-in-Publication Data
Names: Emerson, Don M., author.
Title: Subdivision valuation / by Don M. Emerson, Jr., MAI, SRA.
Description: Second edition. | Chicago, Ill. : Appraisal Institute, [2017]
Identifiers: LCCN 2017043783 | ISBN 9781935328711
Subjects: LCSH: Real property--Valuation--United States. | Land subdivision--United States. | Real estate investment--United States.
Real estate development--United States.
Classification: LCC HD1389.5.U6 E44 2017 | DDC 333.33/820973--dc23 LC record available at
https://lccn.loc.gov/2017043783

Table of Contents

About the Author ix

Acknowledgments xi

Foreword xiii

Introduction 1

Chapter 1   **Overview** 9
Introduction 9
Background and History 10
Defining a Subdivision 10
Subdivision Development Phases 14
Subdivision Terminology and the Bulk Sale
Valuation Premise 18
The Valuation Process 20
USPAP Considerations and Lending Industry Issues 20
Steps in the Valuation Process 26

Chapter 2   **Market Analysis** 31
Introduction 31
Absorption and Highest and Best Use 31
The Six-Step Market Analysis Process 33
Levels of Market Analysis 39
Selecting the Appropriate Level of Analysis 42
Market Analysis in Appraisal and Reporting 43
Rationale for Measuring Absorption 45
Mill Pond Case Study: Absorption Estimate 46

Chapter 3	Neighborhood and Market Area Analysis 59
	Introduction 59
	Relationship to Market Analysis and the Appraisal Process. . . .60
	Defining the Market Area 60
	Economic and Governmental Factors 62
	Character of Single-Unit Development. 64
	Location and Time-Distance Linkages. 66
	Conclusion and Reporting. 68
Chapter 4	Site and Improvement Analysis 71
	Introduction 71
	Relation to Market Analysis and the Appraisal Process 72
	Land Considerations 72
	Improvement Analysis. 81
	The Marketing Concept and Price Points 84
	Conclusion 85
Chapter 5	Highest and Best Use 87
	Introduction 87
	The Role of Market Analysis in Highest and Best Use 88
	Applying the Four Criteria 89
	Highest and Best Use of Existing Lots 92
	Highest and Best Use of Proposed Developments 93
Chapter 6	Profit and Timeline Concepts 95
	Introduction 95
	Timeline and Profit 95
	Typical Value Reference Points 98
	Typical Value Reference Points for Lending Clients 100
	Raw Land Value by Subdivision Analysis 103
Chapter 7	Income Capitalization Approach 107
	Introduction 107
	Timeline Overview 109
	Applying the Income Capitalization Approach 109
	Mill Pond Case Study. 112
	Retail Lot Value Estimate 114
	Absorption Period Estimate. 122
	Holding and Sales Costs 123
	Mill Pond Income Capitalization Approach 129
	Sugarbush Case Study: Analysis with Presales of Lots 132
	Sugarbush Case Study: Analysis with Mortgage Financing 144

Chapter 8	**Cost Approach**	153
	Introduction	153
	Timeline Overview	154
	Applying the Cost Approach	157
	Mill Pond Land Value	158
	Improvement Value	163
	Bulk Value vs. Retail Value Cost Analysis	164
	Other Cost Approach Issues	174
	Valuation of "Common" Land	178
Chapter 9	**Sales Comparison Approach**	185
	Introduction	185
	Applying the Sales Comparison Approach	186
	Mill Pond Value Conclusion	192
Chapter 10	**Yield, Line-Item Profit, and Discounting**	195
	Profit Concepts and the Subdivision Timeline	195
	Madison Square Case Study: Yield Rate Extraction	195
Chapter 11	**Land Value Using the Subdivision Development Method**	227
	Overview	227
	Timeline Concepts	229
	Park View Case Study: Applying the Income Capitalization Approach	231
Chapter 12	**Special Topics**	241
	Common Deficiencies Found in Subdivision Appraisals	241
	Understanding Profit Concepts	245
	Time Zero Profit Dilemma	249
	Developer Risk Reduction Strategies	270
	Lot Sales to Potential Homeowners	275
	Proposed Construction Performance Bonds	275
	Super Pad Sites	276
Appendix	*Frequently Asked Questions on Residential Tract Development Lending* **Memorandum**	279
Glossary		287

About the Author

Don M. Emerson, Jr., MAI, SRA, has been involved in appraisal practice for more than 40 years and is president of Emerson Appraisal Company Inc. in Gainesville, Florida. He received his BSBA and MA in real estate and urban land studies from the University of Florida. Emerson has been involved in advanced appraisal instruction for the Appraisal Institute since 1986 and is an adjunct professor at the University of Florida, Kelley A. Bergstrom Real Estate Center for the Nathan S. Collier MSRE Program. He is past president of the former Gainesville-Ocala Chapter of the Appraisal Institute and has served on many Appraisal Institute education and publication committees over the years. Emerson is also the author of the Appraisal Institute's *Subdivision Valuation* seminar.

Acknowledgments

Many of the examples and observations in this material come from my appraisal practice and field experiences with subdivision valuation over the years. Special thanks to the local real estate development community here in Gainesville where developers, land planners, owners, investors, and home builders have shared their experiences, successes, and tribulations while building future residential neighborhoods. Their insights and experiences are invaluable and are greatly appreciated. Special thanks to Luis Diaz with Dibros Corporation and Svein Dyrkolbotn with Viking Companies for their contributions to this book.

As an instructor with the Appraisal Institute over the past 30 years, I have enjoyed the opportunity to present subdivision valuation topics through the *Subdivision Valuation* seminar and other educational opportunities where various valuation scenarios have been presented, dissected, and discussed with my fellow appraisal instructors and students. All of these contributions have built upon the knowledge base in this material.

I would also like to thank my partners, William Emerson, MAI, and Charles Emerson, for their support, suggestions, and critiques throughout this project. More importantly, I would like to give special thanks to my wife, Debbie, and stepdaughter, Anna, for their encouragement and patience throughout the development of this material. Without their support, this book would not have been possible.

Foreword

Subdivision analysis is a challenging area of appraisal practice because of the complex timeline concepts and value estimates involved. This second edition of *Subdivision Valuation* provides a comprehensive overview of the methodology used in valuing single-unit residential subdivisions.

Both proposed and existing subdivision developments are considered. Specific topics explored include market and neighborhood analysis, highest and best use, profit and timeline concepts, land value, yield, line-item profit, and discounting. This second edition includes new case studies that illustrate lot presales, mortgage financing, bulk sale forecasts, and the time-zero profit dilemma. Special topics including developer risk reduction strategies, lot sales to potential homeowners, proposed construction performance bonds, and super pad sites are also discussed. Finally, common areas of weakness in subdivision appraisal reports are examined to provide guidance on how to avoid some of the common pitfalls associated with this area of appraisal.

This second edition of *Subdivision Valuation* sheds valuable light on a complex topic and will be useful to commercial appraisers seeking to expand their skills and master the challenges of subdivision analysis.

Jim Amorin, MAI, SRA, AI-GRS
2017 President
Appraisal Institute

Introduction

Subdivision analysis is one of the most difficult and challenging areas of commercial appraisal because it involves relatively complicated timeline concepts, and values are estimated for different components of an overall project. This book provides a comprehensive overview of the methodology involved in single-unit residential subdivision valuation and how the process relates to the three approaches to value. While this is an introductory text, it anticipates that the reader has good knowledge and experience in applying discounted cash flow (DCF) analysis to commercial properties. Most situations involving typical suburban subdivisions are explored in the text. All of the examples included have been reduced to their simplest forms to explain the various concepts and techniques involved. While the material is relatively complicated from a mathematical point of view, this book covers only the basic elements of subdivision valuation. Complicated projects such as large developments with regional impact and mixed-use property characteristics as well as projects with multiple marketing concepts are beyond the scope of this book.

Topic Coverage

The primary focus of this book is the valuation of existing and proposed improved subdivisions. This includes the valuation of a group of lots that may be a component of a larger project. The methodology described would also apply to the valuation of a group of units, but for the sake of simplicity, this book focuses on vacant single-family subdivision lots. The *single-unit* termi-

A typical street view in a completed residential subdivision

nology refers to a vacant single-family subdivision lot. In most cases the lot is an improved site ready for construction of a house or other similar residential unit. Secondary emphasis is given to the valuation of raw land using subdivision methodology. In daily practice, most appraisers use subdivision methodology for the valuation of a group of lots or units. A general introduction to subdivision valuation is provided in Chapter 1.

Market Analysis

Market analysis begins early in the appraisal process. The plan of study takes shape when the appraiser is defining the appraisal problem and outlining the scope of work. The values to be reported are established within the context of the intended use, valuation timelines are established, and the process of describing and defining the subject property begins. The data collection process considers market area, subject property, and comparable property data. The property description and market data analysis leads to the highest and best use conclusion, which sets the stage for the valuation process. Within the appraisal framework, market analysis is integral to both highest and best use analysis and the application of the three approaches to value.

Project marketability issues are addressed in the six-step market analysis process and a discussion of the four levels of market analysis. Inferred and fundamental demand analysis methods are explored as they relate to subdivision valuation. Because marketability analysis is critical to the absorption estimate, project marketability and highest and best use are considered early on in Chapter 2.

Market analysis for a subdivision appraisal includes consideration of reported inventories from competing subdivision projects categorized by price points, amenities, and market location. The analyst must be familiar with new subdivision projects entering the market and future forecasts for new household growth in the area. The Mill Pond Case Study is included in this text to illustrate the development of an absorption estimate and the application of the three approaches to value. Components of market analysis such as locational determents and property productivity analysis are considered in Chapters 3 and 4. The absorption forecast for the Mill Pond Case Study property is estimated in Chapter 2 and is applied to the income capitalization approach in Chapter 7.

Neighborhood and Market Area Analysis

Neighborhood and market area analysis are addressed in Chapter 3, in which property productivity and locational attributes are considered in an example of a time-distance linkage.

Site and Improvement Analysis

Chapter 4 considers the appraisal of a proposed subdivision project and addresses the issues encountered in the appraisal of vacant lots. The improvements considered in this chapter are the subdivision's infrastructure improvements. No examples of the appraisal of improved homes or condominium units are provided. Instead, the focus is on typical suburban subdivision projects in which vacant lots are sold. Since the value of vacant lots is directly related to the eventual homes to be built in the project, however, the home marketing concept and price points within the project are analyzed along with their relationship to the site and infrastructure improvements.

Highest and Best Use Analysis

Highest and best use is analyzed in light of all legally permissible, physically possible, financially feasible, and maximally productive uses. The timing of the proposed use is of particular importance to subdivision analysis. Subdivision value is directly dependent on the absorption of vacant lot inventory. The time at which the project enters the market is critical to the absorption of lots, and the current status of supply and demand in the subject market area must be considered in highest and best use analysis.

[margin note: timing and absorption are closely linked]

The lack of sufficient highest and best use and financial feasibility analysis are often cited by typical users of subdivision appraisal reports. Many appraisals are deficient in these areas. Just because a new subdivision is approved by local planning authorities does not mean that there is market demand to support the project or that the project is financially feasible. A proposed project may not necessarily represent the highest and best use of the vacant acreage. Appraisers often make this assumption and fail to conduct an independent supply and demand analysis of the project to address financial feasibility and timing issues.

Chapter 5 provides an overview of highest and best use as it relates specifically to subdivision analysis. Chapter 6 covers profit and timeline concepts as they apply to subdivision analysis.

The Three Approaches To Value

Complete coverage of all three approaches to value can be found in Chapters 7 through 9. Since the income capitalization and cost approaches tend to be more complex in subdivision valuation, these approaches will receive more coverage with numerous examples. The sales comparison approach is especially applicable to subdivision valuation for extracting yield rates and other comparable information. However, finding current sales of a group of lots comparable to a subject property is usually difficult. This tends to reduce the applicability of the sales comparison approach. This section of the book concludes with reconciliation and reaching a final value conclusion for the Mill Pond Case Study.

Income Capitalization Approach

The income capitalization approach is the primary method used in subdivision valuation because the entire approach, especially the DCF analysis component, is designed to measure differences in present value as a result of future cash flow projections. Since all income and profit and, therefore, value comes from the future sale of subdivision lots over time, this approach is the primary valuation method used. Chapter 7 describes the income methodology applied in subdivision analysis and the timeline concepts involved. Most of the DCF examples in this book are based on a total property perspective and discount net income to the property using an appropriate property yield rate. However, Chapter 7 also includes examples of more complicated mortgage-equity methods as well as consideration of lot presales and the impact on developer yield.

The items required to complete the income capitalization approach for an improved subdivision or group of lots (existing or proposed) are:

- The retail lot value estimate
- The absorption period estimate
- The holding and sales costs over the absorption period
- The discount rate analysis or line-item profit analysis used for the present value calculation

The items required to complete the income capitalization approach for an estimate of raw land value are:

- The retail lot value estimate
- The absorption period
- The holding and sales costs over the absorption period
- The discount rate analysis or line-item profit analysis
- Construction costs

- The timeline estimate for permitting and subdivision approval with associated holding costs and expenses

Cost Approach

The cost approach includes three elements:

1. Reproduction or replacement cost new
2. Accrued depreciation
3. Land value

The cost approach is most useful in appraisals of proposed projects or projects that have recently been built. Chapter 8 explains how cost analysis can be performed to reflect the sum of the retail values or bulk sale value for a subdivision project. Two new case studies are presented here to illustrate other issues in the cost approach, including the valuation of excess land for future phases and the allocation of common infrastructure costs among various project phases.

Cost approach conclusions provide a contrast with the information derived from the income capitalization and sales comparison approaches and allow the appraiser to address the feasibility and highest and best use issues inherent in new construction. The cost approach is typically used for proposed projects or groups of lots that make up a substantial portion of an existing project. The cost approach is not particularly useful for valuing a small group of lots in a large planned development. For example, this approach would not be helpful in the valuation of 20 lots in a 500-lot planned development.

The cost approach is not generally used if the objective is to estimate raw land value. In these cases, the sales comparison approach would be used to estimate a current vacant land value. However, one benefit of subdivision valuation methodology is the ability to use the income capitalization approach to conclude a vacant land value when subdivision development is the highest and best use and comparable vacant land sales are not available. In this case, typical subdivision costs are needed to derive raw land value using the income capitalization approach. In any case, if vacant land sales are available for comparison purposes, the sales comparison approach is always the preferred valuation methodology for a vacant tract of land.

Sales Comparison Approach

In the sales comparison approach, a group of lots or units or an entire subdivision is compared to recent market sales of similar projects. Because the objective of the analysis is to obtain the market value for a group of lots under a bulk sale scenario, recent and relevant bulk sales are needed for comparison. This requires the appraiser to research the subject submarket for recent sales of a group of lots. Sales of improved subdivisions or large groups of lots are very limited in most markets. The comparison would involve analyzing sales with a similar remaining absorption period and a similar mix of lots and/or unit types, location, price points, and other characteristics.

If comparable sales are available, then direct comparisons should be made between the market sales and the subject lot inventory. Chapter 9 provides an application of the sales comparison approach to the Mill Pond Case Study using three available methods: the flat discount method, the bulk lot value method, and the retail lot value method. The Mill Pond Case Study concludes with the reconciliation and final value indication presented at the end of Chapter 9.

Profit and Yield Analysis

Chapter 10 provides a detailed explanation of how yield and profit are extracted, analyzed, and reapplied in subdivision valuation. Topics covered include a complete discussion of line-item profit and yield analysis and its significance as well as how this analysis is applied in the income capitalization approach through DCF analysis. The Madison Square project is used as a case study for market extraction and to demonstrate the interaction of line-item profit as a matched pair with selected discount rates. This is reinforced with an example of yield rate extraction from comparable sales. The topics covered in Chapter 10 include

- Profit concepts and the subdivision timeline
- Yield, profit, and the three subdivision phases
- Yield and line-item profit
- Extracting yield rates in the sales comparison approach
- Extracting profit in the cost approach

Land Value Using the Subdivision Method

Chapter 11 provides an overview of estimating acreage land value using the subdivision development method. This is a variation of the income capitalization approach specifically designed to estimate vacant land value when subdivision development is the highest and best use. The Park View Case Study is presented to illustrate the income capitalization approach.

Special Topics

The last chapter of this book delves into four contemporary topics relating to subdivision appraisal and developers' risk-reduction strategies. The first section provides an overview of common deficiencies found in subdivision appraisal reports. This section is based on information gathered from users of appraisal services and reviews several common areas of concern observed in subdivision appraisals. This is followed by an example relating to the concept of profit and how it is measured. The three components of profit–dollar profit, time, and yield–are considered. The example emphasizes that these three components must always be evaluated together rather than separately. Next is a comprehensive discussion of the time zero profit dilemma. The effect of very short absorption periods is considered as it relates to yield rate selection. Placement of sales contracts at time zero in the present value calculation are evaluated within the context of required profit and yield. A sensitivity analysis is performed using the Serenola Hills Case Study, in which required developer profit is contrasted with the present value conclusions and yield to a potential buyer. Yield rate selection with short absorption time frames is problematic, and strategies for selecting an appropriate rate are explored. The last section of Chapter 12 outlines several common strategies used by subdivision developers to reduce or manage risk in the development process.

Additional Materials

Frequently Asked Questions on Residential Tract Development Lending–a memorandum published by the Board of Governors of the Federal Reserve System, the Federal Deposit Insurance Corporation, the National Credit Union Administration, the Office of the Comptroller of the Currency, and the Office of Thrift Supervision–has been included in the back of this book. This memorandum was published in September of 2005 and is available for reference purposes.

This book also includes a glossary of terms. When definitions are available from The *Dictionary of Real Estate Appraisal*, sixth edition, they have been included here.[1] Terms used in this book that do not appear in the *Dictionary* have been defined by the author. Also, *bulk value* has been redefined to accurately describe a specific valuation scenario in which the market value of a group of lots is determined.

---

1. *The Dictionary of Real Estate Appraisal*, 6th ed. (Chicago: Appraisal Institute, 2015).

1 Overview

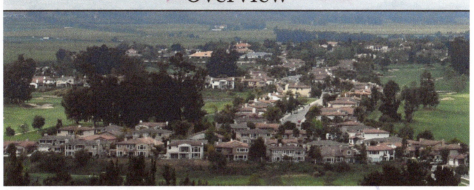

Introduction

Many appraisers recognize that subdivision valuation can be a very complicated process and is one of the most difficult areas of appraisal practice. Applied analysis requires consideration of the three phases of subdivision development, timeline concepts, and related valuation points along the timeline. Project market analysis considering home price points as well as supply and demand conditions is critical; it must be considered for the highest and best use analysis as well as to develop value conclusions. Project holding and sales costs must be projected over a future absorption period with proper recognition of profit and where it occurs along the timeline. To apply the process correctly, the appraiser needs a comprehensive understanding of the methodology involved and how it is applied in the three approaches.

Single-unit subdivision valuation provides a comprehensive overview of the valuation process and the three approaches to value as they relate to typical suburban subdivisions. This text covers existing single-unit subdivision developments as well as proposed projects and considers typical valuation points for lending clients. Most of the examples included in this text involve vacant lots. A basic introduction to vacant land valuation analysis, in which subdivision valuation methodology is employed to support a vacant land value conclusion, is also provided.

Background and History

In the appraisal industry, the income capitalization approach as applied in subdivision development has been identified as the *subdivision development method* and was originally used to estimate raw land value for a parcel of land when subdivision development is the highest and best use. Over time, this method has been adopted for use in a wide variety of valuation assignments involving vacant subdivision lots or home units being sold over time. Today the emphasis has changed, and subdivision valuation is now most applicable to the valuation of proposed subdivision projects for which all three approaches to value are commonly used. When properly applied, the subdivision method produces credible value estimates.

The subdivision development method has proven to be applicable to a wide variety of valuation problems because of its flexibility. The technique is designed to simulate the behavior of typical market participants who are interested in the timing of cash flows and disbursements and in quantifying the risk associated with an inventory of real estate that must be sold over a period of time. The income capitalization approach using discounted cash flow (DCF) analysis allows the appraiser to match the timing of cash flows and disbursements to market expectations. The cost and sales comparison approaches are also integral to the analysis of an improved subdivision. In fact, many of the inputs required for the income capitalization approach are directly related to information developed in the cost and sales comparison approaches.

The unique role of the cost approach in subdivision development relates to the timing of costs over the development period as well as the internal cost accounting that must be considered; it is one of the more difficult approaches to apply. Land value can vary substantially over the development timeline as development entitlements are obtained. In the sales comparison approach, comparable sales can also be analyzed to reflect market value for a group of existing or proposed lots. One of the greatest benefits of the sales comparison approach is the ability to extract market parameters for yield rates, line-item profit, absorption rates, and retail lot or unit values.

Defining a Subdivision

The definition of *subdivision* taken from the sixth edition of *The Dictionary of Real Estate Appraisal* (shown in the accompanying textbox) can apply to a wide variety of valuation issues. Normally, we think of typical suburban subdivisions designed for single-unit residential use where individual lots are sold to end users or homebuilders over time. Subdivision methodology can also be used to solve for a wide range of property types including residential subdivisions, office developments, condominium projects, industrial parks, and other properties in which individual lots, units, or pods are sold over time. The methodology can be applied to an existing group of lots or a proposed project. The common denominator in all subdivision valuation scenarios is the estimation of market value when a group of lots or units will typically be sold over time.

> **subdivision**
> *A tract of land that has been divided into lots or blocks with streets, roadways, open areas, and other facilities appropriate to its development as residential, commercial, or industrial sites.*[1]

A typical residential subdivision. Vacant lots slated for construction appear in the foreground, while homes under construction and completed homes appear in the background.

This process is distinctly different from developing an opinion of market value for a single property. For example, the cost, income capitalization, and sales comparison approaches can be used to value a single office condominium unit in a multiple-unit condominium project. This would be representative of the market value of one unit to one purchaser. However, when valuing a group of 20 units in the same project, the subdivision perspective is typically used. In fact, appraisals performed for lending purposes involving a federally regulated financial institution must address a bulk sale scenario to reflect the market value of a group of lots or units to one purchaser for any valuation of five or more lots or units in a single development. Under certain circumstances it is acceptable to not include a bulk sale scenario for financing on an individual-unit basis if the individual units are likely to be constructed and sold within 12 months (see paragraph 11 of the *Frequently Asked Questions on Residential Tract Development Lending* memorandum in the back of this book).

In subdivision analysis, the market value of a single unit or lot is typically referred to as the lot or unit *retail value*. The market value for a group of lots or units sold in bulk to one purchaser is often referred to as a *bulk sale value*. Actually, this is a market value estimate under a bulk sale scenario. It reflects the present value of a group of lots or units to one purchaser, recognizing that the lots or units must be sold over a period of time. In this example, the market value or "bulk sale" value would be the market value of all 20 units to one purchaser. This value would

---

1. Italicized definitions that appear in textboxes throughout this book have been taken from *The Dictionary of Real Estate Appraisal*, 6th ed. (Chicago: Appraisal Institute, 2015). All other boxed definitions have been provided by the author.

consider the time frame needed to market the unit inventory, holding and sales costs over the absorption period, and typical profit levels needed to attract a purchaser to a group of units that must be sold over time.

General Property Characteristics

All subdivisions have general property characteristics that are considered in the appraisal and scope of work decision.

The primary qualifier that determines when the appraiser should be using subdivision methodology is the number of lots involved. Subdivision valuation methodology is designed to report the market value of a group of lots or units that must be sold over a period of time. This can be a group of existing lots with a valuation date as of the current time period or a group of proposed lots with a date of valuation at a future point in time when the subdivision infrastructure is built and the lots are ready for new building construction. This is commonly referred to as the *when complete* date.

General Characteristics of Subdivisions

- Subdivisions consist of lots or parcels that are subdivided from a larger ownership. A subdivision is typically a group of many lots or units.
- The lots or parcels can be vacant subdivision lots, improved home units, condominiums, or a mix of lots and/or units.
- The inventory can be a group of existing or proposed lots or units.
- For existing lots or units, the date of value is usually time period zero or the current date.
- In the case of vacant lots, proposed projects require a construction phase in which site infrastructure is installed to support the construction of future building units.
- In the case of new units, proposed projects require a construction phase in which site infrastructure and building units are completed.
- The construction of lots and/or units may be phased over time.
- Typically, proposed projects have a future valuation date as of the date of completion of the proposed improvements.

Subdivision Valuation Characteristics

The characteristics of subdivisions and the "product" that is generated by a real estate subdivision development distinguish subdivision analysis from other types of commercial appraisal assignments.

Property characteristics and related valuation characteristics make the appraisal of subdivision projects a unique problem. For example, compare a subdivision appraisal assignment with the appraisal of a typical commercial office property. In a typical commercial transaction, the investor purchases an office building with the expectation of receiving net income from rentals over time and profit from the eventual resale of the office at the end of the investment period. The investor will pay mortgage interest over time, which along with depreciation is deductible for income tax purposes and benefits the cash flow position. Also, if a mortgage is involved, income generated from rentals will eventually pay off the mortgage and increase the equity yield in the project. When the building is sold at the end of the holding period, the resale income is generally treated as capital gains income and has a beneficial impact on the eventual yield or profit generated from the investment.

With a subdivision property, an investor will purchase either a group of lots or vacant land and build a new subdivision. The only way that funds invested can be returned to the investor is through the eventual sale of subdivision lots or completed units. All profit and reimbursement for any expenses can only come from income generated by lot sales. Typically, any income generated from lot sales is classified as "ordinary" income and does not receive the same favorable tax treatment as capital gains income. The absorption period or rate of sale is critical to the actual profit received over time. The shorter the holding period, the lower the costs and the greater the profit. Unlike the office property example, there is no advantage to holding the subdivision property for a longer period of time to allow the mortgage balance to be reduced. In fact, the only way to reduce the mortgage is to sell more lots or units. The goal is to sell the lots as quickly as possible. Increasing the absorption period or holding period does not have any advantages in subdivision development, unless for some reason the lots were expected to increase substantially in value at a future time. A longer absorption period is usually a negative consequence for the investor.

In summary, a typical commercial property and a subdivision are two entirely different types of investments. The appraisal of a subdivision must recognize the property's unique characteristics and apply the appropriate methodology in all three approaches to value. An understanding of the development process and related valuation issues sets the stage for the following discussion of the valuation process and the common problems that can arise in subdivision valuation.

Characteristics of Subdivision Valuation
- Subdivision valuation involves a group of lots, units, or parcels that are typically sold over an absorption period.
- There is no reversion value; when the last lot is sold, the value goes down to zero.
- Income is usually ordinary income rather than capital gains income for income tax purposes. This fact plus the lack of a reversion partially explains the high yield rates typically found in this type of analysis.
- All income and profit must be received through cash flow from lot or unit sales.
- Subdivision valuation involves timeline concepts.
- The cost approach requires the consideration of land value at various stages of development, the cost of infrastructure over time, and any depreciation or obsolescence.
- The income capitalization approach involves the use of DCF analysis in which income, expenses, and profit are considered over the absorption period.
- The sales comparison approach includes analysis of market sales of a group of lots or units that were sold as a single transaction.

Subdivision Development Phases

The three major development phases for any subdivision development are shown in Exhibit 1.1. Each phase of any new project has an associated time frame, and all three phases and associated time frames may be considered directly in the analysis. An appraisal of existing lots would only consider the remaining absorption period needed to market the lot inventory because the permitting phase and construction phase have already been completed.

Exhibit 1.1
Subdivision Development

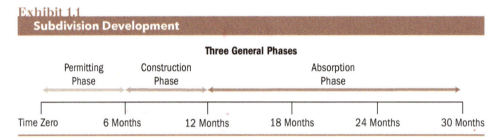

Permitting Phase

The *permitting phase* is the time period when vacant raw land goes through an approval process by local governmental authorities to achieve the appropriate land zoning, permitting, and final site plan approval. Once full "entitlements" are achieved, development can begin. Exhibit 1.1 shows a six-month time frame for the permitting phase. Depending on the "development environment" in a community, the permitting phase can be a relatively easy process with a short time frame and minimal costs or a very expensive undertaking that requires a longer time frame and numerous surveys, environmental audits, and other studies. Typically, vacant land will have a significantly higher value after final site plan approval has been attained. However, depending on the stipulations required for development and the development environment in the area, land values can vary. Once permitting has been achieved, the land has full entitlements.

Entitlements are the legal arrangements and governmental approvals that are required by a community to develop a property. The entitlement process usually requires that subdivision drawings, environmental audits, topographical surveys, wetland surveys, demand studies, traffic counts, and other studies be submitted for consideration by local governmental authorities. This can be a very lengthy, complicated process, especially if rezoning or changes in local land use plans are required. When the project has achieved all approvals, the developers can immediately obtain the necessary permits to start construction. At this point in time, the property has achieved full entitlements and the permitting phase has been concluded.

Stipulations required by the community can include off-site infrastructure that must be completed by the subdivision developer to achieve permitting. Such infrastructure can include acceleration or deceleration lanes along a main thoroughfare, sewer lift stations, or the donation of land for parks, schools, or other public uses. In nearly all cases, some required stipulations must be completed to develop a property. Troublesome or high-cost stipulations can reduce the value of a property for development purposes. Also, the status of any wetlands, floodplain areas, or other environmental factors can reduce usable land area.

An area of land with entitlements. This will be the future site of a subdivision.

In many communities, vacant land that has not gone through a final site plan review process is extremely difficult to appraise because the actual use density, the character of uses, and the stipulations for development are unknown until the final site plan review process has been completed.

The development environment surrounding real estate can vary from community to community. For example, it may be very easy to achieve rezoning and take vacant land through the permitting process in communities that are encouraging new development. In this type of environment, it is relatively easy to bring new inventory into the market.

Conversely, other communities have more stringent requirements. The permitting review process may involve a wide range of studies including archeological, environmental, habitat, traffic, and topographical studies as well as surveys, preliminary site plans, and market studies of future demand. In these communities, vacant land will typically achieve a significantly higher value when permitting has been achieved, all entitlements are obtained, and near-term market demand supports new construction.

Construction Phase

The construction phase is the time period when subdivision site infrastructure is installed on the land. This could include underground utilities, streets, storm drainage, water retention facilities, open space, common amenities, and other improvements that make the individual subdivision lots ready for the construction of homes or units. After construction, the site is an improved subdivision. Phased projects may have a mix of improved subdivision land

and vacant excess or surplus land reserved for future phases of development. Completed units may also be built as part of the initial construction, such as in a proposed condominium project. Most of the examples in this text relate to vacant subdivision lots. However, the methodology employed for completed units would be very similar. Exhibit 1.1 shows a construction phase of about six months.

An appraisal assignment may be conducted at any point along the subdivision development timeline. The most common valuation points will be discussed in further detail.

Streets and sidewalks under construction on a future subdivision site

Slab on grade with attached garage

Subdivision site construction

A detached home with frame construction

An improved site in a subdivision ready for home construction

A two-story custom home

Absorption or Sell-Off Phase

The absorption or sell-off phase begins immediately after the project is built. The absorption period is the amount of time required for the market to absorb the vacant lot or unit inventory.

> **absorption period**
> The actual or expected period required from the time a property, group of properties, or commodity is initially offered for lease, purchase, or use by its eventual users until all portions have been sold or stabilized occupancy has been achieved.

The definition of *absorption period* provided specifically defines the time period as starting at the time of the initial offering of the lots until all the lots are sold. More importantly, the absorption period is an estimate of the time frame needed to market the inventory to the eventual end users as required by lending institutions. This has an impact on the absorption analysis, especially in markets where lots are not typically sold to end users and are instead sold in groups to homebuilders who build speculative and/or custom homes for the eventual end users. Keep in mind that sales to builders can skew the absorption period estimate in comparison with the end user criteria. This may require that multiple values be reported for lending purposes. [important] The required analysis considers the "end user" absorption forecast for the bulk-sale valuation, and additional bulk-sale value conclusions consider presales of lots.

An appraiser may at this point in time consider presale contracts on lots or units within the project, and the actual marketing effort may begin well before the construction phase is completed. However, the actual absorption does not begin until the lots are 100% completed. Normally, the absorption period is estimated using market analysis techniques that will be described in Chapter 2. Both inferred and fundamental demand analysis methods can be used to estimate the subject's absorption period. Usually, demand is estimated as the number of lots sold per month, quarter, or year.

A subdivision project has its highest value and greatest risk at the beginning of the absorption period because construction has been completed and the greatest amount of capital and labor has been invested in the project. This is also the point of greatest risk to the developer, who has a full inventory of vacant lots that must be sold over a period of time. Typically, the initial valuation and absorption forecast ignores any presale contracts and only considers the market absorption characteristics to eventual end users. However, it is quite possible to perform additional forecasts and

A subdivision in the absorption phase

bulk sale value conclusions considering presale contracts when there is an initial burst of sales at the beginning of the absorption period and lot construction is complete. An appraisal under the presale scenario considers the specific presale contracts, lot prices, and closing schedules and their impact on the absorption of remaining lot inventory as part of the analysis.

Ultimately, the goal of the developer is to sell lots or units as quickly as possible. There is no advantage to a longer marketing period. In fact, a longer marketing or absorption period only increases the costs associated with holding the lot inventory over time and reduces value as well as profit.

Subdivision Terminology and the Bulk Sale Valuation Premise

A brief review of the terminology used in subdivision appraisal is needed before the valuation process and application of the three approaches can be discussed.

In subdivision valuation, two specific terms—*bulk value* and *gross sell-out value*—have historically been used, along with many synonyms. However, both of these terms are misnomers and do not describe a specific type of value. Instead, they describe a valuation scenario applied to achieve market value in the unique application of subdivision valuation.

Subdivision analysis is designed to derive a market value for a group of lots to one purchaser. Obviously, this could be two lots or thousands of lots. Common appraisal assignments include the valuation of proposed subdivisions or the valuation of an existing group of lots.

In all of these valuation scenarios, subdivision valuation considers the value of the entire group of lots to one purchaser and recognizes that the only way the purchaser can recoup the initial investment and make a profit is to eventually sell the lot inventory over time. The analysis must consider appropriate deductions and discounts as well as the profit that is expected to be earned by the buyer. Accordingly, bulk sale value really is the *market value* for a group of lots. If the appraisal assignment is to appraise three lots, then there may be minimal, if any, deductions and discounts associated with a sale. In this case, market value under the bulk sale scenario may be very close to the individual retail values of the lots themselves.

In subdivision valuation, the *retail value* is the market value of one lot or unit. The sum of the retail values of all lots within the inventory under study has been historically called the *gross sell-out value*. Today, the preferred terms are *aggregate of the retail values* or *sum of the retail values*, which is the term used in the examples in this book. For simplicity, market value under a bulk sale scenario is referred to simply as the *bulk sale value*. However, the reader should always recognize that the bulk sale value is not a separate type of value; rather, it is a *market value* for a group of lots, which reflects a bulk sale scenario. The bulk sale scenario considers the holding period or absorption period needed to market the lot inventory over time, appropriate deductions for the holding and sales costs required, and the expectation of profit. Profit is represented in the income capitalization approach by the discount rate used for the present value calculation. Hence, the analysis considers appropriate "deductions and discounts" when a buyer is purchasing a group of lots that must be sold over time.

The term *absorption period* also has several synonyms. These include *holding period*, *sell-out period*, and *project marketing period*. These terms describe the time period needed to market the lot inventory given supportable absorption rates for the property under consideration.

In summary, the term *sum of the retail values* is used to describe the aggregate of the individual retail values of the lots considered in the analysis. The term *bulk sale value* describes the bulk value scenario used to arrive at a market value conclusion for a group of lots.

The following chapters describe various valuation scenarios along the timeline for existing lots and proposed subdivision projects. Historically, the lending industry has used terms like *"as is" value*, *value when complete*, and *value when stabilized* to describe the property status for a proposed project and common valuation points along the timeline. The term *stabilized value* is not appropriate in subdivision valuation. *"As is" value* typically represents land value in its current state at the time of the appraisal. If an existing group of lots is appraised, *"as is" value* would be the market value under a bulk sale scenario for the group of lots. It would include appropriate deductions and discounts for the bulk sale scenario as well as profit considerations. In addition, the analysis would consider the absorption period required for the market to absorb the lot inventory over time.

Typically, the future value as of the point in time when the proposed project has subdivision infrastructure that is 100% built is referred to by lenders as the *market value when complete*. In subdivision valuation, this term refers to the market value using the bulk sale valuation scenario. The *bulk sale value* is the market value "when complete" for a proposed project. Historically, many terms have been used to describe this value. They include *"as built" value*, *value when complete*, *value at completion*, and other terms. In appraisal reports, *market value when complete* is the preferred terminology, and the date the value applies is usually stated when a prospective value is reported.

A value conclusion for any proposed project usually involves the use of hypothetical conditions or extraordinary assumptions. Typically, the market value when complete requires an extraordinary assumption that the project is complete at the time when the value estimate is being made. It is also possible to provide a value of a proposed project "as if it were complete today." In this case, since the project is not complete today, the appraisal is based on a hypothetical condition. When reviewing the timeline concepts and values presented in the following chapters, keep in mind that the term *bulk sale value* refers to the market value of a group of lots under a bulk sale scenario. Be aware of the significance of values along a timeline and how they are reported to communicate the appraisal clearly and concisely.

The Valuation Process

The valuation process begins when the appraiser agrees to take on an appraisal assignment and ends when the conclusions of the appraisal are reported to the client. The process used in subdivision analysis is the same as that used in any other appraisal. It involves a systematic set of procedures an appraiser follows to provide answers to a client's questions about real property value. The most common appraisal assignment is performed to render an opinion of market value. The ultimate goal of the valuation process is a well-supported value conclusion that reflects all the pertinent factors that influence the market value of the property being appraised.

Traditionally, specific appraisal techniques are applied within the three approaches to derive indications of real property value. One or more approaches to value may be used depending on their applicability to the particular appraisal assignment, the nature of the property, the needs of the client, and the available data. Application of the appraisal process, the analysis considered, and the reporting formats are defined in modern appraisal practice by the provisions of the Uniform Standards of Professional Appraisal Practice (USPAP).

USPAP Considerations and Lending Industry Issues

The Uniform Standards of Professional Appraisal Practice (USPAP) establish minimum requirements for real estate appraisal practice and requirements for the appraisal process as it relates to all assignments. These requirements should be very familiar to all professional appraisers and will not be reiterated here. Particularly applicable to subdivision valuation are Advisory Opinions 33 and 34. Also, Advisory Opinion 30 addresses appraisal assignments prepared for federally regulated financial institutions and includes guidance that is applicable to subdivisions. While advisory opinions are not mandatory as part of USPAP, they clarify provisions of USPAP and provide advice. The following information is from the 2016-2017 edition of USPAP.[2]

Advisory Opinion 33 (AO-33) addresses the issues involved in DCF analysis and the appropriate steps to be considered by the appraiser to avoid misuse of the DCF technique. Some of the more significant provisions of AO-33 are as follows:

- DCF analysis has become a requirement of many real property clients and other intended users.
- DCF techniques may be applied in the valuation or analysis of proposed construction, land development, condominium development or conversion, rehabilitation development, and income-producing assets of various types.
- DCF methodology is based on the principle of anticipation of future benefits and requires the appraiser to make rational and supportable assumptions.
- To avoid misuse or misunderstanding when DCF analysis is used in an appraisal assignment to develop an opinion of market value, it is the responsibility of the appraiser to ensure that the controlling input is consistent with market evidence and prevailing market attitudes.
- Market value DCF analysis should be supported by market-derived data, and the assumptions should be both market- and property-specific.
- Market value DCF analysis, along with available factual data, is intended to reflect the expectations and perceptions of market participants. The analysis should be judged on the support for the forecasts that existed when the forecasts were made, not on whether specific items in the forecasts are realized at a later date.
- An appraisal report that includes the results of DCF analysis must clearly state the assumptions on which the analysis is based (per Standards Rule 2-1) and must set forth the relevant data used in the analysis.
- Computer printouts showing the results of DCF analysis may be generated by readily available means such as an appraiser's own spreadsheet, a commercially available spreadsheet

---

2. *2016-2017 Uniform Standards of Professional Appraisal Practice* (Washington, DC: The Appraisal Foundation, 2015).

template, or specialized DCF software. Regardless of the method chosen, the appraiser is responsible for the entire analysis, including the controlling input, the calculations, and the resulting output.

- If using commercial software, the appraiser should cite the name and version of the software used and provide a brief description of any assumptions and/or methodology unique to that software. Standards Rule 1-4 requires that projections of anticipated future rent and/or income potential and expenses be based on reasonably clear and appropriate evidence.

- Discount rates applied to cash flows and estimates of reversion should be derived from data and information in the real estate and capital markets. Surveys of investor opinion and yield indices are also useful in the rate selection process, but only when the type of and market for the asset being appraised is consistent with the type of and market for the asset typically acquired by the investors interviewed in the survey. Primary considerations used in the selection of rates are risk, inflation, and real rates of return.

- The results of DCF analysis should be tested and checked for errors and reasonableness. Because of compounding effects in the projection of income and expenses, even slight input errors can be magnified and produce unreasonable results.

Advisory Opinion 34 (AO-34) addresses the issues involved in an appraisal assignment in which prospective value conclusions are being made for proposed construction or other purposes. A prospective value opinion is a value expressed as of a future effective date. The issues addressed in this statement deal with how to prepare and present an appraisal in a manner that is not misleading when a prospective date of value is used. Some of the more significant provisions of AO-34 include the following:

- Prospective appraisals (effective date of the appraisal subsequent to the date of the report) may be required for valuations of property interests related to proposed developments, as the basis for value at the end of a cash flow projection, and for other reasons.

- The use of clear and concise language and appropriate terminology in appraisal reports helps to eliminate misleading reports.

- To avoid confusion, the appraiser must clearly establish the date to which the value opinion applies. In prospective value opinions, use of the term *market value* without a modifier such as *forecasted* or *prospective* and without future verb tenses is improper (i.e., "the prospective market value is expected to be…" rather than "the market value is….").

Subdivision Valuation

- Prospective value opinions, along with available factual data, are intended to reflect the current expectations and perceptions of market participants. They should be judged on the market support for the forecasts when made, not on whether specific items in the forecasts are realized at a later date.
- It is appropriate to study comparable projects for evidence of construction periods, development costs, income and expense levels, and absorption.
- Items such as rental concessions, commissions, tenant finish allowances, add-on factors, and expense pass-throughs must be studied to develop realistic income forecasts.
- All value conclusions should include reference to the time frame when the analysis was prepared to clearly delineate the market conditions and the point of reference from which the appraiser developed the prospective value opinion.
- It is essential to clearly and accurately disclose any appropriate assumptions, extraordinary assumptions, and/or limiting conditions when citing the market conditions from which the prospective value opinion was made.

Advisory Opinion 30 (AO-30) addresses issues that are unique to the lending industry for appraisal assignments used by federally insured depository institutions in federally related transactions, including most appraisals performed for lending purposes:

> Appraisers must identify and consider the intended use and intended users in an assignment to understand their USPAP development and reporting obligations. The agencies' [i.e., federally regulated financial institutions] appraisal regulations and guidelines contain assignment conditions that are part of competent performance when they apply in an assignment. Therefore, compliance with USPAP requirements for proper development and reporting **require** adherence to those assignment conditions that apply in an assignment. [emphasis added]³

Failure to recognize and adhere to applicable assignment conditions violates one or more of the previously identified USPAP requirements.

AO-30 is comprehensive and includes sections on the recognition of assignment conditions, USPAP applicability, and appraiser obligations for performing appraisals for federally regulated financial institutions. The section on appraiser obligations contains provisions relating to appraiser independence, appraisal development and reporting, and the market value definition; it also provides answers to commonly asked questions. Specific appraisal, development, and reporting issues are outlined as follows:

> The agencies' appraisal regulations state, in part:

---

3. *USPAP Advisory Opinions 2016-2017* Edition (Washington, DC: The Appraisal Foundation, 2015), 178.

"For federally related transactions, all appraisals shall, at a minimum:

(a) Conform to generally accepted appraisal standards as evidenced by the Uniform Standards of Professional Appraisal Practice (USPAP)…

(b) Be written and contain sufficient information and analysis to support the institution's decision to engage in the transaction;

(c) Analyze and report appropriate deductions and discounts for proposed construction or renovation, partially leased buildings, nonmarket lease terms, and tract developments with unsold units;

(d) Be based upon the definition of market value as set forth in this subpart; and

(e) Be performed by State licensed or certified appraisers in accordance with requirements set forth in this subpart."[4]

AO-30 also requires that the appraiser be aware of the agencies' appraisal regulations and guidelines, which expand and clarify the five previously described reporting and development issues. The *Interagency Appraisal and Evaluation Guidelines* are part of these regulations and expand on item (c) with the following minimum appraisal standard:

> The appraisal must…analyze and report appropriate deductions and discounts for proposed construction or renovation, partially leased buildings, non-market lease terms, and tract developments with unsold units…
>
> This standard is designed to avoid having appraisals prepared using unrealistic assumptions and inappropriate methods in arriving at the property's market value. For federally related transactions, an appraisal is to include the current market value of the property in its actual physical condition and subject to the zoning in effect as of the date of the appraisal. For properties where improvements are to be constructed or rehabilitated, the regulated institution may also request a prospective market value based on stabilized occupancy or a value based on the sum of retail sales. However, the sum of retail sales for a proposed development is not the market value of the development for the purpose of the agencies' appraisal regulations. For proposed developments that involve the sale of individual houses, units, or lots, the appraiser must analyze and report appropriate deductions and discounts for holding costs, marketing costs and entrepreneurial profit. For proposed and rehabilitated rental developments, the appraiser must make appropriate deductions and discounts for items such as leasing commission, rent losses, and tenant improvements from an estimate based on stabilized occupancy.[5]

Tract development is defined in the *Frequently Asked Questions on Residential Tract Development Lending* memorandum, provided in the back of this book, as follows:

> The agencies' appraisal regulations define a "tract development" as a project with **five or more units** that is constructed or is to be

---

4. Ibid., 180.

5. *Interagency Appraisal and Evaluation Guidelines* (Office of the Comptroller of the Currency, Federal Deposit Insurance Corporation, Federal Reserve Board, Office of Thrift Supervision, October 27, 1994), paragraphs 19-20, www.federalreserve.gov.

constructed as a single development…a "unit" refers to: a residential building lot; a detached single-family home; an attached single-family home; or a residence in a condominium building. [emphasis added][6]

The same publication references a time frame of 12 months that may be applicable for appraisals of less than five units or of individual units if the units are likely to be constructed and sold within 12 months.

These provisions make clear that the sum of the retail values is not the market value for subdivision tract developments. The requirements stated above also establish a threshold provision in which the bulk sale valuation scenario must be used for any group of five or more lots or units. Keep in mind that bulk value is not a *type* of value. The type of value is market value, which must consider appropriate discounts and deductions to reflect the value to one purchaser of a group of lots. This is reinforced by historical regulation over time consistent with bulletins published by various federal agencies, who clarify the issue as follows:

> The sum of retail sales for a proposed development is **not** the market value of the development for the purpose of the agencies' appraisal regulations. For proposed developments that involve the sale of individual houses, units, or lots, the appraiser must analyze and report appropriate deductions and discounts for holding costs, marketing costs and entrepreneurial profit. For proposed and rehabilitated rental developments, the appraiser must make appropriate deductions and discounts for items such as leasing commission, rent losses, and tenant improvements from an estimate based on stabilized occupancy. [emphasis added][7]

> Report the market value to **a single purchaser** as of the date of completion for all properties, wherein a portion of the overall real property rights or physical asset would typically be sold to its ultimate users over some future time period. Valuations involving such properties must fully reflect all appropriate deductions and discounts as well as the anticipated cash flows to be derived from the disposition of the asset over time. Appropriate deductions and discounts are considered to be those which reflect all expenses associated with the disposition of the realty, as of the date of completion, as well as the cost of capital and entrepreneurial profit. [emphasis added][8]

For lending purposes, federal regulators want lenders to obtain a market value (as defined) of the bulk of the lots as though sold together to one buyer. According to AO-30 and other provisions, the appraiser must consider appropriate deductions and dis-

---

6. *Frequently Asked Questions on Residential Tract Development Lending* (Board of Governors of the Federal Reserve System, Federal Deposit Insurance Corporation, National Credit Union Administration, Office of the Comptroller of the Currency, Office of Thrift Supervision, September 8, 2005), paragraph 4, www.fdic.gov.
7. *Commercial Real Estate and Construction Lending Comptroller's Handbook* (Comptroller of the Currency, Administrator of National Banks, November, 1995), 81, www.occ.gov.
8. *Memorandum R 41c* (Federal Home Loan Bank Board Office of Examinations and Supervision, September 11, 1986), 7, www.ots.treas.gov.

counts when there are five or more units or when it will take longer than 12 months to sell all the units. Appropriate deductions and discounts for less than five lots or units is probably not a concern because it will most likely take less than 12 months to sell the lots, and any deductions and discounts would be relatively minor as a percentage of total value. From a valuation standpoint, the five-unit/less-than-12-month absorption period criteria has no unique significance. If an appraiser is valuing three lots as though sold to one buyer or 20 lots that will all sell within three months, USPAP requires the appraiser to consider appropriate deductions and discounts regardless of the number of lots or units.

Most previous references refer to appropriate deductions and discounts for holding and marketing costs as well as entrepreneurial profit. Only the oldest source, Memorandum R 41c from 1986, references cost of capital as an expense deduction. If mortgage interest and principal are deducted as an expense in the DCF analysis, mortgage-equity analysis is being used and the equity yield rate, rather than the property yield rate, is used for discounting. In contemporary appraisal practice, appraisals and the discounting process often take the "total" property perspective, the property yield rate is used for discounting purposes, and mortgage interest and principal are not deducted as an expense in the DCF analysis.

While appraisers generally analyze historic data in the valuation process, it is important to recognize that the value of a property is dependent on the future benefits. Future benefits include the rights to use, occupy, and enjoy the property as well as the right to receive any income it may produce. Market values are therefore forward-looking, and market analysis is a critical step in the appraisal process. Appraisers are not expected to be prognosticators, and no one can predict the exact occurrence of future events. However, the analysis must be supported by market-derived data that includes not only buy/sell market participant data (i.e., sales and other data that is part of inferred analysis), but also fundamental data analysis like demographic forecasts and the six-step process described in the next chapter.

Steps in the Valuation Process

The first component of the valuation process is the identification of the problem and the scope of work determination. This involves identifying the following elements of an appraisal assignment:

- Client and intended users
- Intended use of the appraiser's opinions and conclusions
- Type and definition of value

- Effective date of the opinions and conclusions
- Property characteristics that are relevant to the type and definition of value and intended use of the appraisal
- Any extraordinary assumptions necessary in the assignment
- Any hypothetical conditions necessary in the assignment

Next, the appropriate scope of work necessary to produce credible assignment results is determined.

Identification of the Client and Intended User

Proper identification of the client and intended users helps to determine the values to be considered in the assignment and the audience for the assignment results. The client is the party or parties who engage the appraiser. Intended users are parties who the appraiser intends will use the appraisal report. The appraiser determines who the intended users are through an understanding of the client's needs. USPAP requires the appraiser to specifically identify the intended users of the assignment results either by name or type at the time of engagement. The client is always considered an intended user.

Intended Use of the Appraisal

The intended use of an appraisal is the appraiser's intent with regard to the manner in which the intended users will employ the information contained in the appraisal report. Again, the appraiser determines the intended use by understanding the client's needs. Because an appraisal provides the basis for a decision regarding real property, the nature of the decision affects the scope of work for the assignment and the appraisal report. Possible intended uses include a buy or sell decision and the determination of a loan amount or current asset value.

Intended Use and Lending Clients

The client for appraisal services involving a group of lots (existing or proposed) is often a lender, and the assignment is part of a federally related transaction. In this case, the appraisal requirements of the Financial Institutions Reform, Recovery and Enforcement Act of 1989 (FIRREA), as explained in AO-30, are applicable to the scope of work decision and defined values to be delivered as part of the appraisal assignment. Lending clients usually require a current *as is* value for the property and a future *value when complete* for any proposed construction of subdivision lots or units. Accordingly, the needs of the client establish which values need to be developed and reported and the appropriate valuation date(s).

Type and Definition of Value

The type and definition of value is determined with the client. The purpose of an appraisal is to develop an opinion of a certain type of value. Many definitions of value are available, including *market value, use value, investment value*, and others. The definition that USPAP provides for *market value* is a description of the characteristics common to all market value definitions and is not a definition that could be used in an appraisal. In a specific appraisal assignment, *market value* is defined by a specific client's needs, by jurisdiction (e.g., a court or regulatory body or public agency with legal authority), or by a client group (e.g., a bank or other lender). USPAP's AO-30 contains the definition of value required by lending clients.

The definition of value in an appraisal assignment establishes specific conditions. These conditions impose parameters on appraisal assignments that are necessary to ensure that the assignment's results are meaningful in the context of that definition of value.

The definition of *market value* in the accompanying text box incorporates the concepts most widely associated with the term, provides the appraiser a choice among three bases, and requires increments or diminutions from the all-cash market value to be quantified in terms of cash.

> **market value**
> The most probable price, as of a specified date, in cash, or in terms equivalent to cash, or in other precisely revealed terms, for which the specified property rights should sell after reasonable exposure in a competitive market under all conditions requisite to a fair sale, with the buyer and seller each acting prudently, knowledgeably, and for self-interest, and assuming that neither is under undue duress.

Date of the Opinion of Value

The date of the opinion of value must be specified because the forces that influence real property value are constantly changing. Past (retrospective), current, and future (prospective) dates are considered in any appraisal assignment. Most often, subdivision appraisal practice considers two time periods. Values are expressed as of the current date and represent *as is* value, or values are reported as of a prospective date for proposed construction.

Relevant Property Characteristics

The appraisal problem cannot be properly defined without certain information about the property characteristics that are relevant to the assignment. This identification process relates to the unique characteristics of the subject property and the real property interests to be valued. These characteristics include physical attributes as well as the legal and land zoning attributes of the subject property. The legal description identifies the specific parcel and hopefully identifies any easements that may benefit or encumber the property. The presence of easements, encroachments, and leases may require a refinement in the property interest to be appraised or reveal conflicts between the property interest requested by the client and the actual status of the property to be appraised. Essential physical items include location, parcel size, and other physical characteristics. Physical characteristics can influence the usability of the site for subdivision development purposes. An unusual shape, access problems, or the presence of wetlands can limit the site's uses. Input from other professionals, such as surveyors or environmental engineers, may be required before an accurate appraisal can be made. Depending on the limitations imposed by these factors, the scope of work required may vary or the use of hypothetical conditions or extraordinary assumptions may be required to provide a credible opinion of value.

Extraordinary Assumptions and Hypothetical Conditions

A *hypothetical condition*, which is defined by USPAP as "a condition, directly related to a specific assignment, which is contrary to what is known by the appraiser to exist on the effective date of the assignment results, but is used for the purpose of analysis,"[9] may involve conditions external to the property, such as access characteristics, or may relate to the integrity of data used in the analysis (i.e., preliminary plans). Typically, any appraisal of proposed construction would recognize that the proposed plans are "hypothetical" and would include an extraordinary assumption that it is reasonable to presume that the project can be built within the future time frame allowed and be completed as of the date of completion. At the time of completion (*when complete* valuation date), the construction is an accomplished fact and no longer hypothetical.

An *extraordinary assumption* is an assumption directly related to a specific assignment which, if found to be false, could alter the appraiser's opinion or conclusions. An extraordinary assumption may be a presumption that a new subdivision phase can use the common infrastructure installed in previous subdivision phases (swimming pool, clubhouse, etc.).

Scope of Work

Certain issues must be addressed with the client to determine the scope of work. *Scope of work* is defined by USPAP as "the type and extent of research and analysis in an appraisal or appraisal review assignment."[10] Typically, the scope of work is modified or

---

9. 2016-2017 *Uniform Standards of Professional Appraisal Practice*, 3.
10. Ibid., 4.

tailored to the specific aspects of the property to be appraised. USPAP recognizes that the appraiser's scope of work may differ significantly for different assignments. The Scope of Work Rule in USPAP provides flexibility in determining the scope of work. However, the competency necessary to determine an appropriate scope of work within the allowed flexibility resides with the appraiser. Therefore, while it is common and reasonable for the client to provide input to the appraiser regarding a desired scope of work, the responsibility for determining the appropriate scope of work is the appraiser's.

The Scope of Work Rule also recognizes that the scope of work actually performed may differ from the scope of work initially planned. Determining the scope of work is an ongoing process in an assignment. Information or conditions discovered during the course of an assignment may cause the appraiser to reconsider the scope of work. The appraiser must disclose the type and extent of research and analysis that were actually completed in the development process. Additionally, any information required to allow intended users to understand the scope of work may include the disclosure of the research and analyses that were *not* performed.

After the scope of work has been determined, the data collection and analysis begins. This includes consideration of the market area data, subject property data, and comparable sales data to use in the analysis. Market analysis includes demand studies, supply studies, and marketability studies relating to the subject subdivision. The character of the project will determine the types of analyses to be employed for the valuation. The property description data includes the site description, a description of all relevant zoning issues, the subdivision marketing concept, related price points, and other pertinent property information, as well as any proposed construction plans. This data is discussed in more detail in Chapter 4. Consideration is given to the application of the three approaches to value both as part of the scope of work decision and in the application of the analysis. An initial preview of the available data and analysis facilitates the highest and best use conclusion.

2
Market Analysis

Introduction

Market analysis is the identification and study of the market for a particular economic good or service. In real estate, this typically is a study of the market conditions for a specific type of property or a specific subject property. Market analysis in real estate appraisal has two basic functions. First, market analysis provides the data input to identify the highest and best use of a property. Second, it provides data input and identifies the key property or market attributes that influence value to be measured by applying the three approaches to value. Market analysis can be a separate study from appraisal, but an appraisal cannot be completed without market analysis. This chapter provides an overview of the market analysis six-step process used in real estate appraisal and how it relates to subdivision valuation. A detailed market analysis example is provided for the Mill Pond Case Study. This information is then applied in Chapter 7, when the income capitalization approach is applied to develop the market absorption estimate for the Mill Pond subdivision.

Absorption and Highest and Best Use

Market analysis has a dual role in the appraisal process. It can be used primarily as a forecasting tool in the highest and best use section of the appraisal or it can be used to support a market absorption forecast. Market absorption can take the form of a lease-up estimate for a proposed commercial building or a sell-out analysis for a proposed subdivision or condominium project. A sell-out analysis is an estimate of the future time frame needed to market the lot or unit inventory to end users.

In the highest and best use scenario, the six-step market analysis process is used to analyze the future timing and volume of demand for a specific use. This process is then applied to a variety of uses identified as financially feasible in the highest and best use analysis to determine the use that generates the highest present value. Accordingly, the six-step process is repeated for each identified use with a supported supply and demand forecast unique to each use being tested. This results in a comprehensive analysis for a property in search of a highest and best use.

In most appraisal assignments, the existing use is being appraised or a specific proposed use is being evaluated. In this case, the market analysis six-step process is applied to the specific use to be considered in the appraisal. The use is tested against the maximally productive criteria. After the use satisfies the criteria as the highest and best use, the primary function of the six-step process is to support application of the three approaches to value.

In the appraisal of a specific property, market analysis must show how the interaction of supply and demand affects the property's value. Through the investigation of sales transactions, offerings, listings, and the behavior of market participants for other subdivision properties, an appraiser can ascertain supply and demand relationships and investigate the reasoning behind the prices paid for lot or subdivision projects. If current market conditions do not indicate adequate demand for a particular property, the market analysis may identify the point in time when adequate demand for the project will likely emerge.

Market analysis flows from the overall market for a specific market segment to a specific property and its capture of that market demand. When a specific property is the focus of the analysis, the term *marketability analysis* is used. At the beginning of the market analysis process, the appraiser must clearly identify the real estate product and the real estate market in which the project competes. In nearly all subdivision valuation, this is not a national or state market. Typically, the analysis considers a local market or submarket as the primary focus of the analysis. This

absorption
In subdivision analysis, the process whereby lots or units in a subdivision are sold off.

absorption rate
In subdivision analysis, the rate of sales of lots or units in a subdivision. See also **capture rate**.

absorption period
The actual or expected period required from the time a property, group of properties, or commodity is initially offered for lease, purchase, or use by its eventual users until all portions have been sold or stabilized occupancy has been achieved.

capture rate
The percentage of total market demand a specific property or group of properties is expected to capture, which is derived by comparing the competitive attributes of the specific property to the attributes of all the competitive properties in the area; also called market share.

sell-out
To dispose of entirely by sale.

is accomplished as part of the review of the development plan, governmental restrictions, and subdivision marketing concept. These property-specific components are then compared with the surrounding market to determine the economic environment and status of supply and demand as it relates specifically to the subject project. By analyzing the characteristics and attributes of the real estate project, the appraiser can identify competitive properties that constitute the applicable market. Defining the real estate market for the subject property clearly enhances the appraiser's understanding of how externalities affect the property. Through market analysis, the appraiser breaks down a specific real estate market into consumer submarkets or market segments. The submarket is evaluated within the context of the proposed marketing concept for the subject project, which identifies the price points for the subdivision and the price points and location of competing product inventory. The ultimate goal is to forecast a supportable absorption estimate for the subject property based on the supply and demand at the point in time when the project lot inventory enters the market.

Before undertaking the marketability study, the appraiser accurately defines the price points, the mix of units and their attributes, and supporting amenities in the subject subdivision. This establishes the marketing concept for the project. Once the characteristics and position of the subject property within the market are quantified, the comparison begins.

To measure the market support for a property, the analyst must identify the competitive supply and demand in the subject real estate market both now and in the future. This relationship indicates the degree of equilibrium or disequilibrium that characterizes the present market and the conditions likely to characterize the market over the forecast period. This analysis supports the absorption forecast for a group of existing lots or a proposed subdivision project. For subdivision valuation, especially for a proposed project, this would usually be as of the *when complete* date, which is a future point in time. The absorption would begin as of the *when complete* date and continues throughout the eventual sale of the subdivision lot inventory. The relationship between supply and demand is considered as part of the subject "capture" estimate and may vary over the absorption period.

The Six-Step Market Analysis Process

In appraisal practice, two general methods are used to make current and future forecasts concerning value, absorption, or other market conditions: inferred analysis and fundamental analysis. These methods are related, and fundamental analysis includes all of the components of inferred analysis plus future forecasting using economic base analysis. Both methods use the six-step process to arrive at a market-supported absorption forecast.

The six-step process is designed to answer the following questions:

- What attributes does the subject property offer the market?
- Who are the most likely users of these attributes?
- Is the property use needed? (demand analysis)
- What is the competition? (supply analysis)
- What is the condition of the market? (comparing supply and demand)
- How much of this market can the subject capture?

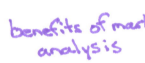
benefits of market analysis

It is impossible to estimate the market value of a property without considering the supply of and demand for the property within a specific time frame. This is especially critical for proposed subdivision projects. Market analysis links value theory and valuation techniques and documents the supply and demand relationship on which the value estimate is based. Market analysis is also used to identify which use among alternative uses the market supports, and thus helps determine the highest and best use of a property.

The six-step market analysis process for appraisal is summarized in Exhibit 2.1.

Step 1. Property Productivity Analysis (Determine the Product)

The appraiser begins the market analysis by investigating the legal, physical, and locational attributes of the subject subdivision. This involves defining the market segment consistent with the subject marketing concept and recognizing the multiple price points or product mix within the project. Mixed-use projects would require a separate study for each property type (i.e., office, apartment, single-unit residential, etc.). Most of this information is already available from the property analysis performed as part of the initial property data collection and analysis for the subject project. The subject marketing concept and other characteristics are ranked in terms of their desirability in comparison with competing projects. In many cases, the property has already gone through the zoning and plan review process with the local planning department and has received a specific site plan approval with full entitlements. However, if a highest and best use analysis is required as part of the analysis (which is required for most appraisals), then the analysis of alternative price points and marketing concepts other than the proposed plan is required. The

Exhibit 2.1
The Six-Step Market Analysis Process

Step 1. PROPERTY PRODUCTIVITY ANALYSIS (Determine the Product)
    A. Physical attributes
    B. Legal and regulatory attributes
        1. Private
        2. Public
    C. Location attributes
        1. Identification of economic attributes - the association between land uses and their linkages
        2. Identification of the movement of demand in relation to the direction of urban growth

Step 2. DELINEATE THE MARKET (Determine the Market)
    A. Market area delineation concepts
        1. Identification of demand sources and their location
        2. Area over which equally desirable substitute properties tend to compete with the subject
    B. Consumer profile concepts
        1. Identification of characteristics of most probable user
        2. Segmentation of consumer groups

Step 3. DEMAND ANALYSIS (Measure Demand)
    A. Inferred demand forecast
        Forecast demand based on historical growth and absorption data
    B. Fundamental demand forecast
        Submarket-specific demand forecast
        Major demand drivers
        1. Population creates households.
        2. Income creates retail buying power.
        3. Employment creates office/industrial users.

Step 4. SUPPLY ANALYSIS (Measure Competition)
    A. Existing stock of competitive properties
    B. Properties under construction
    C. Potential competition
        1. Proposed construction
        2. Probable additional construction
    D. Attributes and characteristics of competitive properties
        1. Economic and financial
        2. Locational
        3. Site
        4. Structure

Step 5. MARKET CONDITION ANALYSIS (Determine Market Environment)
    A. Residual demand studies and forecast (compare supply to demand over time)
    B Market cycle concepts (analyze the interaction of supply and demand)

Step 6. SUBJECT MARKETABILITY ANALYSIS (Determine Market Capture)
    A. Inferred capture methods
        Comparison of subject to general market indicators
        · Comparable property data
        · Secondary data surveys and forecasts
        · Subject historical performance
        · Local economic analysis
        · Other
    B. Fundamental capture methods
        Estimate subject capture potential of fundamental demand forecast by methods such as:
        · Share of market
        · Adjust by quantifiable rating techniques
        · Subject historical capture rate
        · Other
    C. Reconcile subject capture indications derived by analysis of inferred and fundamental methods (market penetration concepts)

USE OF STUDY PROCESS (SIX-STEP) CONCLUSIONS
    · Economic demand data for financial testing of highest and best use alternatives
    · Economic demand data for the valuation models

Source: Stephen F. Fanning, *Market Analysis for Real Estate: Concepts and Applications in Valuation and Highest and Best Use*, 2nd ed. (Chicago: Appraisal Institute, 2014), 15.

project as proposed may or may not be the highest and best use of the property. If it is not the highest and best use, hopefully it is within a group of financially feasible uses for the site. Also, it is entirely possible that the site could have multiple layouts and price point configurations that could have a similar present value.

Defining the product involves the following components:

- Physical attributes
- Legal and regulatory attributes
    - Private
    - Public
- Location attributes
    - Identification of economic attributes—the association between land uses and their linkages
    - Identification of the movement of demand in relation to the direction of urban growth

Step 2. Delineate the Market

Step 2 of the market analysis process is the delineation of the property users with a focus on the specific marketing area of the subject project. Typically, this would be the same area where homebuyers would shop for a home with the same characteristics as the property being appraised. This step involves identifying the neighborhood or group of neighborhoods that make up the primary competing market. The appraiser also identifies the characteristics of the likely users (i.e., owner or renter, occupational profile, and income level), which indicate the likely users' ability to afford housing within specific price points. This step begins the segmenting process by targeting subject-specific submarket demand characteristics. Location and time-distance linkages are studied to determine the locational attributes of the subject project within the market area. The subject project is ranked with competing subdivisions in the area. Most of this information is contained in the neighborhood and market area analysis in an appraisal report, which is discussed in detail in Chapter 3.

Step 2 involves the following components:

- Market area delineation concepts
    - Time-distance relationships and standards
    - Area over which equally desirable substitute properties tend to compete with the subject
- Market delineation techniques
    - Gravity models
    - Customer spotting

- Market delineation by location of consumers and demographic data
- Market delineation by substitute properties

Step 3. Demand Analysis

In Step 3 of the market analysis process, the appraiser estimates or measures existing and anticipated market demand by examining population growth (historical and future estimates) and household demand. The analysis can start with the projected population level and estimated household growth using average household size. Alternatively, the analysis can start at the household demand level if household growth information is available. New household demand over time is quantified and the subject segment criterion is applied. Typically, subdivision analysis uses housing type (owner-occupied vs. renter-occupied) as one segmentation factor. The ability to pay (income level) is often the second segmentation factor. The objective is to transition from aggregate population growth and/or household demand for all unit types to demand for the subject-specific unit type. For example, if the subject project is targeting the high-end residential market, the segmentation criteria would define the percentage of homebuyers in the high-end price range. The income level must match the marketing concept and targeted price range of the subject project. The last component of demand analysis is the consideration of frictional vacancy. If appropriate, the appraiser adjusts the market segment demand for frictional vacancy. The goal of this step is an estimate of "new demand" for the subject unit type for the foreseeable future.

[annotation: growth factors]

Demand analysis includes

- Demand segmentation
  - Identification of the characteristics of the most probable user (consumer profile)
  - Tastes and preferences: behavioral, motivational, and psychological factors
- Inferred demand analysis
  - Analysis of historical growth and absorption data
- Fundamental demand forecast
  - Submarket-specific demand forecast
  - Major demand drivers
    * Population creates households
    * Income creates retail buying power
    * Employment creates office/industrial users

Step 4. Supply Analysis

Step 4 provides an inventory of existing competition and a forecast of new competition to emerge in the immediate future. The timing of future competition is considered in Step 5, in which the current status of market supply and demand for the subject unit type is evaluated. Future supply is difficult to quantify and may be researched by studying recent zoning and/or development applications by subdivision developers and the pattern of historical new project development in the area.

[margin note: future analysis]

Supply analysis involves the following components:

- Existing stock of competitive properties
- Properties under construction
- Potential competition
    - Proposed construction
    - Probable additional construction
- Attributes and characteristics of competitive properties
    - Economic and financial
    - Locational
    - Site
    - Structure

Step 5. Market Condition Analysis

Step 5 is an analysis of the interaction of supply and demand, also known as *residual demand and supply analysis*. In this step, supply and demand are compared over time to determine the status of the market now and at any given time period in the future. When demand exactly equals supply, the market is in equilibrium. This is rarely the case in real estate markets; usually at any given time the market is experiencing oversupply or pent-up demand.

Step 5 involves the following components:

- Residual demand studies and forecasts (compare supply to demand over time)
- Market cycle concepts (analyze the interaction of supply and demand)

Step 6. Subject Marketability Analysis (Forecast Subject Capture)

Step 6 of market analysis results in a property-specific estimate of market capture considering the subject-specific property attributes and the market that it is designed to serve. The property may be a pioneer project with no competing subdivisions or may be comparable to identifiable competitive projects. If the subject project is described as "about average" in terms of its competitive desirability, then it should "capture" its pro rata share of available supply. A superior rating for location, amenities, or other factors may result in a higher capture. Conversely, a marginal location or marketing concept can impair market acceptance and result in a lower capture forecast. Obviously, the capture rate can vary over the absorption period, depending on the overall status of market supply and demand (residual analysis) at any given period of time.

} capture rate

Step 6 involves the following components:

- Inferred capture methods:
  - Comparison of the subject to general market indicators
    * Comparable property data
    * Secondary data surveys and forecasts
    * Subject historical performance
    * Local economic analysis and expectations of market participants
    * Other
- Fundamental capture methods:
  - Estimate subject capture potential of fundamental demand forecast by methods such as
    * Share of market
    * Adjustment by quantifiable rating techniques
    * Subject historical capture rate
    * Other
- Reconciliation of subject capture indications derived by analysis of inferred and fundamental methods

Levels of Market Analysis

The level of market analysis undertaken in an appraisal is determined by the nature of the assignment and the specific problem confronting the appraiser. Once the intended use, intended users, and property-specific data are identified, the appraiser will select a level of market analysis appropriate to the problem. An appraisal should include a market analysis component that not only fulfills regulatory requirements but also complements the application of the appraisal process. Market analysis using the six-step process can be taken to four different levels, as shown in Exhibit 2.2.

The two inferred analysis levels are Levels A and B. More comprehensive forecasting methods are applied in the fundamental Levels C and D. As the level of analysis increases from A

Exhibit 2.2
Levels of Market Study in Appraisal

Level of Study	Inferred Demand Studies		Fundamental Demand Studies	
	A	B	C	D
Step 1:	Inferred subject attributes		Quantified subject attributes	
Step 2:	Inferred locational determinants of use and marketability by macroanalysis		Quantified and graphic analysis of location determinants of use and marketability by macro and microanalysis	
Step 3:	Inferred demand from general economic base analysis conducted by others; inferred demand by selected comparables		Inferred demand derived by original economic base analysis	
Step 4:	Inferred supply by selected comparables		Quantified supply by inventorying existing and forecasting planned competition	
Steps 5 and 6:	Inferred equilibrium/highest and best use and capture conclusions		Quantified equilibrium - Highest and best use—graphic/map - Timing—quantified capture forecast	
	Emphasis is on: - Instinctive knowledge - Historical data - Judgment		**Emphasis is on:** - Quantifiable data - Forecast - Judgment	

Note: An appraisal without a fundamental demand study (i.e., Levels C and D) is designed to estimate value only in a stable market.

[A — Least detailed]
[D — Very detailed]

to D, each succeeding level includes all of the components of the previous levels.

Inferred Analysis

Inferred analysis is simply the use of historical market evidence, current market trends, and expectations of market participants in the application of the six-step process. These analysis methods, which are described as Levels A and B in Exhibit 2.2, identify trends and patterns and infer expected market behavior. This analysis includes the study of comparable sales for retail lot value estimates and the use of historical absorption trends as a basis for concluding market absorption. Current market expectations based on interviews with participants and stakeholders in the market can provide insight into future expectations. Also, the pattern of lot presales in a market can provide some evidence of market demand expectations. Essentially, inferred analysis describes most of the primary data collection and analysis efforts performed and considered by the appraiser in a typical appraisal assignment. As applied in subdivision analysis and specifically the absorption estimate, inferred analysis usually involves the direct comparison of the subject project with the recent sales volume or absorption experience of competing subdivisions. This study can be done on a subdivision-specific level or on an overall macro-market level. The goal is to determine or estimate a market-supported absorption or sell-out period for the subject unit or lot inventory. The basic steps followed in inferred demand analysis are very similar to the steps used in the sales comparison approach for the selection and analysis of comparable sales.

The appraiser surveys the appropriate market area and selects a group of comparable subdivision projects to use for comparison purposes. These projects should be marketing lots in the same general price range as the subject project, have the same or similar marketing concept and project amenities, and have a history of market absorption or sales. Projects that have recently achieved full sell-out can also be used.

inferred analysis is almost the same as sales comparison approach

Next, the appraiser analyzes and quantifies the observed absorption pattern (e.g., lots per month) for each project, identifies market trends, and concludes market absorption for the subject product category. Then the appraiser determines if any additional features in the subject project or comparable projects require consideration and makes appropriate adjustments in the absorption estimate for the subject project. For example, a comparable subdivision marketing homes at several different price points would probably support a different absorption level than a project with only one price point.

Then the appraiser considers the current supply and demand characteristics as they relate to past trends and comparable projects, reconciles market capture and absorption for the subject project, and forecasts the future absorption period. This would involve consideration of any new projects that may be coming on line in the near future and the timing of any future competition. Also, the absorption estimate may vary on a seasonal basis or in some other way during the sell-off period.

Inferred demand analysis tends to be the most accurate for projects with a relatively short absorption period (less than two to three years) and projects that are relatively small in comparison to the overall market. This type of analysis is especially accurate in stable markets with minimal fluctuations. The application of inferred analysis also relies heavily on current and relevant sales information.

small/short = inferred

Fundamental Analysis

Fundamental demand analysis begins with inferred analysis but goes beyond the inferred trend analysis level by forecasting demand based on the segmentation of broad demographic and economic data to reflect the specific subject market. This market analysis follows the same six-step process and is described as a Level C or D study in Exhibit 2.2.

Fundamental demand analysis tends to be most applicable to projects with relatively long absorption periods (greater than two

long/big = fundamental

Market Analysis 41

to three years) and projects that are relatively large in comparison with the overall market. This type of analysis can be valuable in emerging markets that are driven by new population growth. Fundamental demand analysis relies heavily on accurate population and/or household growth data and, like inferred analysis, generally assumes that past patterns will be a determinant of future demand.

Inferred and fundamental demand methods are not separate, mutually exclusive techniques. Essentially, the fundamental methods are extensions of inferred demand analysis. A more detailed description of the six-step process and the levels of market analysis can be found in *Market Analysis for Real Estate: Concepts and Applications in Valuation and Highest and Best Use*, second edition.[1]

The results from both the inferred and fundamental demand methods are reconciled into a final absorption forecast for the subject project. An example of absorption forecasting using both the inferred and fundamental demand methods is presented in the following section.

Selecting the Appropriate Level of Analysis

The level of analysis to be employed in an appraisal depends on regulatory requirements, client needs, prevailing market conditions, property complexity, and whether the property is proposed or existing. The level of market analysis performed should match the level of information a client needs to reach a decision. This need is reviewed with the client as part of the scope of work criteria. The appraisal may be viewed as a service to help reduce (but not eliminate) risk for the client and the public. Larger proposed projects and new marketing concepts may have greater potential risk, where a more intensive level of analysis is required. Regulatory requirements include USPAP, which requires sufficient market analysis in appraisals to support the use determination and the estimate of value.

In a market characterized by stability or equilibrium, a less intensive analysis may meet the client's needs. A stable or balanced market usually exhibits three features: a steady number of sales in the recent past, the absence of overbuilding or a supply shortage, and available public studies documenting market equilibrium. If these conditions exist, a Level A or B analysis may be acceptable. Otherwise, the more detailed Level C and D fundamental methods should be employed.

---

1. Stephen F. Fanning, *Market Analysis for Real Estate: Concepts and Applications in Valuation and Highest and Best Use*, 2nd ed. (Chicago: Appraisal Institute, 2014).

The level of market analysis also varies with the type and size of the property. For an appraisal of an existing group of lots in a successful ongoing subdivision project with a recent history of sustained market absorption in a stable market, a Level A or B analysis may be appropriate. Risk is typically related to project size and the number of lots being appraised. Small projects or groups of lots usually have shorter marketing periods. Large projects or a large lot inventory typically require a longer absorption time period and can be subject to more market and timing risks. A more detailed market analysis is required with a minimum of a Level C market study.

Inferred demand analysis tends to be most accurate for relatively small projects with relatively short absorption periods (less than two to three years). This type of analysis is especially accurate in stable markets with minimal fluctuations. The application of inferred analysis also relies heavily on current, relevant sales information (see Exhibits 2.5, 2.6, and 2.7).

The most unique aspect of fundamental demand analysis is that it attempts to pinpoint where future demand will come from as well as its timing and quantity. Inferred analysis, on the other hand, generally surmises that all else being equal, future growth will follow the same pattern as historical trends. Both methods are important valuation tools.

Market Analysis in Appraisal and Reporting

Market analysis is conducted throughout the appraisal process. Step 1, defining the product, is an analysis of the physical, legal, and locational attributes of the subject property. In this step, the physical and functional qualities of the site and its size, configuration, access, topography, zoning, available utilities, and improvements are analyzed. This study is sometimes referred to as *defining the product* or *property productivity analysis* and is typically found in the site and improvement description sections of an appraisal report. Information relating to Step 2, market delineation, is typically found in the market area analysis or neighborhood analysis section of an appraisal report. The remaining steps in the six-step process are usually presented in a separate market analysis section of the report just before the highest and best use conclusion. Alternatively, all six steps may be presented in a separate section of the report.

When reporting the results of the market area analysis in an appraisal report, one of two general paths can be taken. One method would be to have a stand-alone market analysis section in the report. This section would include all six steps and would typically come just before the highest and best use analysis section of the report. Inherently, this section will repeat much of the information that has already been developed in the neighborhood and area analysis as well as the site and improvement description sections of the report.

The second method is to develop data and analysis for the six-step market analysis process from the start of the appraisal report, especially the data required for Steps 1 and 2. The remaining Steps 3 through 6 are then reported in a market analysis section just before the highest and best use section or possibly as part of the absorption estimate in the income capitalization approach section. This second method is more efficient because it does not repeat information from Steps 1 and 2 that is presented earlier in the report.

The most important concern is that all six steps and their related components are considered and included in the analysis.

Absorption Forecasting

Absorption forecasting is an analysis of the time frame needed for the market to absorb the inventory of existing or proposed lots to end users. It provides a subject-specific estimate for the sell-out of all lots included in the value estimate. The absorption estimate is made at the conclusion of the market analysis six-step process, when the subject capture rate is applied to new annual demand over the future forecast period or estimated directly from market sales.

For a group of existing lots, the absorption period usually begins at time period zero. For proposed projects, the absorption period begins when the subdivision is 100% built and is a future estimate. For example, a subdivision with construction beginning in January and a six-month construction period will start absorption at the beginning of the seventh month. Lot values and market absorption are estimated at that point in time and are projected into the future. The absorption estimate may or may not reflect any presale contracts, depending on the purpose of the appraisal and whether or not the client wants presale contracts to be considered.

The absorption period is usually described in terms of the number of lots or units to be sold on a monthly, quarterly, semi-annual, or annual basis, depending on the size of the project and the level of detail needed to support the analysis or reveal any seasonal trends in the market data. A small group of lots with a typical absorption of less than one or two years may be expressed on a monthly or quarterly basis. Generally, the longer the absorption period, the greater the time frames considered. The market absorption study concludes with a market-supported estimate of lot absorption and the time period required for the market to completely absorb the vacant lot inventory—e.g., the absorption time required to sell the inventory to eventual end users. (Refer to the definition of *absorption period* at the beginning of this chapter.)

The absorption study for a proposed subdivision or a group of existing lots usually begins with a review of the information available to complete a minimum Level B inferred analysis. For a very small group of lots, it may be possible to support the absorption conclusion adequately using a Level A analysis. However, for proposed development, the minimum level of analysis required is usually a Level C market study that introduces fundamental demand analysis into the supply and demand forecast.

Rationale for Measuring Absorption

Absorption forecasting is an easy concept to understand, but it can be a very difficult appraisal problem. The question of when a vacant lot is absorbed arises. The definition of *absorption period* specifically defines the time period as starting at the initial offering of the lots and ending when all the lots are sold to end users. More importantly, it is an estimate of the time frame needed to market the inventory to the eventual end users. This has an impact on the absorption analysis, especially in markets where lots are not typically sold to end users and instead are sold in groups to home builders who build speculative homes and/or custom homes for the eventual end users. Keep in mind that sales to builders can skew the absorption period estimate.

Subdivision developments can employ a wide range of marketing strategies that may include

- "Closed" developments in which one builder/developer uses all of the lots and only sells completed homes to eventual end users
- "Open" developments in which the subdivision developer sells lots to anyone who wants to purchase a lot, including homeowners or home builders
- A strategy in which the developer sells lots only to a small group of selected home builders and the home builders sell homes to end users
- A strategy in which a developer builds the subdivision and then sells all the lots in bulk immediately after construction to one purchaser or group of home builders who then eventually sell completed homes or lots to end users
- A strategy in which a developer builds the subdivision and then sells lots in groups over time to a group of selected home builders with "take down" or other purchase contracts

The difficulty arises when groups of lots are sold to individual builders or the developer has most of the lots pre-sold to builders or investment groups rather than eventual end users. When sale absorption statistics from these projects are used as part of the inferred absorption analysis, the results can reflect a level of absorption that is substantially different from the normal or typical absorption to end users developed by market analysis as part of the six-step process. In this case, the appraiser may place a greater weight on absorption forecasts from the population-based fundamental demand analysis than the inferred analysis indication. The final criterion is the sales velocity or absorption to eventual end users. For convenience, the demand forecast supported by the six steps is referred to as the "fundamental demand" or "fundamental forecast" in the following examples in this book.

This complication does not prevent the appraiser from reporting several value conclusions in the appraisal report. The initial valuation is made using the typical "end user" absorption criteria and labeled as "market value" within the appraisal. Depending on the needs of the client, additional values can be reported considering presale contracts or any take-down sales agreements. However, these values are not reported as market value; they are conditional values, and the specific valuation premise or scenario must be clearly communicated in the appraisal.

Mill Pond Case Study: Absorption Estimate

The following case study provides an example of a Level C inferred and fundamental demand analysis applied in the appraisal of a proposed subdivision project. The case study property is the Mill Pond Subdivision, which is a proposed subdivision containing 76 lots. This subdivision will be used to illustrate the application of the three approaches to value in Chapters 7, 8, and 9. The case study also provides the absorption period estimate used in the income capitalization analysis.

In this case study, the current date is the point in time when site construction begins. The project has a six-month construction period. The *when complete* date is six months in the future, which is also the date of valuation. Accordingly, the date of value is a prospective date that is six months in the future at the point in time when the subdivision is 100% built–i.e., the *when complete* date.

Exhibit 2.3 provides a summary of the subdivision characteristics. This subdivision will be marketing lots at two price points. The project has a total of 76 lots with a mix of 40 small lots and 36 large lots. The small lots average 8,700 square feet, with a typical width of about 80 front feet. The large lots have an average lot size of 11,000 square feet, with a width of 100 front feet. The marketing concept and price points targeted for the project must be known to estimate lot values accurately within the subdivision development. The marketing concept for this project provides for two separate price points consistent with the associated lot sizes. The small lots support an overall price range for the completed home and lot "package" from a low of about $140,000 to a high of $200,000, with an average of $170,000. The large lots support a single-unit price range from a low of $180,000 to a high of about $220,000, with an average of about $200,000. While this is an appraisal of the vacant subdivision lots, the home price points are needed to accurately determine the vacant lot values.

After the physical, economic, and legal characteristics of the proposed project are defined, the next step in inferred analysis is to survey the market for comparable projects. These projects will be used to develop the absorption estimate and to assist in the retail lot value estimate for proposed lots in the subject project.

Exhibit 2.3
Mill Pond Subdivision Project Data

Project Timing

Current date:	1/1/2018
Construction start:	1/1/2018
Construction period:	6 months
Absorption start date:	7/1/2018

Lot Summary

	Lots	%	Lot Size Sq. Ft.	Lot Size Fr. Ft.
Small lots	40	52.6%	8,700	80
Large lots	36	47.4%	11,000	100
Total	76	100.0%		

Price Points
(Package price for home and lot)

	Low	Average	High
Small lots	$140,000	$170,000	$200,000
Large lots	$180,000	$200,000	$220,000

Inferred Market Data

See Exhibits 2.4 and 2.5 for analysis summary.

Exhibits 2.4 and 2.5 summarize the information obtained in the inferred analysis for the subject subdivision project. Inferred analysis is essentially a critical review of comparable projects in the area to determine the price levels supported within each project in light of the various marketing concepts. The velocity of lot sales in each project will be used as a basis for estimating future absorption for the subject subdivision. Once these absorp-

Exhibit 2.4
Inferred Analysis Market Survey

Comparable Projects	Single-Unit Price Range		
	Low	High	Average
1. Kensington	$107,900	$223,400	$160,008
2. Hyde Park	$131,300	$285,773	$188,999
3. St. James Park	$138,704	$188,594	$153,054
4. Baywater	$104,000	$250,731	$167,713
5. Chelsea Lane	$195,000	$325,000	$250,000
6. Nine Elms	$124,000	$173,200	$142,852
7. Lupus Road	$155,000	$190,270	$168,932
Analysis			
Low	$104,000	$173,200	$142,852
High	$195,000	$325,000	$250,000
Average	$136,558	$233,853	$175,937

Inferred Market Data Overview

The 7 subdivisions used for comparison represent a subset of the total subdivisions in the subject's market area. These were the only subdivisions marketing lots in the subject's price range in 2017. In this market, there are typically 7-10 subdivisions marketing lots in the targeted price range for the subject project at any given time. The average project size is about 100 lots per subdivision. This trend is more or less expected to continue for the foreseeable future.

---

tion levels have been quantified, existing competitive supply and probable future competition are reviewed to ascertain the supply and demand in the market at the time of the appraisal and the future absorption period for the subject project.

A search of comparable sales in the subject market area determined that there were seven subdivisions marketing homes in the same targeted price range as the subject project. Information on these subdivisions is summarized in Exhibit 2.4.

The results of the comparable absorption analysis are shown in Exhibit 2.5. The pattern of historical absorption for each project is analyzed on a quarterly basis. All of the subdivisions with small lots have two price points. The three projects used for the large lot comparison have a single price-point category. More price points in a project generally means higher market absorption because lots and/or units are being sold over a wider economic range and the project appeals to a broader market segment.

At any given time, most markets have subdivisions that are just starting their initial absorption, subdivisions that are in the middle of their absorption periods, and subdivisions in which the last lots are being sold. The absorption is typically analyzed from the point when the first lot is sold to the point when the last lot is sold, and may include the effect of presales as part of the absorption analysis. For example, it may be common to have an initial burst of lot sales during the initial marketing of the project; these are presale contracts within the development that

Exhibit 2.5
Inferred Absorption Analysis

Project	Price Points	Total Lots	2015 Q1	2015 Q2	2015 Q3	2015 Q4	2016 Q1	2016 Q2	2016 Q3	2016 Q4	2017 Q1	2017 Q2	2017 Q3	2017 Q4	Total Sales	Remaining Lot Inventory	Average Lots/Quarter
Small Lots - Multiple Price Points																	
1. Kensington	2	145				11	21	18	9	11	23	16	11	12	132	13	14.7
2. Hyde Park	2	64					22	16	12	14					64	0	16.0
4. Baywater	2	112								14	25	18	13	9	79	33	15.8
5. Chelsea Lane	2	115				7	18	14	8	9	21	17	9	12	115	0	12.8
Totals		436	0	0	0	18	61	48	29	48	69	51	33	33	390	46	59.3
Average		109	n/a	n/a	n/a	9	20	16	10	12	23	17	11	11			14.8
Large Lots - Single Price Point																	
3. St. James Park	1	38										7	5		12	26	6.0
6. Nine Elms	1	62	10	9	5	8	11	8	6	5					62	0	7.8
7. Lupus Road	1	48									12	9	9	6	36	12	9.0
Totals		148	10	9	5	8	11	8	6	5	12	9	16	11	110	38	22.8
Average		49	10	9	5	8	11	8	6	5	12	9	8	6			7.6

are "closed" at the start of the absorption period and may or may not involve end users. If this is common in the subject market, then presale absorption should be considered part of the absorption forecast for the proposed subdivision. Examples involving presales contracts are presented in Chapter 7.

However, some clients (especially lending clients) may require a corollary analysis, and two separate forecasts are required for the subject subdivision—one considering presales and one based on a typical sell-out scenario considering the fundamental absorption forecast to end users without consideration of presales. This is common when presales involve home builders and not individual end users. In this case, it may be appropriate to provide two different sell-out scenarios. One value would be labeled as "market value ignoring presales" and the other would be labeled as "market value considering presale contracts." Any lot presales are typically analyzed at the actual presale price and considering the exact timing of the lot sales scheduled in the contracts.

The ultimate goal of absorption forecast is to provide an estimate of the time period needed to market the lot inventory of the subject project to eventual end users. The appraiser also analyzes market sales to determine if any trends in the analysis must be considered for the subject property. For example, the absorption histories of the seven subdivisions used for comparison purposes indicate that there are seasonal trends in lot absorption for most of the subdivision projects. There are typically more lot sales in the first and second quarters of each year and fewer sales in Quarters 3 and 4. In this market there appears to be a definite seasonal trend. The first two quarters generate a higher absorption than the

Market Analysis

remaining two quarters in each year. This seasonal trend should be considered in the absorption forecast for the subject project.

The periodicity used for the absorption forecast depends on project size, price points, and trends within the marketplace. Typically, absorption is analyzed either on a monthly, quarterly, semi-annual, or annual basis. The time periods used are often selected to explain or reveal any seasonal trends like those observed in Exhibit 2.5. If this same analysis were done on an annual basis, the seasonal trend would probably be lost in the analysis and not revealed over the longer forecast period. For this reason, it is imperative to perform a sensitivity analysis to reveal any trends within the absorption forecast that should be considered in the analysis.

The level of analysis required for the absorption study depends on the scale of the project in comparison with the overall market and the available market data. In this example, the subject subdivision is a relatively small 76-lot project in an active market area where 7 to 10 projects are competing in this price category at any given time. If this was a stable market where population trends and/or growth were expected to continue for the foreseeable future, then the inferred demand analysis by itself would most likely be sufficient to support the absorption estimate for the subject property. The comparable subdivisions were used to quantify historical absorption in the subject market for the price points found in the subject project. This information is then compared with the available supply in the subject market segment to make an absorption forecast for the subject project. This forecast would be supported by the inferred supply and demand analysis.

The subject market capture is estimated by studying the historical trends from the inferred analysis as well as by reviewing current competing projects and probable future supply in the market.

Expanding the analysis would include consideration of the fundamental supply and demand aspects and constitute a Level C market analysis of the subject project. A fundamental demand analysis is typically employed when the scale of the project is relatively large in comparison to the overall market and the absorption typically takes place over a longer marketing period. A fundamental analysis would also be required in areas where there is more volatility in the market with respect to population growth trends and subdivision development absorption patterns.

Fundamental analysis includes consideration of population growth and/or household growth. The underlying goal is to determine where growth is coming from in the market and the magnitude and timing of growth in the future. The analysis starts with a study of basic demographic information in the subject's market area. The market data is then segmented to reflect the appropriate price points and marketing concept characteristic of the subject project.

Exhibits 2.6 through 2.9 provide an elementary fundamental demand analysis for the subject market area. As part of the fundamental analysis, population growth over time is considered to make a future demand forecast. The demand forecast is tailored to the subject market segment (which in this case is single-unit residential) and the economic segment (price points) within the subject project. Once the demand has been quantified over time, future subdivision supply is also analyzed to forecast the residual supply and demand characteristics for the subject submarket. Essentially, the residual demand analysis is made to determine the status of supply and demand in the immediate future. The information in Exhibit 2.6 is applied in the fundamental demand analysis grid in Exhibit 2.7.

The data needed to perform the fundamental demand analysis is shown in Exhibit 2.6. The first two steps of the market analysis process are described in detail in Chapters 3 and 4. Chapter 3 provides a discussion of the determinants used to define the market area and includes a location-time-distance linkage example. Chapter 4 covers the site and improvements analysis in which the property

Exhibit 2.6
Mill Pond Subdivision Absorption Study

Property Productivity Analysis (for Steps 1 and 2)

Step 1: Conclusions

　The Mill Pond market area was determined and is the same geographic area used for the census population and supply data in Steps 3 and 4.

Step 2: Conclusions

　The market delineation defined the Mill Pond project as "average" in comparison with competing projects. Accordingly, it is expected to capture an appropriate pro rata share of new demand.

Fundamental Demand Data (for Steps 3 through 6)

Population:	Market area census population
	Year 2013 = 80,000
Population growth:	3% per year compounded
Household size:	2.15 persons
Single-unit ratio:	70.0%
Home market range:	Home prices of $140,000 to $220,000
Economic segment:	Lower middle economic segment
	30.0%
Frictional vacancy:	3%

Future Subdivision Projects:	Year	Projects	Number Lots
	2018	2	235
	2019	3	300
	2020	3	300
	2021	3	300
Vacant inventory beginning 2014:	100 lots ±		

Exhibit 2.7
Fundamental Demand Analysis

Description	2013	2014	2015	2016	2017	2018	2019	2020	2021
Population	80,000	82,400	84,872	87,418	90,041	92,742	95,524	98,390	101,342
Avg. household size	÷ 2.15	÷ 2.15	÷ 2.15	÷ 2.15	÷ 2.15	÷ 2.15	÷ 2.15	÷ 2.15	÷ 2.15
Households	37,209	38,326	39,475	40,660	41,880	43,136	44,430	45,763	47,136
New households		1,117	1,149	1,185	1,220	1,256	1,294	1,333	1,373
Single-unit ratio		× 0.70	× 0.70	× 0.70	× 0.70	× 0.70	× 0.70	× 0.70	× 0.70
New single-unit households		782	804	830	854	879	906	933	961
Subject economic segment		× 0.30	× 0.30	× 0.30	× 0.30	× 0.30	× 0.30	× 0.30	× 0.30
New households in subject segment		235	241	249	256	264	272	280	288
Adjustment for frictional vacancy 3%		÷ 0.97	÷ 0.97	÷ 0.97	÷ 0.97	÷ 0.97	÷ 0.97	÷ 0.97	÷ 0.97
New households in demand subject segment		242	248	257	264	272	280	289	297
Available Supply									
Existing vacant lots		-100	-58	90	84	148	185	165	154
Add: New projects (excluding subject)		– 200	– 100	– 263	– 200	– 235	– 300	– 300	– 300
Residual Demand/Supply		-58	90	84	148	185	165	154	151
Negative = oversupply									
Positive = pent-up demand									
Estimated Capture—Mill Pond						12.5%	11.0%	10.0%	10.0%
Lots per year (capture rate × new household demand)						34	31	29	30

Note: The residual demand/supply status each year is used to estimate subject capture. The capture rate is applied to new household demand.

Subject Capture Analysis

Number of projects						2018	2019	2020	2021
Old						5	5	6	6
New						2	3	3	3
Total						7	8	9	9
Subject pro rata share						12.5%	11.1%	10.0%	10.0%

productivity issues relating to site and improvements are analyzed to determine the relative desirability or "position" of a property in relation to current and future competition. For this example, the Mill Pond project is rated as average in comparison to competing projects in the subject market area, as shown in Exhibit 2.6.

The next data set needed is a supportable estimate of the population at a specific point in time and the future population growth in the subject market area. This is Step 3 of the market analysis process. Population information for most states and communities is readily available through government-sponsored research centers and published census data. The fundamental demand analysis can start either with population growth data or household unit data. The example in Exhibit 2.7 uses population as a starting point and estimates household growth using an average household size factor of 2.15. Household size data is regularly published along with population data and is easily obtained in most areas. If good household data is available with supportable household growth estimates, then the analysis can start with households and skip the population estimate. One of the most difficult aspects of working with population or household data is relating the data to the subject property's geographical market area. The subject's market area is often a subset of a larger area for which population or household data is available. There are many private demographic providers who can perform an analysis of population and households using concentric rings or other methods to obtain subject-specific geographical boundaries and relevant data.

The next two data sets in Exhibits 2.6 and 2.7 relate to subject segmentation criteria. They are the single-unit ratio of 70% and the lower-middle economic segment of 30%. Both of these criteria are also found in demographic data sources. Typically, the single-unit ratio is given in published governmental data sources or can be calculated from household occupancy characteristic data. This ratio tends to be consistent over a large geographical area, but some submarket fine-tuning may be necessary depending on the area of study.

The economic segment percentage is an estimate of the number of single-unit homebuyers in the economic segment directly related to the price points offered in the subject subdivision. In the Mill Pond project, the marketing concept calls for single-unit homes priced at $170,000 to $220,000 for the total home and lot package. It is common for governmental and private demographic sources to publish data on the housing market by home price range. In this case, the subject segment percentage can be taken directly from published data sources. If this data is not available, the economic segment percentage can also be calculated from household income data.

Using household income data, the typical monthly mortgage payment that meets the market underwriting criteria (27% of income in Exhibit 2.8) is used to calculate the ability to pay for new housing. Exhibit 2.8 delineates the household income segments for the subject market area from published demographic data. Typical loan underwriting criteria is used to establish the maximum mortgage payment for each level of household income. The mortgage terms are shown at the bottom of Exhibit 2.8. The mortgage payment information is then used to calculate the total amount of the mortgage supported at each monthly payment level. The mortgage amount is then divided by the loan-to-value ratio to establish the supported home price range for each household income segment. In this example, the subject subdivision is selling homes at prices that range from $170,000 to $220,000. Income segments D and E are supported at this price level and make up 30% of the total occupied housing in the subject market area. This percentage is used for the economic segment calculation in Exhibit 2.7.

Exhibit 2.8
Analysis of Potential New Homebuyers' Ability to Pay

Income Segment	Subject Market Area Household Income Range		Percent of Households	Monthly Mortgage Payment at 27% of Income			Supported Home Price Range at 85% Loan-to-Value Ratio		
	Low	High		Low	High	Average	Low	High	Average
A	Under $25,000		5.0%	$563		$563	$107,479	n/a	$107,479
B	$25,001 to	$30,000	3.0%	$563	$675	$619	$107,483	$128,974	$118,229
C	$30,001 to	$40,000	7.0%	$675	$900	$788	$128,979	$171,966	$150,472
D	$40,001 to	$50,000	13.0%	$900	$1,125	$1,013	$171,970	$214,957	$193,464
E	$50,001 to	$60,000	17.0%	$1,125	$1,350	$1,238	$214,962	$257,949	$236,455
F	$60,001 to	$70,000	17.0%	$1,350	$1,575	$1,463	$257,953	$300,940	$279,447
G	$70,001 to	$80,000	21.0%	$1,575	$1,800	$1,688	$300,945	$343,932	$322,438
H	$80,001 to	$95,000	9.0%	$1,800	$2,138	$1,969	$343,936	$408,419	$376,178
I	$95,001 to $105,000		6.0%	$2,138	$2,363	$2,250	$408,423	$451,410	$429,917
J	$105,001 and over		2.0%	$2,363		$2,363	$451,415	n/a	$451,415
Total			100.0%						

Mortgage terms are 6.25% interest, 30 years, monthly payments, with an 85% loan-to-value ratio.

The last adjustment criterion is frictional vacancy. This step recognizes that in a balanced market, some vacancy for move-ins, move-outs, and short-term growth is necessary to maintain unit prices at a competitive level.[2] Economists sometimes refer to normal vacancy as *frictional vacancy*, or as the *normal* or *balanced market vacancy*. New household demand is divided by 100% less the appropriate frictional vacancy level. The frictional vacancy is 3% in the case study, so new demand is divided by 0.97.

In subdivision valuation, some analysts do not use the frictional vacancy calculation. The rationale is that this forecast is to be used in a DCF analysis for valuation. In the market, the actual income to the developer of the lot or home is realized when the house is occupied or the lot is sold. Under this rationale, no frictional vacancy is applied. Alternatively, if cash to the developer is realized at the beginning of house construction and/or if

---

2. See pages 159-162 of *Market Analysis for Real Estate*, 2nd ed., for more detailed discussion of frictional vacancy.

speculative housing is typical, the additional demand created by frictional vacancy should be considered; thus, frictional vacancy would be considered in the analysis.

The objective of the fundamental demand analysis presented in Exhibit 2.7 is to determine when demand will occur in the future and the timing of that demand as it relates to the subject property. When appraising a group of existing lots or a proposed subdivision, the forecast considers determinants of future demand, competitive supply, and future supply to describe supply and demand in the foreseeable future. This is referred to as a "residual" demand and supply analysis.

In summary, Exhibit 2.7 provides an analysis of demand created by population growth. In this example, total population growth is divided by household size to estimate growth in the number of households. New household demand each year, quantified over the eight-year study period, ranges from 1,117 new households in 2014 to 1,373 new households in 2021. In this market, single-unit homes make up about 70% of total households. Applying this segmentation factor to overall demand for all households (single-unit, multiunit, mobile home, etc.) indicates the single-unit household growth over time (see Exhibit 2.7). The new demand for the single-unit sector is 782 households in 2014, increasing to 961 households per year in 2021.

The subject property is in the lower middle economic segment for the subject market area. Economic segmentation is essentially fine-tuning overall single-unit household demand to the specific economic segment for the proposed project. In this example, the project is in the lower-middle economic segments, which accounts for about 30% of total households in this market. Accordingly, 30% of overall single-unit household demand is applicable to the subject project. This ratio is usually determined by comparing the marketing concept and targeted price range for the subject project with the overall economic character of the subject market area. The typical mortgage loan required to purchase the property may be analyzed for the price range applicable to the subject project and compared with the income stratification for the subject marketing area to estimate this percentage.

Applying the frictional vacancy to the population forecast over time indicates a new household demand for the subject segment type of 242 units in 2014, which increases to 297 units in 2021. This new demand is then compared with the existing status of vacant lots available on the market and probable new construction that would occur over time. This part of the analysis is called the *residual demand and supply calculation*.

The intent of "residual" analysis is to determine the relative status of supply and demand over the eight-year projection period. In 2014, the market is oversupplied by 58 units. In 2015, there is new demand for 248 units, a vacant supply of 58 units, and 100 new units that have come online. Accordingly, there is an ample demand for the available units, and the market has a pent-up demand for 90 units that has not been satisfied. Most markets tend toward equilibrium over time, but rarely are supply and demand exactly at equilibrium in real estate markets. Year 2016 also shows a slight pent-up demand, which continues through 2021. The subject project is anticipated to enter the market in 2018. Application of a pro rata share model results in a capture ratio of about 12.5% in 2018, 11.0% in 2019, and 10.0% in 2020 and 2021. The pro rata share model indicates that the subject project would receive its equal share of capture among new competing projects in the area.

For example, if there are 9 competing projects, there are 10 total projects including the subject subdivision. In the pro rata model, each project would receive about 10% of new demand. The capture estimate is made considering project amenities and the marketing concept of the subject property. The subject property may have a superior location, amenities, or other elements, which could generate a higher market share in comparison with the average product in the market. These property-specific characteristics are considered as part of the capture estimate for the subject property. Conversely, the subject property may have inferior amenities and may be expected to achieve a lower absorption than a typical pro rata allocation.

The greatest strength of fundamental analysis is that it provides a supportable estimate of demand over time based on population and/or household growth in a given market area. Also, this analysis addresses the timing of supply and demand, which is integral in estimating market capture and unit absorption over time. It should be recognized, however, that the information used for fundamental demand analysis tends to be based on historical trends, similar to the information used in inferred demand analysis. Information relating to population growth, household size, and the single-unit ratio are typically developed from historical trends projected into the future. The best source for population growth, household size, and other demographic data are government-supported research centers. Information from the local chamber of commerce should always be compared with data from other reporting sources.

The final absorption forecast for the Mill Pond Project is made by reconciling information developed in the inferred and fundamental analyses. The inferred analysis revealed several trends relevant to the absorption forecast for the Mill Pond Project. The inferred analysis was able to isolate a seasonal trend in the local market and also provided an analysis of absorption "velocity" for the different price points within the project. This trend is considered in the absorption forecast for the Mill Pond project.

As shown in Exhibit 2.9, the Mill Pond Project enters the market in the third quarter of 2018. Total absorption for both price points is estimated at about 12 lots in 2018. Both the inferred and fundamental results are considered in estimating the subject absorption. In the Mill Pond example, fundamental demand supports the available capture of 34 lots in the subject project in 2018. However, the property doesn't enter the market until the third quarter. If the absorption was evenly distributed on a quarterly basis, the subject project should absorb about 17 units (34 lot capture in 2018 ÷ 2). However, the inferred analysis clearly reflects a seasonal trend, with higher absorption in the first two quarters each year and lower absorption in the last two quarters. Accordingly, the results of both the inferred analysis and fundamental analysis are used as a guideline in projecting absorption for the subject project in Exhibit 2.9. The absorption for the last two quarters of 2018 is estimated at six units per quarter because of the seasonal trend effect. A similar process is employed to develop the remaining absorption forecast over a total absorption period of 10 quarters. Elements of both the fundamental and inferred methods were used in forecasting overall absorption.

As mentioned, inferred analysis typically reveals seasonal trends and differences in absorption velocity between price points—subtleties that are often lost in the fundamental demand analysis. The fundamental demand analysis is valuable because it provides a residual demand and supply forecast over time, which is used in conjunction with the inferred analysis to antic-

Exhibit 2.9
Mill Pond Subdivision Absorption Estimate

Year	Quarter	Lot Absorption
2018	1	n/a
	2	n/a
	3	6
	4	6
2019	1	12
	2	10
	3	8
	4	8
2020	1	10
	2	7
	3	5
	4	4
Total		76

ipate the supply and demand status of the market at any given point in time for the foreseeable future and supports the subject capture estimate. Both methods tend to be based on historical trends and, as such, are subject to variability—especially as the time frame increases from the date of valuation.

Obviously, no one can predict the exact occurrence of any event in the future. The objective of inferred and fundamental analysis is to provide a market-supported absorption estimate for the property under consideration. The level of analysis depends on the size and scale of the property, the status of the market (stable or rapidly changing), and the current economic climate.

3
Neighborhood and Market Area Analysis

Introduction

Neighborhood analysis is a study of the locational, social, economic, governmental, and environmental forces that influence property values in the vicinity of a subject property. The first step is to delineate the boundaries of the area of influence. Although physical boundaries may be drawn, the most important boundaries are those that identify factors influencing property values. Residential subdivisions have unique characteristics that must be considered in the appraisal process. Delineation of the appropriate market area provides a basis for the selection of comparable properties and a focus for supply and demand analysis.

The area of influence is commonly called a *neighborhood*, which can be defined as a group of complementary land uses. A residential neighborhood, for example, may contain single-unit homes and commercial properties that provide services for local residents. A district, on the other hand, has one predominant land use. Districts are commonly composed of single-unit homes, apartments, or commercial, industrial, or agricultural properties. In broader terms, appraisers must analyze the market area within which a subject property competes for buyers and sellers in the real estate market.

A market area can encompass one or more neighborhoods and/or districts. For single-unit subdivision projects, the market area is typically the same area where homebuyers shop for competing homes or lots. The neighborhood and market area section of an appraisal defines the immediate neighborhood of the subject property and establishes the physical extent and economic characteristics of the neighborhood and competing market area.

This analysis provides input for the value conclusions and directly addresses the second step of market analysis—delineating the market area for the subject property.

Relationship to Market Analysis and the Appraisal Process

Market analysis extends to all parts of the appraisal process. Chapter 2 provided a detailed explanation of the six-step process used in market analysis. In appraisal assignments, especially assignments for proposed construction in which a lease-up or market sell-out forecast is required, the six-step process is used to support the highest and best use conclusion and provide an indication of supply and demand for a defined real estate product. Residual supply and demand status is concluded in the market analysis process and used to estimate market capture as well as provide a supportable absorption forecast for an inventory of subdivision lots over time.

[*important for forecasting*]

When a separate market study is made for an assignment, the six-step process is employed and each step is clearly identified and performed. The steps are usually performed in a specific sequence, and appropriate conclusions are drawn. **Step 1**, defining the product, is an analysis of the physical, legal, and locational attributes of the subject property. This information is usually contained in the site and improvement analysis sections of an appraisal report. **Step 2**, market delineation, is a study of the subject market area where locational, social, economic, governmental, and environmental forces and time-distance relationships are explored and the market area is delineated. This information and analysis is typically found in the market area or neighborhood analysis sections of an appraisal report. The remaining steps in the six-step process are usually found in the market analysis section of the appraisal report, just before the highest and best use conclusion.

The six steps can appear throughout the report or in a separate identifiable market analysis section. The critical issue is that all steps are conducted and explained within the analysis and provide input to both the highest and best use and the lot absorption conclusions.

Defining the Market Area

For single-unit residential properties, the market area is the area where most of the properties that can be considered competitive to the subject property are located. This is the same geographical area where a homebuyer would shop for competing properties in the same price range. The analysis identifies the primary area from which comparable lot sales, home sales, and historical absorption data is collected. Information can be compiled from published data sources such as census data, utility line maps, land use district maps, multiple listing sales websites, or public records data sources.

The boundaries of the market area may coincide with observable changes in land use or demographic and socioeconomic characteristics. Physical features such as structure types, street patterns, terrain, vegetation, and lot sizes help to identify land use districts. Transportation arteries (highways, major streets, and railroads), bodies of water, and changing elevations can also be significant boundaries.

There are three general techniques that may be considered when defining the market area:

- Delineation of the market area in relation to customer location
- Identification of the market area by location of substitute properties
- Specification of the market area based on analogs or analogous situations

The first two methods may be used in subdivision analysis. Analogous situations tend to be used for retail stores but may also be applied to subdivision analysis.

The first method, delineation of the market by customer location, may employ census tract information to represent the area from which the subdivision will draw prospective homebuyers. The second method applies the principle of substitution in defining the market area for comparable properties, assuming that a residential buyer will purchase the least expensive or most suitable unit among equally desirable substitute units. The appraiser delineates the market area by identifying substitute properties and their geographic distribution in relation to complimentary population areas and employment centers. The geographic distribution of the subdivisions defines the market area. Then the appraiser identifies the census tracts that correspond to the defined market area.

Identification of the market area can be achieved by

1. Examining the subject property and related characteristics
   The process of defining a market area must start with an analysis of the subject property and its related amenities and home price points.
2. Examining the area's physical characteristics
   The appraiser then explores the area to develop a sense of place, noting the degree of similarity in land uses, structure types, architectural styles, home price points, and maintenance or upkeep. Using a map, the appraiser identifies points

Neighborhood and Market Area Analysis

where these characteristics change and notes any physical barriers that coincide with these points.
3. Drawing the preliminary boundaries on a map
4. Determining how well the preliminary boundaries correspond to available demographic data

The market area boundaries are often overlaid on a map of geographical areas including zip codes, census tracts, land use zoning, and utility infrastructure to determine available data sources that may be used to quantify growth and development trends in the area. While the appraiser's preliminary boundaries may not match up perfectly with some published data sources, the boundaries may be modified. Most data providers have websites that facilitate interactive geographical maps corresponding to specific areas defined by the appraiser.

It should be recognized that market delineation is more than drawing lines on a map. Market area delineation has two major purposes. It identifies the customers for the subject property type and where these customers come from. The results of the market delineation lead into the next step, which is measuring the depth of the demand from this market segment.

Economic and Governmental Factors

The economic overview provides data that describes the local economy in general and the market area of the subject property in particular. The issues addressed in an economic overview for a valuation appraisal must relate to economic and demographic trends that affect the use and value of properties in the same category as the property being appraised. Accordingly, the subject price points, marketing concept, and amenities are analyzed to determine the typical homebuyer and household income needed to support homes in the subject project. Population growth is quantified from reliable public data sources to forecast new growth over time and future support for new development in the subject market area.

Economic considerations relate to the financial capacity of the market area's occupants and their ability to rent or own property, maintain it in an attractive and desirable condition, and renovate or rehabilitate it when needed.

Economic characteristics may include

- Population growth and distribution
- Mean and median household income levels
- Household size and size trends over time
- Per capita income

- Income distribution for households
- Extent of owner occupancy
- Property rent levels and trends
- Property value levels and trends
- Vacancy rates for various types of properties
- The amount of development and construction

The physical characteristics of the area and individual properties may indicate the relative financial strength of area occupants and how this strength is reflected in local development and upkeep. Ownership and rental data can also provide clues to the financial capability of residents.

The presence of vacant lots or acreage suitable for subdivision development in an area may indicate further development and growth potential or the lack of current demand. Relatively high growth and property "flipping" may indicate speculative or unstable markets. Current construction and sustained absorption in existing projects may create trends that affect the value of existing lots and improved properties as well as reflect stable market growth. It is imperative that the appraiser study these trends to help forecast future desirability and market demand.

Governmental influences can have a far-reaching impact on current and future growth patterns. These influences relate to the laws, regulations, and property taxes that affect properties in the market area. Also included are the administration and enforcement of zoning regulations and the administration of utility districts, building codes, and housing codes. Land zoning regulates the land use density of development. Communities may regulate zoning to halt or slow growth. To encourage new development, they may expand capital improvements such as sewage treatment facilities, fire stations, streets, and public recreational amenities.

The value of subdivision land is influenced by environmental regulations, which can affect the amount of time required to develop and sell the sites. Environmental regulation can have an impact on land use and the density of development that may be achieved. In some cases, buffer areas must be provided or land must be set aside in protected areas before new subdivision development can begin.

Governmental influences may include

- An unusual property tax burden relative to the services provided and compared with other areas in the community
- Special assessments and community development taxing districts (CDDs)
- Zoning, building, and housing codes

- Policies regarding development growth
- The availability and quality of public services such as fire protection, law enforcement, schools, and other governmental services
- Environmental regulations and impact fees

The goal of economic and governmental analysis in an appraisal is to identify the current status of a defined area, analyze market and submarket trends, and provide a supportable economic trend forecast. This forecast is a component of the six-step market analysis process and is a subject-specific analysis used for the highest and best use conclusion and the subdivision absorption forecast.

Character of Single-Unit Development

Value influences in a market area often include physical, legal, locational, and other tangible characteristics revealed by economic analysis. However, amenity benefits and intangible elements also help define the relative desirability of an area. These intangibles may include the appearance of properties, architectural diversity, the age and design of the homes, reputation, and the popularity of existing residential developments. Some residential areas may be very desirable just because they are near a favorite restaurant district. Fortunately, most of these intangible characteristics can be revealed by studying market trends. Subjective ranking analysis can be used by the appraiser when specific market or demographic data is not available.

The topographical and climatic features of land in a residential district are generally analyzed as possible amenities or potential hazards. Access to a body of water can increase a home's value if the location provides a scenic view, but the same lake or stream may reduce value if flooding occurs frequently. Sometimes a river, lake, hill, park, or other natural feature may act as a buffer between a residential district and commercial or industrial areas and thereby reinforce the residential appeal. Proximity to preservation lands can provide a beneficial and secluded view but may require setbacks that decrease the land area useable for development. Subdivision developers almost always face trade-offs between the density of use per acre, project configuration, and amenity benefits while at the same time trying to satisfy all of the required zoning or other governmental site plan criteria. Many of these issues

A subdivision with a retention pond water feature. A water feature may increase a home's value if it enhances the view or acts as a buffer between the residential area and other land uses, or may reduce value if flooding occurs frequently in the area.

are reviewed in the site description and improvement description sections of an appraisal. The market area analysis summarizes the relative appeal of the subject market area in comparison to competing districts of the city.

In some cases, the amenities provided by an individual project or proposed subdivision development can offset neighborhood deficiencies, creating a self-contained environment or supplementing missing elements. Large regional developments and mixed-use projects covering hundreds or thousands of acres may be able to create their own town centers with new shopping and recreational areas. The appraisal of large, mixed-use developments can be very complicated, and this topic is not covered in this book.

Single-unit residential areas are defined by the predominance of owner-occupied homes. Subdistricts found in residential areas and typical value influences are shown in the following list:

Defining characteristic:

- Predominance of owner-occupied homes

Subdistricts:

- Custom-built subdivisions
- Entry-level tract developments
- Attached housing (e.g., condominiums, townhouses)
- Senior housing
- Rural housing
- Mixed-use housing
- New urbanism

New townhomes in a residential subdistrict

Value influences:

- Access to workplaces
- Transportation access and adequacy
- Access to shopping centers and cultural facilities
- Quality of local schools
- Reputation of area
- Residential atmosphere, appearance, and protection from unwanted commercial and industrial intrusion
- Proximity to open space, parks, lakes, rivers, or other natural features
- Supply of vacant land likely to be developed, which could make present accommodations more or less desirable
- Private land use restrictions (e.g., conditions, covenants, and restrictions)

Subdistricts are typically defined by a specific housing style, such as the patio homes in this subdivision.

Subdistricts are typically defined by a specific housing style. Each style has its associated price points and a specific marketing concept that will be effective and financially feasible in a particular market area. Values are often sustained when there is a mix of residential housing districts in a given market. While individual neighborhoods may have a predominance of one or several styles, the accumulation of many submarkets and related commercial and employment centers help ensure the continued appeal of a defined area.

Location and Time-Distance Linkages

Proximity to employment opportunities, shopping, recreation, and regional transportation significantly influences property values in a residential district.

The appraiser should be sensitive to factors that can influence the homebuyer's decision process. The subjective distance of a neighborhood or market area can be an influential factor. *Subjective distance* refers to the perceived convenience of access to the neighborhood in terms of *time-distance*. *Time-distance* is the actual amount of time it takes to travel to a selected destination during typical travel periods. For example, a five-mile distance from a major employment center may not be a beneficial marketing factor if it typically takes one hour to transverse those few miles in rush hour traffic. Time-distance rather than physical proximity becomes the deciding factor. A variety of subjective factors can be considered in defining desirability in relation to time-distance and in establishing the market area boundaries.

Exhibit 3.1 is an example of a subjective land use linkage analysis. A subject subdivision is compared to competing projects in the same market area to determine its relative desirability. In Exhibit 3.1, the subject subdivision is compared to six competing projects that are marketing homes and/or lots in the same price category. Travel time to selected land uses, or destinations, is estimated for each location. The land uses identified as destinations are uses that are typically important to single-unit occupants and would be considered by the typical homebuyer. This analysis gives the same relative weight to each destina-

location

The relative position of a property to competitive properties and other value influences in its market area; the time-distance relationships, or linkages, between a property or neighborhood and all other possible origins and destinations of people going to or coming from the property or neighborhood.

tion, and the average travel time is calculated for the subject property and all six competing projects. The subject has an average travel time of 22.9 minutes to all 18 destinations. This is just below the average of 23.8 travel minutes for the six competing projects, which is a favorable marketing factor. The subject project in this example is just above average in terms of locational linkages as compared to the competition. This factor may be reflected in a higher absorption or market capture for lots in the subject project.

A similar analysis can also be performed to ascertain the relative desirability of the subject project's physical characteristics and project amenities as compared to the competition.

Exhibit 3.1
Time-Distance Land Use Linkage Analysis

| | | Drive Time in Minutes | | | | | |
| | | Competitive Subdivisions | | | | | |
Selected Destination	Subject	1	2	3	4	5	6
Shopping and Entertainment							
Regional mall, eating, and entertainment	30	35	40	25	15	50	30
Community grocery	10	15	15	5	5	5	10
Community restaurants	10	15	15	5	5	5	10
Convenience shopping	7	7	5	3	4	5	5
Regional Transportation							
Community airport	25	22	30	35	40	22	25
Regional airport	70	80	60	65	60	80	70
Interstate access point	5	3	2	10	35	2	5
Bus route	1	3	1	10	10	5	1
Subway access point	n/a	n/a	n/a	n/a	n/a	n/a	n/a
Employment							
CBD office district	25	30	35	30	5	30	25
West Point office district	10	15	15	5	5	15	10
Regional office park	35	40	45	40	15	45	35
R & D industrial park	40	45	35	35	30	45	40
Electronics manufacturer	30	20	30	35	40	20	30
Other							
Football stadium and sports complex	45	35	45	55	60	15	45
West Side park	15	5	20	20	30	5	15
Grade schools	10	13	6	10	15	10	10
High schools	25	12	30	30	36	5	25
Country club and golf	20	25	5	30	40	40	20
Average drive time	22.9	23.3	24.1	24.9	25.0	22.4	22.8
Subject	22.9		Low	22.4			
			High	25.0			
			Average	23.8			

Exhibit 3.2 provides a similar analysis with a refinement to address the appeal of the project for senior retired occupancy. For a subdivision targeting retired seniors, relative weights can be given to the land uses that are most important to seniors. This table gives a greater weight to shopping, entertainment, regional transportation, and recreational activities. Under this scenario, the senior appeal of the project is well above average, with a time-distance score of 78.3 minutes for the subject project as compared to 83.0 minutes on average for the six competing projects. This refinement may be used for other occupancy classes including empty nesters or families with children.

The time-distance linkage analysis used in these examples was applied to a relatively narrow market consisting of the subject subdivision and six nearby competing projects. The subject property and all six competing projects were located in the same residential market area or district. A similar analysis could also be conducted in which the subject residential district is compared to other districts rather than individual projects. This analysis would assess the relative desirability of the subject market area as compared to other residential areas in the community.

Conclusion and Reporting

Neighborhood and market area analysis is needed to accurately define the subject property's market area. The market area is delineated by studying a host of factors, including economic, governmental, and physical boundaries. Observable changes in land use or demographic and socioeconomic characteristics and a review of amenity benefits all assist in describing the market area and future trends. Economic data and projections of future population or household growth are reviewed and used to support population-based demand calculations. Time-distance linkages are explored to determine the relative desirability of a subject project as compared to competing subdivisions in the area. This exploration sets the stage for the three approaches to value and the capture conclusions derived from the absorption estimate.

When reporting the results of the market area analysis in an appraisal report, two general paths can be taken. One method is to present the neighborhood and market area section simply as a descriptive analysis of the subject market area, identifying boundaries and describing the area without a future forecast or locational analysis. When this method is used, the forecasting and subject locational analysis components are presented in the market analysis section of the appraisal, usually just before the highest and best use analysis. Under this scenario, part of Step 2 of the market analysis process is covered in the neighborhood section

Exhibit 3.2
Time-Distance Land Use Linkage Analysis - Weighted for Senior Retired Occupancy

| | | | Drive Time in Minutes | | | | | |
| | | | Competitive Subdivisions | | | | | |
Selected Destination	Relative Weight	Subject	1	2	3	4	5	6
Shopping and Entertainment								
Regional mall, eating, and entertainment		30	35	40	25	15	50	30
Community grocery		10	15	15	5	5	5	10
Community restaurants		10	15	15	5	5	5	10
Convenience shopping		7	7	5	3	4	5	5
Subtotal	35.0%	57	72	75	38	29	65	55
Regional Transportation								
Community airport		25	22	30	35	40	22	25
Regional airport		70	80	60	65	60	80	70
Interstate access point		5	3	2	10	35	2	5
Bus route		1	3	1	10	10	5	1
Subway access point		n/a	n/a	n/a	n/a	n/a	n/a	n/a
Subtotal	30.0%	101	108	93	120	145	109	101
Employment								
CBD office district		25	30	35	30	5	30	25
West Point office district		10	15	15	5	5	15	10
Regional office park		35	40	45	40	15	45	35
R & D industrial park		40	45	35	35	30	45	40
Electronics manufacturer		30	20	30	35	40	20	30
Subtotal	0.0%	140	150	160	145	95	155	140
Schools								
Grade schools		10	13	6	10	15	10	10
High schools		25	12	30	30	36	5	25
Subtotal	0.0%	35	25	36	40	51	15	35
Other								
Football stadium and sports complex		45	35	45	55	60	15	45
West Side park		15	5	20	20	30	5	15
Country club and golf		20	25	5	30	40	40	20
Subtotal	35.0%	80	65	70	105	130	60	80
Weighted average drive time	100.0%	78.3	80.4	78.7	86.1	99.2	76.5	77.6

Subject	78.3			
		Low	76.5	
		High	99.2	
		Average	83.0	

of the report and part is incorporated into the market analysis section of the report. This is the option used by most appraisers.

The second option is to perform the complete Step 2 analysis within the neighborhood and market area section of the appraisal and possibly also include several of the demand analysis procedures from Step 3. The neighborhood analysis may include the population forecasting data and income segmentation analysis, which is an extension of the economic analysis conducted in the neighborhood section.

4

Site and Improvement Analysis

Introduction

Subdivision development is the process of converting vacant land into smaller lots, thus creating a greater utility of the site to support building improvements. Horizontal site infrastructure is added, and land, labor, capital, and management are combined to support an economic enterprise. Profit is earned if the marketing concept and development plan are successfully received. The development plan may support one or multiple lot categories or design concepts and may include proposed homes or units and common amenities in addition to the vacant lots. Subdivision valuation requires an understanding of the development plan for the physical characteristics of the subdivision as well as the targeted marketing concept, home price points, timing of construction, and other economic criteria.

The site and improvement analysis portion of the appraisal report provides a detailed description of the subject property and any existing or proposed improvements. Its goal is to accurately describe the project and to convey the strengths or weaknesses of the subdivision property in relation to competing projects in the market area. Subdivision development transforms raw land into smaller sites for a specific defined purpose or marketing plan. Even when vacant subdivision lots are being appraised, the marketing plan for the eventual home units to be placed on the lots must be

raw land
Land that is undeveloped; land in its natural state before grading, draining, subdivision, or the installation of utilities; land with minimal or no appurtenant constructed improvements.

site
Improved land or a lot in a finished state so that it is ready to be used for a specific purpose.

land (or site) analysis
A study of factual data relating to the characteristics of undeveloped land or a site that create, enhance, or detract from the utility and marketability of that parcel.

considered. The marketing plan includes single-unit price points for the eventual home and lot package to be sold to end users. Accordingly, the marketing concept and home price points must be studied in relation to the proposed lot sizes, the subdivision layout, the amenities offered, and other project characteristics.

The analysis starts with the overall locational and physical characteristics of the raw land and then addresses the existing or proposed improvements in relation to the land and the subdivision marketing concept. Site and improvement analysis provides direct input into market analysis.

Relation to Market Analysis and the Appraisal Process

Like the neighborhood and area analysis, site and improvement analysis is part of the six-step market analysis process described in Chapter 2. In an appraisal assignment, especially for the valuation of proposed construction where market absorption is required, the six-step process is used to support the highest and best use conclusion and provide an indication of supply and demand for a defined real estate product. Residual supply and demand status is concluded when the six-step fundamental process is used to estimate market capture and provide a supportable absorption forecast for an inventory of subdivision lots over time. In order to support this conclusion, the product must first be defined.

Land Considerations

Whether a property is raw land available for future subdivision development or a group of sites (subdivision lots) with infrastructure already installed, the appraiser must consider the overall physical, governmental, and economic characteristics of the property.

Legal Description, Deed Restrictions, and Access

Every parcel of real estate is unique. To identify individual parcels, appraisers rely on legal descriptions, surveys, or other descriptive information typically provided by the client or found in public records. A legal description identifies a property in such a way that it cannot be confused with any other property. The legal description specifically identifies the parcel size, location, and other site data. It may identify easements and other restrictions within the document or may simply refer to existing "easements and encumbrances of record." Preferably, the client will have a current survey and title search information available to be reviewed by the appraiser. The appraiser will then verify the data to ensure that it corresponds to the subject land parcel and accurately describes the property being appraised.

Title search information may reveal the existence of deed restrictions that limit how a property is used and prevent subdivision development or specific uses or densities. Easements are grants of partial ownership of part of a property to others (typically public utility providers) for underground utilities, overhead transmission lines, or other purposes. Preexisting easements may have an adverse effect on a proposed subdivision design. The orientation of easements within the subdivision can impair the usability of lots, reduce the usable lot area, or affect the placement of homes. It may be necessary to incorporate additional landscaping or a buffer area to reduce the visual impact or other effects associated with an easement.

Property desirability may be reduced or enhanced by easements. For example, off-site access easements can provide access to a major highway, which will facilitate development. Proposed subdivision plans must also be analyzed so that new easements can be placed in the development to deliver water, sewer, electric, and other services to individual lots.

Ownership Information

Ownership information is obtained from local public records maintained by a county clerk or another official source. The status of ownership for subdivision development purposes is typically fee simple. In this case, the current owner of record is reported with a statement describing the fee simple ownership status. Any exceptions to the fee simple status, such as the presence of easements, will be itemized in the legal description portion of the site analysis. It may be possible to have a development with leased fee or leasehold ownership status. If a leasehold or land lease is involved, the appraiser should describe the terms of the relevant lease and report its effect on the marketability of the project and its value.

USPAP requires that the appraiser consider and analyze any current agreement for sale, option, or listing of the subject property and any prior sales that have occurred within three years prior to the effective date of appraisal. Prior sales are typically analyzed in conjunction with the current appraised value of the vacant acreage.

Zoning and Land Use

Thorough analysis of zoning and land use regulations is critical for subdivision properties, especially when raw land for a proposed project is evaluated. Land zoning consists of commu-

nity land use plans that call for general uses such as residential, commercial, or industrial. Zoning districts coincide with the land use plan and specify uses and their associated use density. A list of allowed uses is usually provided with associated density, minimum lot sizes, required setbacks, and other criteria.

Zoning and land use regulations often control the following:

- Height and size of buildings
- Lot coverage ratio
- Street and utility requirements
- Required landscaping or open space
- Number of units allowed
- Parking requirements
- Water retention requirements
- Sign requirements
- Building setbacks
- Provisions for future street widening or interconnectivity with adjoining projects
- Other factors of importance

Although zoning ordinances and maps are public records that are available at planning offices, an appraiser may need help from planning and zoning staff to understand the impact of zoning regulations. An appraiser must often contact several agencies such as water management districts, state and regional planning offices, or the army corps of engineers. Zoning and land use restrictions are not usually listed in the recorded title to a property, so confirmation from controlling agencies is necessary.

For a group of lots in an existing subdivision project, zoning and land use analysis can be fairly simple and lead to an obvious conclusion. However, for proposed projects, zoning and land use issues can be very complicated and have a host of interlaced components that must be considered. Land development regulations (LDRs) may have provisions for mandatory setbacks from creeks, significant woodlands, or other physical characteristics defined in the regulations that limit the usability of a parcel. Overlay zoning districts may require specific housing types and project orientation as well as the use of new urban design characteristics.

Zoning and land use regulations often control factors such as street and utility requirements and building setbacks.

When appraising vacant raw land, the appraiser should recognize that properties may not achieve the maximum allowed zoning density. For example, it may be common that parcels zoned for a single-unit density of one to four units per acre in a community only achieve a density of two to three units per acre when all the other zoning requirements for streets, open space, and on-site water retention are considered.

> **entitlement**
> In the context of ownership, use, or development of real estate, governmental approval for annexation, zoning, utility extensions, number of lots, total floor area, construction permits, and occupancy or use permits.

Once a property has gone through the site plan review process and has all the necessary permits and governmental approvals to build a proposed subdivision, the property has full entitlements. Entitlements typically relate to a specific site plan and may be transferable on a sale of the property. Also, site plan entitlements may expire over a period of time if subdivision construction and development are not started and completed within the time frames specified in the land use regulations.

Properties that require rezoning or a change in the land use plan represent a significantly more difficult appraisal issue. The appraiser must support the probability of a favorable rezoning by doing the following:

- Establishing a pattern of recent change in the area
- Addressing the risk inherent in the process as well as the required time frame and associated costs for appraisals of raw land on an *as is* basis

However, it is not uncommon for appraisers to perform investment consulting, in which various proposed plans are evaluated to ascertain the most beneficial or optimum layout and associated price points. When the ability to achieve a specific plan, use, or layout is unknown, a hypothetical condition may be required to explain the specific hypothetical forecasts or assumptions.

Environmental Considerations

Environmental issues can have a significant impact on how a property may be utilized from both a regulatory and a site contamination perspective. A contamination issue may relate to on-site or nearby environmental hazards that may result in delayed development or an expensive clean-up process. Performing appraisals under these circumstances is very problematic and requires the input of environmental engineers or other professionals to ascertain the extent of contamination and a remediation program with associated costs. Depending on the magnitude of the problem, a parcel may be rendered unmarketable.

Environmental issues more commonly affect existing and new development because the government's environmental regulations affect real estate development in proximity to identified areas of environmental concern.

Environmental regulation may impact values and use via the following:

- Required setbacks or buffer areas for developments near parks, wetlands, creeks, animal habitats, or other defined areas
- Required relocation of endangered species or the dedication of preservation land for new development
- Floodplain regulations and coastal control zones
- Water consumption regulations
- Regulation of wetland destruction
- Air quality regulations
- Impact on fish and wildlife
- Proximity to earthquake zones, faults, and known slide or avalanche zones
- Requirements for developers to provide environmental audits, studies of historical and archaeological significance, watershed studies, or other types of studies to reveal any environmental issues that should be considered

Like land zoning and use regulations, environmental issues often require an appraiser to contact several agencies such as water management districts, state and local environmental and planning offices, and the army corps of engineers. Vacant land that has not gone through a zoning and site plan review process with local, regional, or state departments is usually very difficult to appraise because the actual use density, character of uses, and any stipulations required for future development are unknown at the time of appraisal. An appraisal under these circumstances may require extraordinary assumptions, and the rationale for the assumptions must be fully explained in the analysis.

Tax and Assessment Data

Property taxes in all jurisdictions are based on ad valorem assessments, and taxation levels are significant in considering a property's potential uses. Current taxes and assessed value can be determined from present assessment data. Future trends can be evaluated from past tax increases over time and used to estimate future taxes applicable to vacant acreage or a group of vacant subdivision lots.

Lot assessments can be set at current market value or at the ratio used in the local taxing district. Comparable vacant lots and assessment ratios and taxes should be studied to ascertain the tax liability for a proposed subdivision project. Taxes are one of the more significant holding costs to consider as part of the DCF analysis on a proposed project or existing group of lots. Taxes will probably increase over time, which should be projected over the absorption period.

The fairness of assessments on existing lots and anticipated future taxes must be thoroughly analyzed. Recently completed lots may have higher assessments and resulting higher taxes than existing nearby vacant lots. The assessment pattern for new subdivisions should be studied to reveal any patterns.

When looking at tax and assessment data, the appraiser also considers the possibility of special assessments or the creation of community taxing districts that may be specific to a particular subdivision project or geographical area.

Size, Shape, and Excess Land for Future Phases

The size and shape of an acreage parcel or individual subdivision lot have an impact on the usability and value of the land for a subdivision project or the construction of an individual home on a single lot. Land size is measured and expressed in different units depending on local custom.

Large tracts of land are usually measured in acres. Individual lots are usually measured in square feet or front feet along the frontage street. Lots abutting a creek, lake, or golf course may be measured in terms of frontage along the water or golf course amenity. Amenity view has value in residential markets, and subdivision projects are usually designed to make maximum use of amenity views, open space, and proximity to parks or nature preserves. The most valuable lots are typically adjacent to these features. Cul-de-sac locations or corner lots may command higher prices because of their larger size, increased utility, or secluded nature. Lot setbacks and utility easements and configurations are studied for consistency with the marketing plan for the project and the adequacy of the site to support homes in the targeted home price range for the project. The appraiser should be aware of the characteristics that affect value and apply appropriate adjustments when appraising the subject lot inventory.

Many developers have a lot pricing schedule that has a base price for the typical lot and a schedule of higher prices or adjustments to the base lot prices based on "lot premiums." For example, the base price may be $60,000 per lot for a typical or regular lot. The added premium for a wooded lot might be $6,000. A fairway frontage lot may add $30,000, and cul-de-sac larger lots may add $10,000. A wooded cul-de-sac lot may add $16,000. These pricing schedules must be verified by supporting market

excess land
Land that is not needed to serve or support the existing use. The highest and best use of the excess land may or may not be the same as the highest and best use of the improved parcel. Excess land has the potential to be sold separately and is valued separately.

surplus land
Land that is not currently needed to support the existing use but cannot be separated from the property and sold off for another use. Surplus land does not have an independent highest and best use and may or may not contribute value to the improved parcel.

A subdivision of detached homes in a cul-de-sac location. Lots on cul-de-sacs may be more desirable and thus command higher values due to their larger size, increased utility, and more secluded locations.

evidence and considered in the retail lot values reflected in an appraisal.

The size and shape of acreage parcels will impact the design of the project and determine how many lots can be built. Road frontage, width, and depth are reported and considered within the context of overall parcel size. Frontage should be adequate but not excessive, and depth should be sufficient to allow for efficient project design and support the required open space needs and spacing of proposed lots. Location within the submarket area, especially for protection from nuisances and detrimental conditions such as heavy traffic, is important for residential acreage. The land must have access that is suitable for residential development and would preferably have direct frontage or access to public paved roads so that traffic can enter and exit in both directions along the roadway.

Large tracts of land may support subdivision development that is phased over time, which introduces the need to address excess or surplus land in the appraisal analysis. Land is considered to be excess land if it can be sold separately from the initial phase and has a separate highest and best use. Land may be treated as surplus land if it cannot be separated and sold separately. In either scenario, the land can add value. Common infrastructure, roadways, basic utility systems initially installed for the future development of extra land, and permitted entitlements will all affect the value of land after the initial phase is built. When near-term demand is present, the value of excess or surplus land can increase significantly over raw land value.

Topography

Because the topography of a site can have an impact on appeal and the cost of development, topographic characteristics should be considered. Topographical studies provide information about contour, grading, natural drainage, soil conditions, view, and general physical usefulness. Sites may differ in value due to these physical characteristics. Steep slopes often impede building construction. Natural drainage can be advantageous. However, if a site is located downstream from other properties or is a natural drainage basin for the area, it may have severely limited use.

Subsoil conditions can influence the cost of development in areas where wetlands must be crossed or poor land must be removed and in-fill land placed for road systems. The construction of roads and central utilities on hillsides or in areas with substantial rock can greatly increase the cost and configuration of internal roadways within a project.

When describing topography, an appraiser must employ the terminology used in the area. What is described as a "steep hill" in one part of the country may be considered a "moderate slope" in another. Typically, descriptions of properties' topographies are taken from published sources such as topographic maps.

Utilities and Services

Subdivision development requires utilities to support the construction of new single-unit homes. These utilities may be minimal in rural areas where individual subdivision lots have access to overhead electric service and make use of on-site well and septic systems. Local and regional agencies regulate the minimum lot sizes needed to support these utilities and determine whether they will be allowed in specific areas.

Suburban development, on the other hand, requires significantly more infrastructure. The typical infrastructure needed includes

- Sanitary sewers
- Domestic water (i.e., portable water for human consumption)
- Types of raw water (grey water) for lawn irrigation or other uses
- Natural gas
- Electricity
- Storm drainage
- Telephone service
- Cable television and/or Internet services

Although market area analysis generally describes the utility systems that are available in an area, the site analysis should provide a site-specific description. The subdivision plans should clearly identify how sewage generated by the property will be handled within the development. In addition, the capacity of municipal utilities may limit the intensity of development for a specific site and should be considered to determine if utility access would have any impact on the number of lots that could be built, the number of units that could be supported within the project, and the timing of the development. Any high connection or impact fees and their effect should be noted. The rates for utility services and the burden of any bonded indebtedness or other special utility costs should also be considered.

Utilities and services are studied to determine how they will be provided for any proposed project, their cost relative to competing projects or vacant land, and their impact on highest and best use and the value conclusions.

Governmental Restrictions and Legal Framework

Subdivision projects, whether proposed or existing, may be subject to governmental restrictions, private restrictions, and unit owner associations that require financial support from lot owners.

Governmental restrictions usually have the most important impact on proposed projects. These restrictions relate to traffic volume and control, the capacity of utilities, and any concurrency limitations that prohibit or otherwise delay project development. *Concurrency* is a general term used to describe a set of land use regulations that local governments are required to adopt by state-mandated legislation. The purpose of this legislation is to ensure that new development does not outstrip the local government's ability to support new development. For a development to be "concurrent" or "meet concurrency," the local government must have enough infrastructure capacity to serve each proposed development. Specifically, concurrency regulations may require that local government has the capacity in terms of storm water, solid waste, sewer, water, mass transit, and park facilities to serve each proposed development. Together, these public services are typically known as *concurrency facilities*.

Local governments are usually required to maintain a management system to track the impact of new development on concurrency facilities and determine if there is sufficient capacity to support new development. If capacity is not available, then the proposed development cannot be approved. For example, concurrency infrastructure may consider the adequacy of public road systems to support new development along a major highway. The local government must establish a specific traffic capacity (concurrency limit) that the road is able to support–such as an average daily traffic of 40,000 cars per day. If the current traffic level is greater than 40,000 cars per day, then no new development will be approved along the roadway. If the road has a traffic count less than the concurrency limit, then new development may be approved.

Concurrency problems with respect to transportation, available utilities, school capacity, and other issues may limit the timing of a project as well as the intensity or number of lots or units that can be supported within a development. These issues also contribute heavily to governmental stipulations. The developer may be required to invest in off-site public infrastructure to achieve permitting approval for new development. This investment may include reconfiguring public road systems, donating private land for public use, or contributing to the capital infrastructure for water or sewer expansion or similar activities. Nearly all projects have some stipulations and cost associated with development. However, troublesome or high-cost stipulations could have a negative impact on land value as well as the project's ability to support financially feasible new development and deliver lots at an acceptable price.

Land zoning and use regulations are considered and establish general limitations with respect to unit density and the character of homes or units that may be built on a particular property. These regulations are one of the first factors considered in the appraisal and highest and best use estimate. Also, consistency must be maintained between the proposed plans and the current zoning and land use for the property. However, even with known zoning and land use criteria, there is never a guarantee that a proposed project can be built until the project has gone through the final site plan review process and has been approved by the appropriate governmental authorities.

For a proposed project, the appraiser is typically provided a set of plans with specifications and employed to provide a value estimate for the proposed development. This type of assignment, which assumes that the project can be permitted exactly according to plans provided to the appraiser, involves a series of hypothetical conditions and/or extraordinary assumptions within the appraisal. Values, development costs, and project design can change depending on the outcome of the approval process. Appraisals based on preliminary information may be subject to variability, which should be communicated as part of the scope of work and in the initial engagement letter to the client.

For both proposed and existing projects, the ownership status and the necessity for a unit owner association or a system of private deed restrictions can influence the types of homes that may be placed in the project, the location of the homes, and the price points. Subdivision restrictions may be comprehensive and control almost all aspects of the appearance of homes as well as their size and other characteristics. These restrictions may or may not be beneficial, depending on market acceptance in the area. By contrast, a subdivision with relatively minimal restrictions could allow for a very heterogeneous mix of properties, which could have a negative consequence. The overall goal of governmental and legal analysis is to review the physical, legal, and economic framework of the subject property for consistency and compatibility with similar projects in the area. This analysis precedes the highest and best use conclusion for the property and sets the stage for a detailed valuation analysis.

Improvement Analysis

Once the land analysis has been completed, the appraiser begins to focus on the development plan. The development plan is

especially critical if the appraisal involves a proposed project that is not physically complete at the time of valuation. Available plans must include sufficient detail so that the relevant costs, lot sizes, individual lot amenities and configurations, and installed infrastructure can be accurately determined from both a cost and market analysis perspective. Conceptual plans or artist renderings are rarely adequate, and a lack of detailed data will impact the scope of work decision. The improvement analysis includes a review of the physical characteristics of the subdivision, the legal framework for the subdivision project, and the economics of the units to be placed on the various lots.

The physical components start with the development plan, which is usually prepared by a professional architect or engineer. The development plan should specify the number of lots, lot sizes, and orientation within the project as well as the locations of roads, utility lines, and easements. The plan should provide a full listing of the project specifications and any amenities provided as part of the subject subdivision or available in the larger planned development if the subject subdivision is a component of a larger community. Amenities such as buffer zones, pools, playgrounds, clubhouses, parks, golf courses, lakes, or other recreational facilities should be clearly identified, as should any required off-site public improvements that are part of the required stipulations for development.

For an existing project, the appraiser would perform a similar analysis with or without detailed plans from the prior construction of the development. In this case, the same information is ascertained from physical observation of the property or available public records, such as recorded plats. If the appraisal assignment is to value a small component of a larger subdivision project, it may not be possible or appropriate to provide a cost approach analysis. However, the cost approach should be applied to all proposed projects to explore the issue of financial feasibility–i.e., so that the results of the cost approach can be compared with the conclusions of the income capitalization and sales comparison approaches.

A meaningful site plan review for a proposed project is based on detailed plans and specifications for the development. In addition, the appraiser must obtain information on anticipated costs, project timing, completion dates, and the marketing concept for completed homes or units to be built within the project. The project marketing concept, which is especially important, may have multiple price points and/or design concepts with a mix of attached, detached, or other types of units. A proper understanding of each element is essential for the valuation and defines the economics inherent in the project design. The lot design, front footage, and other physical characteristics should be consistent with the home price point for each group of lots.

The physical layout of the project is reviewed in light of the physical real estate to be improved with the subdivision infrastructure, the orientation of existing wetlands, the usable land area, natural amenities, access, and other characteristics. These characteristics are examined to determine if the layout makes efficient use of the available site area. Any negative factors should be considered and evaluated.

The boundaries, dimensions, and area of all lots should be clearly identified on the development plan, along with the location(s) of all easements. Sufficient detail should be supplied to allow the analyst to determine the impact of easements and lot dimensions on the effective usable area of the site as well as how access to each lot will be obtained. The road system (private vs. public) and access points to the public road system or surrounding subdivision projects are examined. The design concept should match the legal status of the property and the intended form of ownership.

For example, a private gated community may require private roads and a unit owners or homeowners association (HOA) to maintain the roads. This type of development may require a planned development zoning designation. More typical subdivisions without private gated access may require interior roads dedicated to the community, and a specific road construction criterion must be followed. The project's road system should be engineered to provide for safe traffic flow and surface water runoff. The project plan should provide detailed descriptions of the proposed installation of curbs, gutters, and sidewalks as well as the treatment of storm water runoff and how it will be managed.

Project amenities available to the subdivision can have a significant impact on the price levels commanded by lots within the development and on the eventual absorption of the lot inventory over time. Amenities may assume many forms and can have positive or negative design characteristics that affect the marketability of the subdivision lots. Common amenities include clubhouse buildings with swimming pools, natural buffers used as privacy screening, and recreational amenities such as tennis courts, basketball courts, golf courses, and water features. These amenities usually enhance the value of lots adjacent to them. The scale of amenities must be consistent with the size of the project and the marketing concept. For example, a clubhouse facility with a swimming pool may be very beneficial to a project designed for homes in the lower to lower-middle price range, but may be an unused benefit in a subdivision with high-priced homes that typically feature private swimming pools. The scale of amenity infrastructure should be consistent with the number of lots in the project and the economic benefit added to the underlying lot value. A comprehensive amenity package in a project with only 100 lots may not be financially feasible, while the same amenity package in a development with 400 lots may be well supported.

Passive recreational amenities such as trails, open space, and buffer areas usually require minimal upkeep and minimal unit owner association dues. Projects with more extensive amenities will require larger budgets and must be maintained as part of each unit owner's dues. Some amenity packages require relatively burdensome costs that may actually impair the marketability of a project. All of the elements must be in balance with the physical site plan and layout, the marketing concept employed in the project, and the home price points.

Common amenities in residential subdivision developments include recreational features such as the volleyball court and clubhouse shown here.

Passive recreational amenities, such as the common area park with walking path shown here, require less upkeep and unit owner association dues.

The Marketing Concept and Price Points

The economic characteristics of a subdivision project must be examined along with its physical and legal characteristics because most subdivisions are designed to meet specific target price ranges for proposed homes or other living units. To accurately value the vacant subdivision lots, the appraiser must also define and analyze the marketing concept.

The appraiser first determines the marketing concept for homes in the subject project because lot value is usually directly related to the eventual unit (home and lot package) that will be placed on the lot. For example, a one-acre lot located in a subdivision designed for detached single-unit homes in the $250,000 price range would command a different price than a one-acre lot in a development designed for the $500,000 price range. Each project must have amenities that support that particular marketing concept.

For a proposed project, the marketing concept is usually defined by the project developer, and lot value is estimated within the context of the proposed home price range. Appraisal reports typically include a section explaining the marketing concept and how it relates to the valuation, the proposed subdivision layout, and the highest and best use. Consistent with USPAP guidelines, an extraordinary assumption is typically included in appraisal reports. This extraordinary assumption explains the marketing concept and makes the value estimate contingent on the concept being followed through to the eventual marketing and sale of the lots. The extraordinary assumption is included because a change in the marketing concept could have an impact on the values estimated for the vacant lots. Many large subdivision developments have multiple price points, and the project may be marketing lot inventory designed for both attached and detached units as well as a full stratification of detached lots in multiple price points within the development. A firm understanding of how these price points relate to lot value and the layout and orientation of the project is important in estimating the project's eventual retail lot values as well as its absorption characteristics. It is quite possible to have a project with multiple price points and absorptions within a comprehensive marketing concept.

At a minimum, the appraiser should define the targeted price range within each price point for completed housing units and the typical building size associated with the price range. The appraiser should also study the relationship between lot sizes and the targeted price range for consistency within the project. This will also help identify comparable projects to use for comparison purposes in estimating the retail lot value and forecasting absorption. The marketing concept is integral to valuation. It must be defined within the appraisal as well as considered in the highest and best use analysis and, ultimately, the valuation of the property. In brief, the appraiser must be able to fully answer the following questions:

- What is the marketing concept?
- How does it relate to the physical and legal characteristics of the project?

Conclusion

The site and improvement analysis provides a detailed description of the subject property and any existing or proposed improvements. The goal of this analysis is to achieve an understanding of the strengths or weaknesses of the subdivision property in relation to competing projects in the market area. The legal description, owner of record, tax data, size, shape, topography, and available utilities are all considered to establish the suitability of the land for subdivision use. Since subdivision development is the transformation of raw land into smaller sites for a specific defined purpose, the economics of the marketing plan must be analyzed in relation to the physical site and zoning and governmental regulations. The site plan layout is then considered in light of the marketing plan and the residential price points supported within the project. All of these elements directly relate to the highest and best use analysis and value conclusions.

5
Highest and Best Use

Introduction

In all valuation assignments, opinions of value are based on use. The highest and best use for a property to be appraised provides the foundation for the value conclusion. A thorough investigation of the competitive position of the property in the minds of market participants is made. The highest and best use of a specific parcel of land or group of lots is not determined through subjective analysis by the property owner, the developer, or the appraiser. Rather, highest and best use is shaped by competitive forces within the market where the property is located. Therefore, the analysis and interpretation of highest and best use is an economic study and a financial analysis focused on the subject property.

The definition of highest and best use provides four tests or criteria that are used for the property as though vacant and as improved. The highest and best use must be

1. Physically possible
2. Legally permissible
3. Financially feasible
4. Maximally productive

These criteria are often considered sequentially. The tests of physical possibility and legal permissibility must be applied before the remaining tests of financial feasibility and maximum productivity. A use may be financially feasible but irrelevant if it is legally

highest and best use
The reasonably probable use of property that results in the highest value. The four criteria that the highest and best use must meet are legal permissibility, physical possibility, financial feasibility, and maximum productivity.

prohibited or physically impossible. The initial market analysis and land use regulations usually limit the number of property uses to a few logical choices.

The four criteria must be considered for the land as though vacant and the property as improved. In the case of subdivision lots, the property as improved consists of improved subdivision lots where all site infrastructure has been installed to make the vacant lots ready to accept building improvements. Alternatively, the property may be a vacant tract of acreage, and the highest and best use analysis includes an investigation of the timing and support for single-unit residential development.

The Role of Market Analysis in Highest and Best Use

Market analysis in appraisal has two basic functions. First, market analysis identifies the highest and best use of a property in terms of property use, market support (economic demand), timing (absorption rates), and market participants (probable users and buyers). The second major function of market analysis is to identify the key factors of value that are to be measured and to provide data input for applying the three approaches to value once the highest and best use has been determined. Chapter 2 provided a comprehensive description of market analysis and how it is applied to support an absorption estimate for a subdivision project and the three approaches to value. Market analysis also provides the necessary support for a highest and best use conclusion, especially when the timing of current and future demand is integral to the use determination. Market analysis will provide an overview of residual supply and demand over time for the specific use category (i.e., home price points) under consideration. Depending on the timing of demand and existing supply characteristics in a market, highest and best use may sometimes be an interim use, especially if vacant acreage is not ripe for immediate development.

As indicated in Chapter 1, one of the major deficiencies in subdivision appraisals reported by review appraisers is a lack of support for the highest and best use conclusion, particularly a lack of evidence to support market absorption. Documented evidence that there is an appropriate level of market support for the existing or proposed use of a site is a fundamental component of market analysis. Through supply and demand analysis, the appraiser identifies and tests the level of market support, which is critical in the analysis of highest and best use for a proposed subdivision project.

Applying the Four Criteria

Legally Permissible

To apply the criterion of legal permissibility, the appraiser considers the uses that are supported by existing legal constraints on the property. Land zoning is a major legal consideration and often limits land to specific classes of uses. For residential development land, allowed uses are typically expressed on a unit-per-acre basis, with density per acre defined within specific ranges. For example, vacant acreage in rural areas may support a density of one residential unit per five acres; suburban residential land may support a density of one to four units per acre or higher.

The test of legal permissibility helps the appraiser determine which uses are permitted by current zoning, which uses could be permitted if a zoning change were granted, and which uses are restricted by private restrictions on the site. Private restrictions, deed restrictions, and long-term leases relate to the covenants under which some properties are acquired. These restrictions may prohibit certain uses or specify building setbacks, heights, and types of materials. If deed restrictions conflict with zoning laws or building codes, the more restrictive guidelines usually prevail.

In addition to analyzing zoning and private restrictions, testing the legal permissibility of a land use also requires the appraiser to investigate other applicable codes and ordinances including building codes, historical district ordinances, environmental regulations, and zoning overlay districts. Zoning may encourage, restrict, or require specific land uses through overlays, linkages, and transferable development rights (TDRs).

The investigation of legally permissible uses includes uses that are legally permitted at the time of appraisal and uses for which there is a reasonable probability that permission will be granted upon application. In the latter case, the appraiser considers the risk that the application will be denied. In addition, there are likely to be costs associated with the permitting process, including the amount of time required to complete the process, carrying costs for the property while the permitting application is in progress, costs for the engineering and site concept plan drawings, legal fees, and any other costs required to facilitate the permitting process.

When investigating the reasonable probability of a zoning change, the appraiser must consider the history of and trends in zoning requests in the market area as well as documents such as the community's comprehensive or master land use plan. Uses that are not compatible with the existing land uses in the area and uses for which zoning changes have been requested but denied can usually be eliminated from consideration as potential highest and best uses. On the other hand, a zoning change from agriculture to a higher-density, residential use may be reasonable if other properties in the market area have recently received a similar zoning change or if a community's comprehensive plan designates the property for some use other than its current use.

In preparing a land development forecast for an area, the appraiser must fully disclose all pertinent factors relating to a possible zoning change, including the time and expenses involved and the risk that the change will not be granted. Appraisers must exercise caution when performing a market analysis that results in the determination of highest and best use. Although a given site may be particularly well-suited for a specific use, there may be a number of other sites that are equally or more appropriate. Therefore, the appraiser must test the highest and best use conclusion to ensure that existing and potential competition from other sites has been fully recognized.

Physically Possible

The test of physical possibility addresses the physical characteristics associated with the site that might affect its highest and best use. The size, shape, terrain, and accessibility of land and the risk of natural disasters such as floods, sinkholes, or earthquakes affect the uses to which land can be put. The utility of a parcel may also depend on its frontage, depth, and shape. Irregularly shaped parcels can cost more to develop and may have less utility than regularly shaped parcels of the same size after development is completed. Residential development in particular is sensitive to its surroundings. Factors such as transmission lines, adjoining uses that emit noise or odors, and excessive highway traffic can adversely affect the appeal and demand for residential uses. Adverse factors may also limit the range of the site's uses and/or necessitate buffer areas, which will reduce the amount of land useable for development purposes. The presence of wetlands, conservation areas, or protected habitat can also limit the amount of land area available for development or may add an amenity value.

The appraiser should also consider the capacity and availability of public utilities. If a sewer main is located in front of a property but cannot be tapped because of a lack of capacity at the sewage disposal plant, that property's use might be limited. When topography or subsoil conditions make development difficult or costly, the land's utility may be adversely affected. If grading and installation costs of subdivision streets and utilities are higher than usual for sites in the area competing for the same use, the subject site may be economically infeasible for the highest and best use that otherwise would be appropriate.

Financially Feasible

Highest and best use in many respects is an elimination process in which a wide range of physically possible uses is narrowed down into a smaller group of probable uses that are legally permissible. Only those uses that meet the first two criteria are analyzed further. These remaining available uses are then studied to determine if they are financially feasible. As long as a potential use supports a value commensurate with its cost with an appropriate market-oriented profit and conforms to the first two tests, the use is financially feasible.

Subdivision development is income-oriented. Determining the timing of potential development and eventual lot sales entails consideration of when the lots will be placed on the market as well as anticipation of supply and demand characteristics. Analysis of supply and demand, market location, and subdivision price points is needed to identify those uses that are financially feasible and, ultimately, the use that is maximally productive. If the present value of the development meets or exceeds the cost with a reasonable profit, the use is considered feasible. If the value falls below the costs or exceeds costs by only a marginal amount, the use may not be financially feasible. Future demand characteristics and the market absorption of lot inventory must be considered. Income and profit can only be generated by the successful absorption of lots over time.

Maximally Productive

When testing for maximum productivity, the appraiser's goal is to determine which use or uses produce a positive return (i.e., are financially feasible) and then identify the ideal improvement for the site. The ideal improvement is the subdivision plan that produces the highest present value. Several development designs could achieve about the same or similar present values that are reasonably supported. The idea that there is one and only one configuration is not always realistic.

Next, financially feasible uses are further analyzed. Market forces of supply and demand may aid in the process of elimination. This final test addresses not only the value created under the maximally productive use but also the costs necessary to achieve the value. Of the financially feasible uses, the highest and best use is the one that produces the highest residual land value consistent with the market's acceptance of risk and the rate of return warranted by the market for that use. For land as though vacant, rates of return that reflect associated project risks are often used to capitalize income from different subdivision layouts and home and lot price points into the residual land value conclusion for each alternative. The use and/or configuration that produces the highest present value is the maximally productive use, and hence the highest and best use of the site as vacant.

The appraiser defines a specific ideal improvement to the greatest extent possible. For vacant land, the ideal improvement analysis should describe the residential land use, subdivision layout, density, home price points, common amenities, and marketing concept needed to achieve the maximally productive use. The plan may encompass multiple price points or pods within a mixed-use building concept, the types of lots (i.e., size, frontage, and square footage) associated with each use, and the subdivision infrastructure and amenity package needed for the project. It is possible that the vacant acreage could have several financially feasible subdivision layouts that would support the same or a similar present land value and be very competitive for the maximally productive conclusion.

For the highest and best use of a property as improved (i.e., existing subdivision lots rather than vacant acreage), the existing lot infrastructure and project amenities, location, and other property characteristics are analyzed in comparison with the ideal improvement and associated marketing concept described for the site as though vacant. The highest and best use of improved lots may be the continuation of the existing subdivision with the same marketing price points and design criteria or the conversion of the lots to a different home building concept.

Determining the highest and best use for a mixed-use parcel of land or existing subdivision lots with commercial, office, or industrial uses can be more complicated and may involve the consideration of a separate highest and best use for each lot or group of lots within the lot inventory. Again, the appraiser's goal is to define the ideal use for the property in order to select appropriate comparable sales.

Highest and Best Use of Existing Lots

Evaluating a group of lots in an existing subdivision may be a relatively simple highest and best use exercise. Still, the ideal use should be defined as specifically as possible. For vacant residential subdivision lots, the appraiser would describe the typical single-unit dwelling to be built on the various lots as well as the marketing price point for the home and lot package, the typical building size range, and other parameters.

The appraiser considers current subdivision amenities, infrastructure, and price points as well as supply and demand characteristics to conclude financially feasible uses and the maximally productive use for the subject lots. There may be different highest and best use conclusions for various lots within the inventory. For example, an appraisal of 20 existing lots that are located in different "pods" within a large subdivision project may require a separate conclusion for the lots in each pod. Ten of the lots may be located in the patio home section of the development, with the remaining ten lots located in the upper-end, custom home section of the project. The patio home lots would have a different highest and best use than the custom home lots, but both types of lots will have a general use for residential development with single-unit homes. Highest and best use analysis would require a defined conclusion describing the specific ideal use for each group of lots. The appraiser describes the home characteristics and targeted home size and price range for each group of lots and ensures that the highest and best use conclusion is consistent with the subdivision restrictions.

Highest and Best Use of Proposed Developments

One common application of subdivision valuation is the appraisal of a proposed subdivision project. For this type of appraisal, the highest and best use addresses the use of the vacant tract of land and the support for its immediate development. Under this assignment scenario, the goal of a highest and best use as vacant analysis is to estimate the ideal subdivision to be placed on the vacant site and the timing of development. Typical subdivision price points, supply and demand, and site adaptability are explored to develop a conclusion of the financially feasible uses and the maximally productive use. The maximally productive use study could identify multiple marketing concepts and/or subdivision layouts while supporting the same or a very similar current vacant land value.

The highest and best use analysis for a proposed subdivision addresses the same considerations for existing lots and vacant acreage. However, when performing the improvement analysis, the appraiser studies the proposed subdivision according to the plans and specifications provided. The appraiser assumes that the plans, specifications, proposed subdivision restrictions, and marketing concept (price points for eventual homes) have been accurately described by the developer. If necessary details are missing, the appraiser may introduce extraordinary assumptions with respect to preliminary plans or other project criteria and may have to discuss these extraordinary assumptions with the client (if the lack of detail and/or complete plans were not already identified as part of the initial scope of work determination).

The appraiser must recognize that the highest and best use conclusion may be directly limited by the marketing concept employed for the proposed subdivision. The appraiser considers the proposed subdivision amenities, infrastructure, and price points as well as supply and demand characteristics to conclude financially feasible uses and the maximally productive use for the proposed subdivision lots within the context of the proposed project. In most cases, the highest and best use as improved is consistent with the proposed subdivision plans and the highest and best use as though vacant.

However, a use or building concept proposed by the developer may not be the highest and best use of the site as though vacant. The proposed project may not be the maximally productive use of the site as though vacant, but it would hopefully be one of a group of financially feasible uses. The appraiser would need to explain this disparity in the highest and best use as improved portion of the appraisal report. Also, this condition may introduce a functional or external consideration into the appraisal analysis. This does not automatically mean that the project would not be financially successful. The developer may have chosen a project design that fits well within that builder's skill level and design concept for other successful projects in the area. The proposed design could be the highest and best use of the project as proposed, but not the optimum use of the site as though vacant.

Under this scenario the appraiser then continues with the appraisal of the proposed project, since that is the assignment at hand. Also, as described in the highest and best use as though vacant, it is possible for different marketing concepts and subdivision layouts to support the same or a similar maximally productive present land value.

6
Profit and Timeline Concepts

Introduction

This chapter provides an overview of the typical timeline concepts involved in subdivision valuation and considers where profit is earned in each stage of the process. Attention is given to the typical valuation points for lending clients and for existing projects versus proposed projects.

One of the most difficult aspects of subdivision valuation is the various timeline concepts that are involved and the many valuation points along the timeline. Subdivision valuation may include excess or surplus land for future phases, common infrastructure, and amenities installed at various points in time. The appraiser may have an appraisal assignment to value a group of existing lots, a proposed project, or a combination of these. A combined appraisal of existing lots, proposed lots, and excess land must be valued at various points along the timeline. All of this can become quite confusing. A good understanding of timeline concepts and where profit is earned at each stage of subdivision development is essential for applying the three approaches to value.

Timeline and Profit

The expectation of profit is common to all real estate markets, including subdivision developments. Different levels of profit must be considered depending on the date of value and where the project is along the development timeline. It is entirely possible that profit can be earned during all three phases of subdivision development—the permitting phase, the construction phase, and the absorption phase. Allocating dollar profit along the timeline is one of the most difficult aspects of subdivision valuation. Part of the problem is assigning risk. To do this, the appraiser must consider when risk is encountered in the completion of a subdivision and when the profit is earned. The earning of profit depends on general market and property-specific characteristics, but it can generally be earned anywhere along the timeline.

Federal lending guidelines indicate specific values to be reported. *As is* market value is always needed, and other valuation scenarios are also allowed. Subdivisions fall under the lending guidelines for tract developments. *Frequently Asked Questions on Residential Tract Development Lending*—a memorandum published in 2005 by the Board of Governors of the Federal Reserve System, the Federal Deposit Insurance Corporation, the National Credit Union Administration, the Office of the Comptroller of the Currency, and the Office of Thrift Supervision—is provided in the Appendix of this book. The memorandum states that "the appraisal should reflect the value of the property in its current condition and existing zoning as well as the market value of land upon completion of land improvements, if applicable. The land improvements may include the construction of utilities, streets, and other infrastructure necessary for future development." Typically, the initial valuation for a proposed development is the *as is* value reported at the current date (time zero), and the *when complete* value is as of the future point in time when construction is finished and the lots are ready to be sold. The *when stabilized* concept is not applicable to subdivision valuation. The values reported are also evaluated within the context of the three phases of development.

Permitting Phase

Profit is typically earned during the permitting phase by successfully permitting a project and achieving the necessary approvals and entitlements for construction when there is market demand to support new development. Markets in which entitlements are difficult to obtain or long-term time frames are required typically support a higher profit upon approval.

Construction Phase

Profit may be earned in the construction phase when there is significant risk in construction (i.e., cost or timing). Risk may first arise from determining an accurate cost to construct the site infrastructure or from an economic environment in which costs are changing rapidly. The construction phase typically produces minimal profit in comparison to the permitting and absorption phases.

Absorption Phase

The profit earned in the absorption phase is directly related to the successful marketing and sale of the entire lot inventory. This profit is the typical amount of money necessary to attract a developer or investor to purchase a group of lots, recognizing the time needed to market the lot inventory as well as the holding and sales costs over the absorption period. A reasonable profit must be allocated to attract capital to a bulk sale lot purchase. The absorption phase can be subject to relatively high risk, depending on market characteristics, and this phase can achieve a relatively high profit return.

Exhibit 6.1 provides a general comparison of two separate markets and how profit may be distributed among the three phases of development.

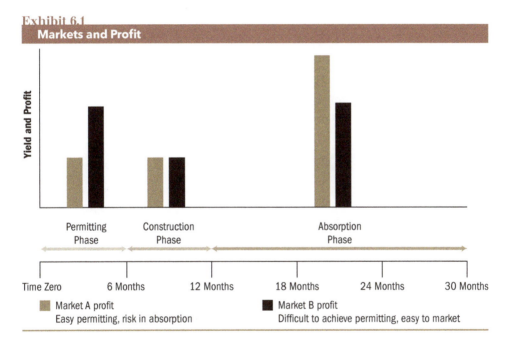

Exhibit 6.1
Markets and Profit

Most of the risk exists in the absorption phase in Market A. The characteristics of Market A include the following:

- The development approval process is relatively easy.
- The time frames for zoning and entitlements are short (up to one year).
- Activity by land planners and attorneys for the permitting process is less intensive.

Profit and Timeline Concepts

- Marketing has more risk because it is easy to quickly bring competing projects online.
- Permitting involves less risk and profit.
- Marketing and the sustained absorption of lots involves more risk and profit.

The appraiser would expect to experience the most risk and the highest profit during the absorption phase in Market A.

Permitting is more difficult to achieve in Market B. Other Market B characteristics include the following:

- Development involves long lead time frames (one to three years) to achieve permitting.
- The front-end costs for land planners and engineers to design preliminary subdivision drawings are high.
- Attorneys, numerous community meetings, etc., are involved.
- The eventual marketing of lots is relatively easy and fast because the supply is limited.

As shown in Exhibit 6.1, Market B would typically have a higher profit expectation for the permitting phase. Since it is so difficult to bring inventory onto the market, the absorption is relatively fast and has minimal risk.

Typical Value Reference Points

Exhibit 6.2 provides a timeline with typical value reference points that may occur during the subdivision development process. It is possible to provide value anywhere along the timeline, and four of the most common value dates or reference points are shown.

**Exhibit 6.2
Valuation Timeline**

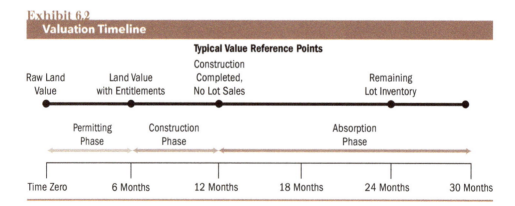

Raw Land Value

The *raw land value* reference point would typically indicate an *as is* value for vacant land that has not gone through a subdivision review or entitlement process and therefore has not achieved a final site plan approval. Vacant sites at this point in time typically do not have any entitlements and are not ripe for immediate development. The land sales comparison approach is usually used at this point in time, and the value indication would be valid at the start of the permitting and entitlement phase. Appraisal assignments undertaken at the *raw land value* point in time are usually very difficult because actual use densities and stipulations required by local authorities for future development may be unknown, which may add variability to the value conclusion.

Land Value with Entitlements: After Permitting Is Achieved but Before Subdivision Construction

The point in time when the proposed project has achieved final site plan approval and has full development entitlements is known as *land value after permitting is achieved but before subdivision construction*. This valuation date occurs just before the construction phase and at the end of the permitting phase. Depending on the development environment surrounding the project, land values can significantly increase at this point. Substantial profit may have been earned by successfully receiving final site plan approval from local authorities. At the *land value after permitting is achieved but before subdivision construction* reference point, the developer has approved subdivision development plans and wants to borrow funds to construct the subdivision. Appraisals for lending clients may be made at this point in time.

Construction Completed, No Lot Sales

The point when subdivision site infrastructure is 100% built and all construction has been completed is referred to as *construction completed, no lot sales*. This date is the *when complete* valuation point for proposed projects. At this point in time, subdivision value is at its highest. The developer has a full inventory of vacant improved lots available for sale for the immediate construction of residential units. The *construction completed, no lot sales* reference point may have relatively high risk, depending on the level of market acceptance for the development concept and the competition for similar projects in the area. If the appraisal is for an existing group of lots, the analysis would reflect an *as is* value as of the current time period.

Remaining Lot Inventory

Groups of remaining lots can be valued anywhere along the absorption timeline. The appraiser considers the appropriate level of remaining profit and expenses to determine the market value of the remaining lot inventory on a bulk sale basis. For an existing group of lots, the estimate would reflect *as is* value.

Typical Value Reference Points for Lending Clients

Many subdivision appraisals are performed for lending clients, and lending clients require specific values. As described in Advisory Opinion 30, the required values always include the *as is* value and may include the *when complete* value for a proposed project (see Chapter 1). The term *stabilized value* is not applicable to subdivision valuation.

Proposed Project

Proposed subdivision appraisals require the determination of an appropriate *when complete* date, which is a prospective value estimate. While a prospective value estimate may appear as a simple determination, there may be multiple *when complete* dates depending on the appraisal problem. For example, a project with multiple phases being built simultaneously may have different completion time frames for the various phases of development. The appraiser must identify the separate phases and consider the appropriate *when complete* dates and time frames.

Exhibit 6.3 illustrates the typical valuation points for lending clients. This exhibit relates to a single-phase project with one *when complete* date and an associated absorption period.

**Exhibit 6.3
Valuation Timeline**

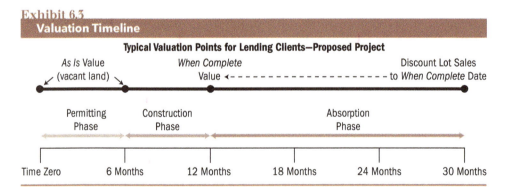

As Is Land Value

The *as is* land value is typically a value for vacant land either as raw land or with some level of entitlements. If land value is estimated at the end of the permitting phase, all permitting (full entitlements) would be in place for immediate construction. Some level of profit may have been earned as part of the permitting process, and the cost to achieve the permitting should be considered. The sales comparison approach is most often used to estimate *as is* land value. Care should be taken when selecting comparable land sales to ensure that these properties have similar levels of entitlements to the subject property.

In some cases, sales with similar levels of entitlements may be very difficult to find. The appraiser may need to revert to using the subject's raw land value and adjusting the land value for any entitlements in place at the time of the appraisal. This can create a relatively complicated appraisal issue for a site with full entitlements. For example, a cost approach analysis of a proposed subdivision would typically include the cost for the permitting process, which includes engineering, surveys, environmental audits, attorney's fees, land planner fees, and other costs. In addition, some level of profit has probably been earned as part of the permitting process. When using land value with full entitlements in the cost approach, it would not be appropriate to also add the cost to achieve these entitlements in reproduction cost new. The cost approach requires the appraiser to perform an internal "cost accounting" to ensure that each level of cost and/or profit is considered only once. The appraiser may use raw land value and include permitting costs and profit as separate line-item cost estimates in the cost approach. Alternatively, a cost approach using land value with full entitlements would exclude the cost needed to achieve permitting and profit over the permitting period because the elements are already considered in the *as is* land value estimate. Either method is acceptable. However, when reporting current *as is* value for lending clients, the full land value with any entitlements in place must be stated.

When Complete Value

The *when complete* value reference point is the point when lots are 100% built and ready to be sold in the local marketplace. This point occurs immediately after construction, when the project has achieved a final completion approval. For proposed projects, value indications at the *when complete* reference point are typically for prospective value, and all values are reported as of the future *when complete* point in time. If the current *as is* value in Exhibit 6.3 is made at the end of the permitting period (six months), then the *when complete* value would be six months in the future (twelve months from time zero). *Time zero* is the current date or the *when complete* date, depending on the appraisal timeline.

Absorption analysis may or may not consider lot presale contracts, depending on client requirements. The retail value of the individual lots less holding and sales costs and the consideration of profit are discounted to the *when complete* date. One of the major misconceptions in subdivision valuation is that the bulk sale value is discounted to time period zero. For a proposed project, the discounting of lot sale proceeds is brought back to the *when complete* date, which is a future point in time. Lending requirements specifically state that values must be reported at the point at which they occur along the timeline. This requirement has significant ramifications for projects that are phased over time.

In summary, two values are typically reported to lending clients for a proposed subdivision project: the market value *as is*, which is typically vacant land value with some level of entitlements, and the future *when complete* value at the point in time when the subdivision construction is 100% completed. All lot sales income and appropriate holding and sales costs and profits are discounted over the absorption period to the *when complete* date.

Existing Project

The appraisal of an existing project or group of lots is more straightforward from a timeline perspective. Exhibit 6.4 provides a timeline scenario for an existing project and typical values reported for lending clients. In an existing project, the lots are already built, and no permitting or construction phase is considered as part of the appraisal. An existing project is essentially an *as is* lot inventory that must be valued as of the current date. Accordingly, the appraisal will provide a bulk sale value of the entire lot inventory and will report an *as is* value. The sum of the retail lot values less holding and sales costs over the absorption period and the appropriate profit and discount rate are used to reflect an *as is* value. In Exhibit 6.4, this value is representative of a lump-sum purchase of all lots to one buyer as of time period zero. Actually, the only difference between this valuation and the one in Exhibit 6.3 is that the *when complete* date is used in the example in Exhibit 6.3. The result is a prospective value under the proposed project scenario. The discounting process is the same in the income capitalization approach, and the presentation of the cost analysis and/or sales comparison approach for a bulk sale would be similar in terms of the methodology employed; the only difference would be the time period involved for the date of value.

Raw Land Value by Subdivision Analysis

Subdivision valuation methodology can also be used to estimate the market value of a parcel of land for which subdivision development is the highest and best use of the vacant site (see Exhibit 6.5). This is one of the original applications of the subdivision development methodology as employed in the income capitalization approach. Most of the examples in this book involve valuing a group of lots that must be sold over a period of time. Some examples of using the subdivision valuation methodology to estimate raw land value are also provided. In these cases, the highest and best use must be for immediate or near future subdivision development. Also, the sales comparison approach would be the most accurate indicator of vacant land value and should always be used as a first choice in estimating vacant land value for a site that is available for development.

The income capitalization approach can be used to estimate raw land value. However, the value conclusion for raw land is usually subject to a higher degree of variability than would be associated with the results of a sales comparison approach because relatively small changes in estimates of absorption, retail lot values, and the time frames involved in permitting, construction, and absorption

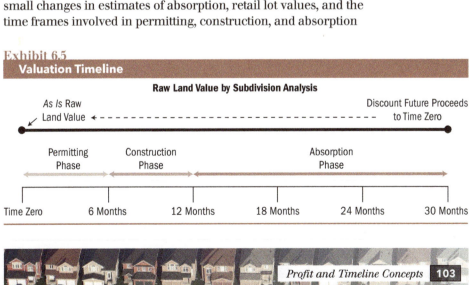

can have a significant impact on raw land value in a DCF analysis. Land value is derived as a residual in the subdivision valuation technique. The income capitalization approach is typically only used to value vacant land when sales of similar vacant tracts are not available or the unique characteristics of the property require subdivision analysis. For example, the income capitalization approach may be needed to value sites in market areas that are almost 100% built up and have relatively few vacant sites. In valuing vacant development sites in "in fill" locations, market sales of vacant parcels are rarely available for comparison purposes, and subdivision analysis using the income capitalization approach is one of the few tools that may be used to approximate an *as is* land value.

The estimation of land value by the income capitalization approach begins at time period zero (typically the current *as is* date) and considers the permitting time, the construction period, and the absorption period needed to market the lot inventory. This type of valuation requires many of the same inputs as the valuation of the subdivision but takes the analysis one step further and provides a residual vacant land value conclusion based on a hypothetical subdivision development scenario. The appraiser must estimate the amount of time required to obtain permitting, the cost associated with the permitting, and any profit earned by achieving a successful site plan approval in addition to the typical elements needed to value a proposed project. All of the cash flows and costs are discounted to time period zero to reflect an *as is* land value. If the intended use of the appraisal is to report raw land value, the costs and profit associated with any entitlements are also subtracted as part of the development cost over time in the discounting process. If the entitlements have been achieved at the date of valuation (time period zero), the costs and profit associated with the permitting process would not be subtracted in the discounting process.

The appraiser should use great care when using this technique to value vacant land. All of the underlying assumptions must be in place for the analysis to reflect an appropriate land value estimate. The primary consideration is that the highest and best use must be for immediate development sufficient to support a financially feasible development scenario. If this is not the case for a vacant parcel of land being appraised, then an alternative valuation method should be used.

Timeline and Value

Exhibit 6.6 illustrates the value timeline for a typical proposed project. This timeline is consistent with Exhibit 6.3, which shows the typical valuation points for a proposed project specified by lending clients. Exhibit 6.6 expands the timeline graph by adding a value line overlay. In this example, time period zero is the point

Exhibit 6.6
Timeline and Value

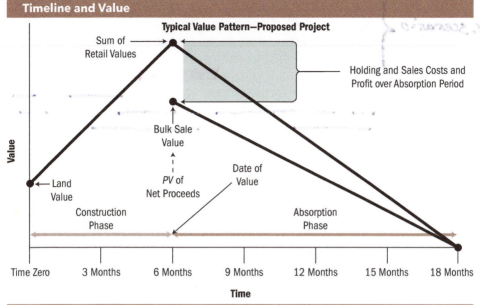

when all entitlements have been achieved, just before the construction of the proposed subdivision. The values actually reported to the client include land value at time period zero and the market value of the proposed project at the point in time when subdivision improvements are 100% built. In Exhibit 6.6, this point in time would be six months in the future. Accordingly, the *when complete* date is a prospective value that will not occur until after the subdivision improvements are 100% built and the lots are made ready to accept residential dwelling units. In this example, construction completion is six months from the current date.

The sum of the retail values indication is the sum of the retail values of each lot as of the *when complete* date. This value is not typically reported to the lending client, but it is needed as a reference value to facilitate the calculation of bulk value. The bulk sale value is the market value of the proposed subdivision as of the *when complete* date. In the example in Exhibit 6.6, the date of value is six months in the future and is a prospective valuation date.

Now, the appraiser focuses on the valuation of a group of lots as of the *when complete* date. One confusing aspect of subdivision analysis is that different terms are often used to describe the same concept. For example, the lending industry uses *when complete*, but the value as of the *when complete* date can also be referred to as *market value under the bulk sale* scenario. Advisory Opinion 30 of USPAP and publications by the lending industry make it clear that the sum of the retail values is not the market value for proposed subdivision projects or tract developments.

Profit and Timeline Concepts

bulk sale scenario — The bulk sale scenario takes the perspective of the lump-sum market value that the lots would have to one purchaser who must market the lots over a required absorption period, pay all holding and sales costs associated with marketing the lots over time, and earn sufficient profit to attract capital to the purchase. Obviously, the bulk sale or *when complete* value must be less than the sum of the retail values because of marketing and sales costs, holding costs over time, and advertising and other promotional expenses, as well as the expectation of profit. The goal of the developer or investor is to sell the lots as quickly as possible. When the last lot is sold, the value of the subdivision goes to zero.

The appraiser can begin the valuation process at any point along the absorption timeline. The bulk sale value will always be less than the sum of the retail values because of the costs associated with the sale and marketing of the lots and the expectation of profit. However, when relatively few lots are left in the inventory, the sum of the retail values and the bulk sale value will be about the same. This similarity is recognized by the lending industry. In fact, a bulk sale value is not required for any inventory of less than five lots. The bulk sale value is the present value of net proceeds. Conversely, the difference between the sum of the retail values and the bulk sale value is the sum of the holding and sales costs and the profit over the absorption period. The net proceeds are discounted over the entire 12-month absorption period to the date of value, which is 6 months in the future in the example in Exhibit 6.6. Estimating present value as of time period zero is one of the common mistakes appraisers make in the subdivision valuation of proposed projects for lending clients. The current value in this example is land value as of time period zero. Land value may be raw land value or land value with some level of entitlements, depending on the status of the site as of time period zero. In Exhibit 6.6, the vacant land is being valued at the end of the permitting phase and would include all entitlements.

Most of the terminology and discussion relating to timeline concepts relate to the income capitalization approach to value and discounting sales proceeds over time to a present value. As described in Chapter 1, the income capitalization approach is a primary valuation tool in estimating the value of proposed subdivisions because the character of a subdivision inherently involves cash flow over time from the sales of lots. The income capitalization approach, and more specifically DCF analysis, becomes a primary valuation tool in estimating the market value of a proposed subdivision or an existing group of lots or units. The cost and sales comparison approaches are also applicable and can be used to estimate the bulk sale value of a proposed or completed subdivision project.

7
Income Capitalization Approach

Introduction

Subdivisions are properties that have irregular income patterns, generate income over relatively short time horizons, and are subdivided for resale at a profit. As a result, the income capitalization approach using discounted cash flow (DCF) analysis is a primary valuation tool for appraisal problems that involve subdivision valuation.

Application of the income capitalization approach requires an understanding of timeline concepts as well as how DCF analysis is applied to irregular income over time to provide an estimate of market value. Subdivision valuation always considers income flows from lot or unit sales over a relatively short absorption period (usually less than five years). While large subdivision developments can have time horizons of more than five years, the development is usually phased so that individual phases span shorter absorption periods. This phasing occurs because long absorption periods can take profit away from the development when holding costs over time erode the profit potential from lot sales. Profit is generally higher when absorption periods are shorter. The investment goal for most subdivision developments is to sell the lots as quickly as possible and at the highest price to maximize profit.

Real estate valuation using the income capitalization approach employs two general methods that can be used to convert income into a value conclusion: direct capitalization and yield capitalization.

Direct capitalization methods are designed to value properties with regular income flows over time in a discernable pattern,

[Direct Capitalization] such as properties with level income or income changing at a constant ratio or a constant amount per period. For example, an office building may have a net income that is increasing over time at 2% per year. In this case, a capitalization rate extracted from current market sales of office properties with similar income and expense structures and similar expectations for future growth would be used. To apply the method, the first year's net income is divided by the capitalization rate to derive a value conclusion. Net income generated by subdivision development is rarely level and usually does not follow any specific pattern, so direct capitalization is not applicable and cannot be used.

The yield capitalization method is designed to value properties that do not have regular or discernable patterns of income over time. These are properties with irregular income patterns, and subdivisions fall into this category. Characteristically, income generated from lot sales is irregular over time, and the income eventually goes to zero when the last lot is sold. For this reason, yield capitalization using DCF analysis is the income method used for subdivision valuation.

This book focuses primarily on the valuation of improved subdivisions with vacant home lots, which are groups of existing lots with valuation as of time period zero or proposed subdivisions with valuation analysis based on *when complete* values as of some future point in time. The costs and time frames considered can vary depending on the appraisal problem and the intended user. Three common valuation scenarios are

- A value estimate for an existing group of lots as of time period zero
- A value estimate for a proposed subdivision as of a future point in time
- An *as is* raw land value estimate considering a subdivision development scenario

All of these valuation scenarios use DCF analysis and yield capitalization to report either a present value or a prospective value for a proposed project. A complete understanding of the timelines involved and the costs and profit considered at each stage of the valuation are critical when developing a DCF analysis.

This chapter provides a complete overview of the timeline concepts involved and the yield capitalization methodology applied to a proposed single-unit residential subdivision. The Mill Pond project is a typical suburban subdivision designed to support detached single-unit homes on individual lots. In this chapter, the income capitalization approach is applied to value the project. The same project is used to illustrate the application of the cost approach in Chapter 8 and the sales comparison approach in Chapter 9. The reconciliation and final value conclusion for the Mill Pond project is provided at the end of Chapter 9. Later in this chapter, the Sugarbush Case Study is used to illustrate subdivision analysis with presales of lots and with mortgage financing.

Timeline Overview

The income capitalization approach using DCF analysis is a very flexible valuation tool. However, some difficulty can arise concerning the timeline and the appropriate point along the timeline when the valuation is taking place.

The Mill Pond project is a proposed subdivision, which is one of the most common valuation scenarios encountered by appraisers. In this scenario, the value to be reported is a prospective value rather than a current *as is* value because a program of building must be conducted to install site infrastructure on a vacant tract of land. The site infrastructure supports completed subdivision lots with installed infrastructure (utilities, roads, water retention, etc.) and facilitates the building of single-unit homes or other building units. Accordingly, the future value reported will not occur until after all the subdivision lots are 100% built and made ready to accept single-unit dwellings.

Applying the Income Capitalization Approach

This section provides a more detailed view of the income capitalization approach process and the required inputs needed to arrive at a value conclusion for the proposed Mill Pond subdivision project. Because the Mill Pond project is a proposed subdivision, the income capitalization approach requires an estimate of the time frame needed to complete construction of the lots to determine the *when complete* date. For the Mill Pond project, the construction timeline is estimated at six months, and the *when complete* date is six months in the future. The prospective value for the subdivision project will be estimated accordingly. The absorption period, which begins when the lots are 100% built, is the amount of time needed to sell out the entire lot inventory. Holding and sales costs are considered over the absorption period to estimate net proceeds, which are then discounted at an appropriate rate to indicate the present value of the net proceeds as of the *when complete* date. This bulk sale value is the market value of Mill Pond as of the *when complete* date reflected by the income capitalization approach.

Four Income Capitalization Approach Components

As described in the Introduction to this book, the income capitalization approach as applied in subdivision valuation has four required components:

- The retail lot value estimate
- The absorption period estimate
- The holding and sales costs over the absorption period
- The discount rate analysis or line-item profit analysis used for the present value calculation

Both the discount rate and line-item profit are a function of overall profit associated with the absorption period. The four components appear in the subdivision DCF analysis as shown in Exhibit 7.1.

Step 1 Exhibit 7.1 shows a typical subdivision DCF analysis. Time is shown in quarters in the first column. The analysis has 10 quarters and covers a 2.5-year absorption period. The four elements of the income capitalization approach are indicated in Exhibit 7.1. All of these elements are required inputs for any DCF analysis for subdivision valuation. The absorption forecast, which is the first element of the income capitalization approach, is represented by the first column and can be expressed either on a monthly, annual, semi-annual, or yearly basis.

Step 2 The retail lot value is the second component needed for the DCF analysis. In Exhibit 7.1, the average lot value is given for each quarter and starts at $41,500 per lot. The lot value increases over time at 4% per year, adjusted on an annual basis. The sum of all retail lot values is $3,240,700. The gross sales represent the gross proceeds that will accrue to the developer who has an inventory of lots that must be sold over a period of time.

Step 3 The third component considered in the DCF analysis consists of any holding and sales costs over the absorption period. These costs include items such as real estate taxes, security, insurance, maintenance, administrative costs, and other expenses that must be covered by the owner or developer over time. Also, as lots are sold, expenses associated with the sales of lots must be paid either to a real estate agent or in-house sales staff. Holding and sales costs are subtracted from the gross proceeds to indicate the net proceeds. In the example in Exhibit 7.1, there is no line-item profit and therefore the net proceeds are equal to the gross proceeds less all holding and sales costs. The total net proceeds are $2,971,044.

Step 4 The last step in any DCF analysis for subdivision valuation is the application of a discount rate to convert the net proceeds into a present value conclusion as of the *when complete* date for the proposed project. In Exhibit 7.1, the discount rate considers

Exhibit 7.1
Mill Pond Discounted Cash Flow—Four Income Components

				Absorption Holding and Sales Costs						Discount Rate	
Quarter	Lots Sold	Average Lot Value	Gross Sales	Sales 6.0%	Tax	Assoc. Dues	Misc. 2.0%	Line-Item Profit 0.0%	Net Proceeds	PV Factor 18.000%	Present Value
1	6	$41,500	$249,000	$14,940	$250	$500	$4,980	$0	$228,330	0.956938	$218,498
2	6	$41,500	$249,000	$14,940	$250	$500	$4,980	$0	$228,330	0.915730	$209,089
3	12	$41,500	$498,000	$29,880	$250	$500	$9,960	$0	$457,410	0.876297	$400,827
4	10	$41,500	$415,000	$24,900	$250	$500	$8,300	$0	$381,050	0.838561	$319,534
5	8	$43,200	$345,600	$20,736	$1,000	$300	$6,912	$0	$316,652	0.802451	$254,098
6	8	$43,200	$345,600	$20,736	$1,000	$300	$6,912	$0	$316,652	0.767896	$243,156
7	10	$43,200	$432,000	$25,920	$1,000	$300	$8,640	$0	$396,140	0.734828	$291,095
8	7	$43,200	$302,400	$18,144	$1,000	$300	$6,048	$0	$276,908	0.703185	$194,718
9	5	$44,900	$224,500	$13,470	$1,000	$100	$4,490	$0	$205,440	0.672904	$138,241
10	4	$44,900	$179,600	$10,776	$1,000	$100	$3,592	$0	$164,132	0.643928	$105,689
	76		$3,240,700	$194,442	$7,000	$3,400	$64,814	$0	$2,971,044		$2,374,945
										Indicated bulk sale value	$2,374,945
										Rounded	$2,370,000

Absorption Period

Retail Lot Value

Holding and Sales Costs

Discount Rate and Line-Item Profit

two components. These components are line-item profit and the actual discount rate used for the present value calculation.

Whenever zero line-item profit is given in the analysis, the discount rate is a "true" internal rate of return (*IRR*) or yield rate for subdivision discounting. In the example in Exhibit 7.1, all profit is reflected in the selection of an 18% discount rate. Discounting the future net proceeds over the 2.5-year holding period on a quarterly basis indicates a present value of $2,374,945, rounded to $2,370,000. This is the market value using a bulk sale scenario of the entire subdivision inventory as of the *when complete* date. Accordingly, this is the market value for the proposed subdivision project anticipated to contain 76 lots at the time of valuation.

A more complete discussion of line-item profit versus discount rate is provided in Chapter 10. The income capitalization approach as applied to the Mill Pond project in this chapter uses an overall yield rate with zero line-item profit. The next section of this chapter provides a detailed description of all four components of the income capitalization approach and the value conclusion determined by the income capitalization approach for the Mill Pond project.

Mill Pond Case Study

The Mill Pond project is a typical, detached single-unit subdivision with a total of 76 residential lots. The construction period is estimated at about six months, which would indicate a *when complete* date of July 2018, as shown in Exhibit 7.2. The subdivision supports two separate price points. The 40 small lots have an average lot size of 8,700 square feet and 80 front feet. The second price point consists of 36 larger lots with an average size of 11,000 square feet or about 100 front feet. Most of the lots are regular interior or corner lots. The eight cul-de-sac lots make up about 10.5% of total lots within the project.

This subdivision has minimal common area amenities: a small playground area with a parking lot and fencing, a typical entrance with landscaping and an irrigation system, and passive open space. There will be a unit owners association for the maintenance of all common areas, including the front entrance and playground area. The association will have minimal fees, which is typical for similar projects in the area. The marketing concept supports an overall approximate price range for home and lot packages on small lots of $140,000 to $200,000. The average price is $170,000. The larger lots support a single-unit approximate price range of $180,000 to $220,000, with an average price of $200,000. In this market, cul-de-sac lots typically sell for about 10% more than regular interior or corner lots. Two types of lot premiums are being considered in this subdivision: lot size category and cul-de-sac location.

The Mill Pond subdivision descriptive information is the same for all three approaches to value. Because this subdivision is a proposed project, the date of value is six months in the future as of the *when complete* date.

The four required components of the income capitalization approach are applied to the Mill Pond project to reflect a market value conclusion for the bulk sale value of all 76 lots as of the *when complete* date. The project data is provided in Exhibit 7.2.

Exhibit 7.2
Mill Pond Project Summary

General Information

Mill Pond is a proposed single-unit subdivision to be built in the immediate future. The project is located in a well-established residential area and will be marketing detached single-unit lots and/or homes with two separate price points and two lot categories.

Project Timing

Current date:	01/01/2018
Construction start:	01/01/2018
Construction period:	6 months
Absorption start date:	07/01/2018

Site Characteristics

	Units	Size (Ac.)	Units/Ac.
Site area	76	28.50	2.67

Lot Inventory by Size Category

	Total Lots	Regular Lots	Cul-de-sac Lots	Avg. Lot Size (sq. ft.)	Avg. Lot Front Feet
Small lots	40	36	4	8,700	80
Large lots	36	32	4	11,000	100
Total	76	68	8		
%	100.0%	89.5%	10.5%		

Subdivision Site Amenities

Front entrance with signage and landscaping
Underground utilities (water, sewer, gas, and elec.)
Underground phone, cable TV
Paved interior roads, concrete curb, public roads
Streetlights, water retention, and open space

Subdivision Common Amenities

Playground area with small parking lot, fencing, and landscaping
Unit owners association

Marketing Concept

Target Price Range for Home and Lot

Lot Category	Lot Size Sq. Ft. ±	Home Size Sq. Ft. ±	Home Price Range		
			Low	Average	High
Small lots	8,700	1,500	$140,000	$170,000	$200,000
Large lots	11,000	2,000	$180,000	$200,000	$220,000

In this market, cul-de-sac lots sell for about 10% more than typical interior or corner lots, and lot value prices are increasing by about 4% per year.

Retail Lot Value Estimate

A retail lot value estimate takes into account the value of individual lots that make up a subdivision or a group of lots under study. For a proposed project, this estimate is the price or market value of the completed lots after all site infrastructure has been installed and the lots are made ready to accept building units.

Define the Marketing Concept

The marketing concept, which was described in Chapter 4, is integral to a conclusion of the retail lot value. The single-unit price points in a subdivision have a great influence on lot values, and the home price points are the single most important determinant of lot value in many markets. For example, a one-acre lot located in a subdivision designed for detached, single-unit homes in the $250,000 price range would command a different price than a one-acre lot in a development designed for the $500,000 price range. Each project must have the amenities to support the various marketing concepts, and the marketing concept must be defined in the appraisal along with the estimate of lot value. The marketing concept is usually described in the site description, improvement description, and highest and best use sections of the appraisal report. Also, new subdivisions may have subdivision restrictions that will match the marketing concept and "regulate" the size of homes for each lot category or section of the project.

For a proposed project, the marketing concept is usually defined by the project developer, and lot value is estimated within the context of the proposed home price range. The appraisal report usually includes a section that explains the marketing concept and how it relates to the valuation, the proposed subdivision layout, and the highest and best use. Consistent with USPAP guidelines, an extraordinary assumption is included in the appraisal that explains the marketing concept and makes the value estimate contingent on the concept being followed through to the eventual sale and marketing of the lots.

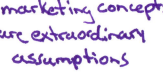
marketing concepts are extraordinary assumptions

While the concept of retail lot value is easy to understand, the actual determination can be relatively complicated, depending on the project and typical lot buyers in the market. For example, many entry-level housing developments are "closed" developments in which only one builder is marketing lots and/or completed housing units. Individual lots may not be sold to eventual homebuyers. In cases like this, the lot allocation method may be used to approximate typical lot prices within a project.

Another project might have a high-priced housing concept in which individual lots are regularly sold to end users and/or small groups of lots are sold at a discount to builders in the area.

Multiple prices for the same lots require the appraiser to anticipate the probable pattern of sales along with the typical purchaser for the subject lot inventory. Average retail lot value may be some combination of sales to different classes of users within the same project. The appraiser's ultimate goal, then, is to estimate the probable sale price and retail market value of each completed lot. This process becomes complicated when appraising a product category in which subdivision developers typically sell large groups of lots to builders for future use. These large group lot sales may approach the level of bulk sale value and not be representative of individual retail lot prices. The retail lot value is the market price supported by selling one lot to a single user.

Sales Comparison Approach

The sales comparison approach is the most common method used to derive vacant lot value estimates. After the marketing concept and targeted price range for the subject project is defined, a comparable sales search is performed. Lot sales in subdivisions that are similar in terms of home price range, marketing concept, and project amenities are selected for comparison purposes. For a proposed project, the lots are valued as of the *when complete* date and assuming all site infrastructure has already been installed. The price per lot, front foot, or other physical unit of comparison is typically used and may be refined to consider subcategories of lots within the project. Lot values are often stratified by size and type (e.g., interior, corner, cul-de-sac, creek front, golf course frontage). Other lot valuation methods are also available and can provide very accurate results. One of the most common alternative methods used in subdivision valuation is the allocation method. The retail lot value estimate for the Mill Pond project is derived using both the price-per–front foot method and the lot allocation method.

The price per front foot is one of the "physical" comparison methods. In subdivision design and layout, lots in each home price point within the project are usually designed to support a specific building footprint or group of footprints. Typically, the lots are grouped by front-foot size to coincide with a specific home product. Builders and developers design the lot sizes and overall subdivision layout to accommodate specific homes and the physical character of the land. A minimum lot depth is needed for each category of lots and should be considered as part of the analysis. The appraiser could also use the price per square foot or some other physical unit of comparison if that unit of comparison shows a higher correlation with lot values.

> **allocation**
> A method of estimating land value in which sales of improved properties are analyzed to establish a typical ratio of land value to total property value and this ratio is applied to the property being appraised or the comparable sale being analyzed.

Available sales are summarized in Exhibit 7.3, which provides an analysis of lot and home sales in seven comparable subdivisions. The seven projects reflect an overall price range for single-unit home and lot packages of approximately $104,000 to $325,000. The average single-unit price range for all seven projects is about $143,000 to $250,000, with an average of about $180,440 (see Exhibit 7.3).

Overall, the sales compare favorably with the targeted price range for the two price points in the subject project. The subject property supports an overall price range from a low of about $140,000 to a high of around $220,000. The average for the small lots is about $170,000 and the average for the larger lots is about $200,000, as shown in Exhibit 7.2. Exhibit 7.3 shows the average lot size for each project, the average front foot size of lots within the project, and the average price per square foot and front foot.

Subdivision analysis requires the appraiser to perform comprehensive research. Exhibit 7.3 provides a historical sales analysis for a group of comparable subdivisions. Exhibit 7.4 provides a history of lot and home sales specifically within one project–the Lupus Road Project–for 2017. Lupus Road provides the best direct comparison with the large lots in the Mill Pond project. Aggregate information, including lot size on a square-foot and front-foot basis, is shown with the indicated price per square foot and front foot for each lot sold within the project. The same analysis is made for all of the comparable projects, with the results summarized in Exhibit 7.3.

Sales activity in the Lupus Road subdivision includes sales of vacant lots to private individuals or builders within the area as well as sales of homes that were built and sold directly by the project developer. This project is an open development that allows homes to be built by individuals or other builders as well as the initial developer of the project. In 2017, a total of 36 vacant lots and/or homes were sold within the project. This number indicates an average absorption of about nine lots or units per quarter. For the absorption estimate, the appraiser quantifies the initial sale of either a vacant lot or an improved lot with a single-unit home. The sales statistics are summarized at the bottom of Exhibit 7.4.

As shown in Exhibit 7.4, the 20 lot sales indicate an average lot price of $3.93 per square foot, or about $450 per front foot. These coincide with the Lupus Road subdivision statistics in Exhibit 7.3. The comparable data shows that cul-de-sac lots are selling for about 10% more than typical interior lots on a price-per-front-foot basis. The average price per front foot for a cul-de-sac lot is $482, compared to $437 for a typical interior or corner lot. Homes in the Lupus Road subdivision range from about $185,000 to

Exhibit 75
Comparable Lot Sales

Project	Single-Unit Price Range			Lot Sales Price Range			Allocation Percentage	Price Points	Average Lot Size		Average Price Per	
	Low	High	Average	Low	High	Average			Sq. Ft.	Fr. Ft.	Sq. Ft.	Fr. Ft.
1. Kensington	$107,900	$223,400	$160,008	$23,738	$49,148	$35,202	22.00%*	2	9,000	98	$3.91	$359
2. Hyde Park	$131,300	$285,773	$188,999	$27,000	$46,219	$32,682	17.29%	2	8,800	100	$3.71	$327
3. St. James Park	$138,704	$188,594	$153,054	$30,515	$41,491	$33,672	22.00%*	1	6,000	60	$5.61	$561
4. Baywater	$104,000	$250,731	$167,713	$25,000	$47,000	$34,396	20.51%	2	10,000	95	$3.44	$362
5. Chelsea Lane	$195,000	$325,000	$250,000	$49,950	$82,500	$64,608	25.80%	2	8,400	85	$7.69	$760
6. Nine Elms	$124,000	$173,200	$142,852	$34,000	$35,000	$34,083	23.86%	1	7,405	75	$4.60	$454
7. Lupus Road	$185,000	$225,000	$200,451	$42,500	$49,000	$44,525	22.21%	1	11,317	99	$3.93	$450
Analysis												
Low	$104,000	$173,200	$142,852	$23,738	$35,000	$32,682	17.29%		6,000	60	$3.44	$327
High	$195,000	$325,000	$250,000	$49,950	$82,500	$64,608	25.80%		11,317	100	$7.69	$760
Average	$140,843	$238,814	$180,440	$33,243	$50,051	$39,881	21.95%		8,703	87	$4.70	$468

* Lot value allocation of 22%

Exhibit 7.4
Comparable 7–Sales History for Lupus Road Subdivision

| | | | Lot Sales History | | | Lot Sales Analysis | | | | Home Sales History | | |
| | | | | | | Regular Lots | | Cul-De-Sac Lots | | | | |
	Lot No.	Lot Type	Sale Price	Size Sq. Ft.	Size Fr. Ft.	Per Sq. Ft.	Per Fr. Ft.	Per Sq. Ft.	Per Fr. Ft.	Sale Price	Home Size Sq. Ft.	Home Price Sq. Ft.
Year 2017												
Quarter 1	1	Interior	$43,500	12,000	100	$3.63	$435					
	2	Corner	$43,500	12,000	100	$3.63	$435					
	4	Interior	$43,500	12,000	100	$3.63	$435					
	6	Interior	$45,500	12,600	105	$3.61	$433					
	7	Cul-de-sac	$49,000	14,000	98			$3.50	$500			
	8	Cul-de-sac	$48,000	13,500	98			$3.56	$490			
	11	Interior	$43,500	10,000	100	$4.35	$435					
	9	Cul-de-sac	$47,000	12,500	100			$3.76	$470			
	5	Interior	$44,000	12,000	100	$3.67	$440					
	10	Cul-de-sac	$47,000	14,000	100			$3.36	$470			
	3	Interior	$43,000	11,640	97	$3.69	$443					
	12	Interior	$44,000	10,500	105	$4.19	$419					
Quarter 2	13	Interior	$42,500	9,900	98	$4.29	$434					
	14	Interior	$43,500	10,780	98	$4.04	$444					
	15	Interior	$43,500	10,780	98	$4.04	$444					
	17	Interior	$43,500	11,000	100	$3.95	$435					
	16	Interior	$44,000	11,000	100	$4.00	$440					
	19	Interior	$44,000	11,000	100	$4.00	$440					
	20	Interior		10,450	95					$185,000	1,667	$110.98
	18	Interior		10,450	95					$195,000	1,750	$111.43
	21	Interior		10,450	95					$195,000	1,700	$114.71
Quarter 3	22	Interior		10,450	95					$191,000	1,680	$113.69
	23	Interior		10,500	95					$193,000	1,680	$114.88
	26	Cul-de-sac		12,500	95					$220,270	1,850	$119.06
	27	Cul-de-sac		12,700	95					$210,600	1,800	$117.00
	28	Cul-de-sac		12,700	95					$225,000	1,935	$116.28
	29	Cul-de-sac		12,500	95					$217,600	1,900	$114.53
	24	Interior		9,500	100					$187,000	1,780	$105.06
	25	Interior		9,500	100					$195,000	1,780	$109.55
	32	Interior		9,500	100					$194,750	1,780	$109.41
Quarter 4	30	Interior		11,000	100					$210,000	1,950	$107.69
	31	Interior		11,000	100					$195,000	1,700	$114.71
	33	Interior		10,000	100					$195,000	1,700	$114.71
	34	Interior		11,000	100					$198,000	1,700	$116.47
	35	Interior	$44,000	11,000	100	$4.00	$440					
	36	Interior	$44,000	11,000	100	$4.00	$440					
Low			$42,500	9,500	95	$3.61	$419	$3.36	$470	$185,000	1,667	$105.06
High			$49,000	14,000	105	$4.35	$444	$3.76	$500	$225,000	1,950	$119.06
Average			$44,525	11,317	99	$3.92	$437	$3.54	$482	$200,451	1,772	$113.13
Lot sales	20		Lot value ratio				22.2%	(average lot value ÷ average home price)				
Home sales	16		Average price per sq. ft.				$3.93	(average lot value ÷ average lot size sq. ft.)				
Total sales	36		Average price per fr. ft.				$450	(average lot value ÷ average lot size fr. ft.)				

Subdivision Valuation

$225,000, with an average of $200,451. Homes in this subdivision compare most favorably with the larger lots in the subject project in terms of lot size and the price range supported for single-unit homes in the development. Accordingly, the Lupus Road Project would be given the most weight in estimating retail lot values for the higher priced lots within the subject project.

The subject project's front-foot values are estimated based on a comparison with front-foot price levels in the Lupus Road project and the remaining six subdivisions used in the analysis. These values are shown in Exhibit 7.5. The prices range from $435 per front foot for large interior lots to $500 per front foot for the smaller cul-de-sac lots.

The allocation method is also used to derive the various Mill Pond lot values. This method, which compares sales of comparable lots to the sale price of the subject home and lot package, is often overlooked by appraisers estimating lot value. The allocation method can be very accurate and can be applied when current lot sales at a particular price point may not be readily available. This method is especially useful for entry-level housing developments and "closed" developments for which comparable vacant lot sales within the project are not available. *[Allocation Method]*

An elementary example employing the allocation method is shown in Exhibits 7.2, 7.3, and 7.4. The Mill Pond project contains 76 lots with two separate price points. This project has small and large lots. The home price ranges supported at each price level are summarized in Exhibit 7.2. The average home price is $170,000 for the smaller lots and $200,000 for the larger lots.

The allocation method begins with selecting comparable sales from projects that are similar to the subject property. In this example, the sales used for the price per front foot method are again used in the allocation method. Available sales are summarized in Exhibit 7.3. These sales include subdivisions marketing homes and lots at both price points. Four projects offer two price points, and three projects offer one price point. There is some overlap in terms of lot size between the projects that support two price points and those that support one price point. Aggregate statistics are accumulated for all seven subdivisions, and individual sales within the subdivision for both lots and homes were tabulated over time. The high, low, and average home and lot sale prices are reported for each project.

In Exhibit 7.3, the lot allocation percentage is calculated by dividing the average lot value by the average home sale price. For example, the lot ratio for the Chelsea Lane subdivision is calculated by dividing the average lot value of $64,608 by the average home price of $250,000, resulting in a ratio of 25.8%. This calculation is made for all seven comparable projects, and the re-

Exhibit 7.5
Mill Pond Retail Lot Value Conclusion

Description	Analysis		
Lot Allocation Method			
Indicated lot value ratio from market sales	Ratio =	22.00%	
Small Lots	Low	Average	High
Target home price range	$140,000	$170,000	$200,000
Supported lot value range	$30,800	$37,400	$44,000
Large Lots			
Target home price range	$180,000	$200,000	$220,000
Supported lot value range	$39,600	$44,000	$48,400
Price per Front Foot Method	Value per Fr. Ft.	Size Fr. Ft.	Indicated Lot Value
Small lots: Regular and corner lots	$460.00	80	$36,800
Cul-de-sac lots	$500.00	80	$40,000
Large lots: Regular and corner lots	$435.00	100	$43,500
Cul-de-sac lots	$480.00	100	$48,000
Estimated Lot Values	Lot Value	No. Lots	Total
Small lots: Regular and corner lots	$37,000	36	$1,332,000
Cul-de-sac lots	$40,700	4	162,800
Average value small lots	$37,370	40	$1,494,800
Large lots: Regular and corner lots	$44,000	32	$1,408,000
Cul-de-sac lots	$48,000	4	192,000
Average value small lots	$44,444	36	$1,600,000
Average retail lot value entire project	$40,721	76	$3,094,800
Adjustment for market conditions - 4% per yr. (6 months or 2%)			$41,535
Rounded (to nearest $100)			$41,500

sults are tabulated in Exhibit 7.3. The range is 17.29% to 25.80%, with an average of 21.95%.

Exhibit 7.3 shows that the Kensington and St. James Park subdivisions each have a lot allocation of 22% as estimated by the appraiser. Because these two subdivisions are "closed" developments and individual lot sales are not available for them, the lot values were abstracted from typical home price levels in the subdivisions. The lot allocation method can be used to approximate typical lot value price levels for comparable subdivisions when recognized patterns exist in the local market area.

The lot allocation percentage can be very consistent over a wide range of price points in markets throughout the country. Typically, retail lot values will range from about 15%-30% of the overall home and lot package, depending on the area of the country and individual project characteristics. In most developments, there is a relatively consistent ratio between home and lot prices. Lot prices do not usually increase unless there is an associated increase in the price of the home and lot package.

Conversely, lot values typically decrease as home price levels decrease due to oversupply.

The application of the lot allocation method in estimating retail lot values for the Mill Pond project is shown in Exhibit 7.5. In this calculation, an average ratio of 22% was used for both price points in the Mill Pond project. Applying a 22% ratio to the targeted price range for the two price points reflects an average lot value range of $37,400 per lot for small lots to $44,000 per lot for large lots. The cul-de-sac lots have an estimated value that is about 10% higher than typical interior or corner lots. Accordingly, the retail values for the cul-de-sac lots are about 10% higher than the typical lot within each category (see Exhibit 7.5).

The appraiser should recognize that a proposed project will require a retail lot value estimate as of the future point in time when the lots will be 100% built. If the construction period is six months and all values in the sales table reflect a market conditions adjustment to time period zero (the current date, or January 1, 2018), an additional market conditions adjustment (time adjustment) must be made to reflect the retail lot value as of the point in time when the lots will be completed six months in the future. The adjustment for the subject project is shown at the bottom of Exhibit 7.5. The average retail lot value is rounded to $41,500.

The DCF analysis should reflect any increase in lot value over the absorption period consistent with observed trends in the market. For example, if a subject market indicates an average increase in lot value of about 4% per year, an appropriate adjustment to the retail lot value should be included in the retail lot sales over time in the DCF analysis absorption forecast. The adjustment may be an average rate of increase over time, or the developer may increase lot values at the construction of each new phase. Typically, this is a flat increase that takes effect as each new phase is built. The method used in the marketplace should be applied or considered in the DCF analysis for the proposed subject subdivision. (The Mill Pond DCF analysis shown in Exhibit 7.8 later in this chapter reflects an annual adjustment of 4% per year.)

The allocation method is a recognized valuation tool in estimating retail lot values for subdivision projects. However, it is always important to compare the results of the allocation method with other valuation methods, including a physical unit comparison or a paired sales comparison, to identify lot value differences for various characteristics. For example, the allocation method may not be a good indicator of the difference between fairway frontage lots and typical interior lots in a project without a fairway view. Obviously, the home and lots on the fairway may sell at a higher price level, but the lot allocation ratio may not be the same for different categories of lots within the project. The results of the lot allocation method should always be compared with other methods for consistency. When a project provides a homogeneous product, the lot allocation method by itself can be a very consistent indicator of retail lot values. When there is a heterogeneous mix of lots, other methods may be better indicators of retail lot value.

Absorption Period Estimate

The absorption period is an estimate of the amount of time required for the market to absorb the lot or unit inventory over time. It provides a subject-specific estimate for the sell-out of all lots included in the value estimate whether the appraiser is considering a group of existing or proposed lots or using subdivision valuation methodology to estimate a vacant land value.

For a group of existing lots, the absorption estimate usually begins at the current date. For proposed projects, the absorption period begins when the subdivision site improvements are 100% built and it is a future absorption estimate (see Chapter 6). For example, a subdivision beginning construction in January with a nine-month construction period will begin absorption at the beginning of the tenth month. Lot values and market absorption are estimated at that point in time and are projected into the future. The absorption estimate may or may not reflect any presale contracts depending on the intended use of the appraisal and whether or not the client wants any presale contracts to be considered.

Proposed developments may have some lot presale contracts. The appraiser should discuss whether to include presale contracts in the initial absorption forecast with the client. Lending clients usually require initial forecasts to exclude any presale contracts. In this case, all lots would be priced at their retail lot values, and the typical fundamental absorption would be estimated ignoring any presales. The client may request several value scenarios with presale contracts. (See the discussion of absorption in Chapter 2 and the Sugarbush Case Study later in this chapter.)

A scenario that includes presale contracts would use the actual presale prices for lot inventory, timing of the presale contracts, and any other unique characteristics of presales as part of the forecast estimate. The value without presales is representative of market value. The value estimate considering presales would typically be labeled as "indicated value considering presales." Depending on the presale prices and the timing of the absorption or "take-down" provisions in the presale contracts, the value considering presale contracts could be greater than, the same as, or less than the value ignoring presale activity. In any case, presale activity should be discussed with the client as part of the scope of work decision, and multiple values may be included in the appraisal with and without presales.

The absorption period is generally one of the most sensitive determinants of profit. Most of the risk and profit associated with the sell-out of a group of lots is considered in the retail lot value estimate and the time period needed to market the lot inventory. Holding and sales costs and typical profit levels usually fall within established ranges in a particular market and are subject to less variability.

The absorption period is usually evaluated as the number of lots or units to be sold on a monthly, quarterly, semi-annual, or annual basis, depending on the size of the project and the level of detail available to support the analysis. For a small group of lots with a typical absorption of less than one or two years, the estimate may be expressed on a monthly or quarterly basis. Generally, the longer the absorption period, the greater the time frame considered. The goal is to form an opinion of market supply and demand over time and present a supportable forecast of capture and absorption for the subject product.

The six-step fundamental Level C market analysis described in Chapter 2 was conducted to estimate the absorption period for the Mill Pond project. The results of the forecast are shown in Exhibit 7.6.

Exhibit 7.6

Mill Pond Subdivision Absorption Estimate		
Year	**Quarter**	**Lot Absorption**
2018	1	n/a
	2	n/a
	3	6
	4	6
2019	1	12
	2	10
	3	8
	4	8
2020	1	10
	2	7
	3	5
	4	4
Total		76

Holding and Sales Costs

Holding and sales costs are typical expenses associated with maintaining and selling the lots over the absorption period. Holding costs include real estate taxes, insurance, project security expenses, sales and marketing costs, management and association fees, and administrative costs. These costs vary considerably depending on project characteristics, size, and location. Typical sales costs necessary to market the lot inventory include promotional costs, advertising, sales commissions, on-site sales staff, closing costs, and other indirect expenses. These costs can be estimated as lump-sum costs per period or based on percentages of gross sales.

Most of the examples relating to holding and sales costs presented in this text are relatively simple. Many of the expenses are expressed as percentages of gross sales. Other expenses such as real estate taxes, insurance, and other fixed expenses are typically expressed as lump-sum amounts per period. Line-item profit is not a "true" expense and is estimated in conjunction with the discount rate used in the present value calculation.

The holding and sales expenses for most of the examples in this book do not include mortgage interest or principal payments. However, several mortgage loan scenarios with equity return considerations are presented at the end of this chapter. All remaining examples are based on a total property perspective and do not directly reflect mortgage financing. It is common in many markets to include mortgage interest only during the construction period as part of the overall construction cost allocation. Under this scenario, construction interest is deducted as an expense for the construction period only and is included as an indirect construction cost in the cost approach. Also, all yield rates used for comparison should have a similar expense structure. If mortgage interest and principal are included in holding and sales costs over the absorption period, a mortgage-equity analysis is being performed and the appropriate equity yield rates should be used for any present value calculations.

Subdivision valuation methodology can be used to estimate the "bulk" value of an improved subdivision or to provide a "raw" land value estimate. The improved subdivision may be a group of existing lots or the proposed construction of a new project. The typical expenses considered in the bulk sale over the absorption period are the same whether the appraiser is dealing with existing or proposed lots. However, the analysis of vacant land requires additional consideration of expenses over the permitting and construction phases in addition to the absorption period.

Bulk Sale Value

When a bulk sale value for a group of lots is the objective of the analysis, holding and sales costs are those costs associated with marketing and inventory management activities over the absorption period only.

Typical holding costs may include

- Real estate taxes
- Insurance
- Project security expenses
- Association dues
- Project administration or sales office expenses
- Temporary utility costs or project maintenance
- Other miscellaneous holding costs

Typical sales costs include

- Legal and closing costs on lot sales
- Real estate commissions
- Profit allocation
- Other allocations
- Other miscellaneous costs

As with most real estate projects, there are always exceptions. There may be some remaining permitting fees, construction costs, or other costs to consider over the absorption period. Obviously, individual project characteristics and local practices dictate what is considered and what is excluded. Expense forecasts typically exclude mortgage financing from expenses unless a mortgage-equity analysis is being performed.

Exhibit 7.7 shows the holding and sales costs estimated for the Mill Pond project. Mill Pond is a relatively small subdivision with 76 lots that will be sold over an absorption period spanning 10 quarters, or 2.5 years. Because this subdivision project is relatively small and has a short absorption period, it would typically have minimal carrying costs. The carrying costs for the project are shown in Exhibit 7.7. Real estate taxes must be paid on the acreage parcel and/or developed lots throughout the absorption period. Typically, real estate taxes are paid for the vacant tract of land prior to the development of subdivision lots. In many communities, developed lots will not appear on the tax roll until about one year after they are actually built, with minimal taxes in the first year of sales.

Real estate taxes for Mill Pond are estimated at about $250 per quarter for the first year and average about $1,000 per quarter during the sell-off period. Taxes can be one of the highest carrying costs for vacant lots. In this example, taxes are estimated on a lump-sum basis. For longer marketing periods, periodic taxes may be estimated by applying the tax millage rate and the typical assessment ratio to any lots remaining in inventory at the end of each period.

The Mill Pond project will have a small recreational facility with a playground. Each lot or unit owner will contribute association dues for the maintenance of the developed common areas. Typically, the developer pays maintenance costs for any common improvements until the improvements are actually transferred to the unit owners association. At that time, the developer becomes responsible for association dues for any remaining lot inventory. However, this could vary from project to project. In this example, carrying costs are estimated at $500 per quarter for Year 1 (the first four quarters), $300 per quarter for Year 2, and $100 per quarter for Year 3. These estimates recognize that owners' association fees are paid over the entire absorption period by the developer, and will decrease over time as lot inventory decreases.

The sales costs associated with marketing the lot or unit inventory can vary substantially depending on whether the project is "open" or "closed." In an open development, lots are marketed to individuals and other builders. In a closed development, one builder will use the entire lot inventory. Even under the closed development scenario, appropriate sales expenses should be considered for typical administrative overhead and/or marketing expenses. The percentage used for the Mill Pond subdivision is 6%, which would include typical commission splits for local real estate brokers and/or sales efforts conducted by an on-site project management team. Sales expenses can vary substantially depending on the marketing concept and how lots are typically sold in the local area. Also, nominal miscellaneous expenses are included in the expense forecast to cover any legal, administrative, insurance, or other costs. These miscellaneous expenses are estimated at about 2% of gross sales for the Mill Pond project. The amounts are summarized in Exhibit 7.7 and will be applied

Exhibit 7.7
Mill Pond Subdivision

Holding and Sales Costs

Holding costs:
    Real estate taxes:
        $250 per quarter for the first calendar year, until the lots appear on the tax roll. Beginning the second calendar year, taxes are averaged at about $1,000 per quarter.
    Unit owners association fees:
        $500 per quarter for Year 1
        $300 per quarter for Year 2
        $100 per quarter for Year 3

Sales costs: Estimated at 6% of gross sales

Miscellaneous: Includes miscellaneous legal, administrative, or other costs. Estimated at 2% of gross sales.

to the income capitalization approach conclusion for the Mill Pond project.

Property Discount Rate Analysis

Discounting to present value is required to bring the future net cash flow from lot sales to the date of valuation. With subdivisions, discount rate analysis can be accomplished using a "true" yield rate or some combination of a line-item profit and discount rate. The second method is commonly called the *split-rate method*.

Two methods may be used to apply appropriate discounting in a subdivision valuation problem. The first method consists of using the "true" yield rate with zero or no line-item profit. The second method is to include line-item profit as an expense and select an appropriate discount rate that considers the line-item profit allocation.

The term *yield rate* has been changed to *discount rate* to reinforce the idea that this rate of return is not a true *IRR* or yield rate because line-item profit has been included in the expense allocation for the split-rate method. The discount rate used under the split-rate method is a "hybrid" rate, which is not a true yield rate. Mathematically, this rate is calculated in the same way as an *IRR* and yield rate. However, because the inputs for the split-rate method do not allow for all of the profit to flow into the calculation of the interest rate, this is a "hybrid" rate labeled as a *generic discount rate* in order to avoid the term *yield rate*. Both yield rates and internal rates of return require that all income, expenses, and profit be allowed to flow through into the calculation of the number. When line-item profit is included as an expense, the term *discount rate* is used instead of *yield rate*.

When line-item profit is employed in a subdivision discounting problem, the discount rate must be selected in conjunction with the line-item profit as a "matched pair." The matched-pair information typically comes from a market sale extraction, and should be reapplied to a subject property when line-item profit is considered in the DCF analysis.

Alternatively, the true *IRR* could be used with zero line-item profit. In the Mill Pond example, a "true" yield rate of 18% is used based on a comparison with rates extracted from market sales and market survey information (see Chapter 8).

If the methodologies for the split-rate method and yield rate method are employed correctly, they should generate similar results. If not, the appraiser is probably making an error. Once the appraiser selects the methodology to use for the discounting process, the next step is to estimate the appropriate yield or discount rate and the line-item profit. Ultimately, the rate selection is derived from market extraction or surveys and interviews with knowledgeable participants in the market.

Market Extraction vs. Survey Techniques

Market extraction is the easiest method to understand. In market extraction, the appraiser performs primary research and extracts yield and profit data from bulk sales. The dollar amount of profit earned, how it is allocated between the phases of development, the discount rate, and the line-item profit should all be extracted from market sales. This process is demonstrated in the Madison Square Case Study in Chapter 10.

One of the greatest advantages of market extraction is that the appraiser has good knowledge of the inputs and ensures that all components are considered in the same manner as they are applied in the valuation of the subject property. Elements to be considered include the basic physical and economic attributes of each bulk sale as well as the overall absorption period inherent in the bulk sale in comparison with a subject property and its absorption period forecast. As explained in the Time Zero Profit Dilemma section of Chapter 12, yield rates are very sensitive to the absorption time involved, especially for holding periods of less than about two years. Accordingly, any analysis of yield rates should consider the absorption time frame associated with the market extraction. Consistency between extraction and application is critical in any valuation assignment, including subdivision analysis.

Several weaknesses of market extraction include the inability to find bulk sales, especially sales that are comparable to the subject property. Also, older sales or historical absorption data may not represent current market rates and trends. However, appraisers can consider proposed developments for which known cost data is available, and the probable lot sale prices and absorption can be estimated. In fact, the results of market extraction using "real time" data considered by market participants provides good support for current market trends.

Market surveys can be used to estimate a yield rate for a subject property. Such surveys are valuable when extraction cannot be applied or sufficient local sales data is not available. Survey data can be obtained from regional and/or national data providers or from surveys and interviews performed by the appraiser. The data should be specific to the subdivision property class, risk, and geographical location. The data provider should explain how the rate was calculated, including the holding expenses considered in the rates. For example, some reporting sources may allow mortgage interest expenses to be considered as a holding expense in the rate calculation, essentially reporting an equity yield rate and not a property yield rate. Again, consistency is important for the subject comparison. Consideration should be given to ensure that the yield rates and/or profit levels collected from various sources are consistent with how the appraiser plans to apply the data to the valuation problem and the timelines involved. This includes consideration of the absorption time involved for the various data points. This is problematic for most reporting services, as often very limited information is available to make an informed rate selection.

For example, an appraiser may canvas developers to ascertain a property yield rate with zero line-item profit. One developer may state that his or her last project reflected an *IRR* with no line-item profit in expenses of 37% and that most other developers in the area use the same criteria. Upon further questioning, however, the appraiser may learn that this rate was an equity yield rate after project financing expenses were considered. This is not the same as a property yield rate ignoring financing. As a result, it would not be appropriate to use this rate.

Mill Pond Income Capitalization Approach

The income capitalization approach conclusion for the Mill Pond project is shown in Exhibit 7.8.

Exhibit 7.8 shows a DCF analysis with zero line-item profit using a yield rate of 18%. The yield rate was chosen based on a comparison of market surveys and market extraction techniques, which will be described in more detail in Chapter 10. In this spreadsheet presentation, the average retail lot value for both the small and large lots is provided from the retail lot value conclusion. The absorption period was estimated based on a Level C market analysis. A quarterly absorption forecast was used for the Mill Pond project to reflect the seasonal trends observed in the absorption analysis. Also, lot values were estimated to increase by 4% per year throughout the absorption period. Holding and sales costs were deducted from gross proceeds to indicate net proceeds. The net proceeds were then discounted at a rate of 18% per year, expressed on a quarterly basis (4.5% per quarter). The present value of the sell-out is $2,374,945, rounded to $2,370,000. This amount is reported as the market value of the subdivision as of the *when complete* date. Since no line-item profit is considered as part of the expenses, the discount rate of 18% is a "true" yield rate. In summary, the income capitalization approach reflects a market value of $2,370,000 for the Mill Pond project as of the *when complete* date.

Care must be taken when performing a DCF analysis to ensure that the appropriate discount factor is used with the associated interest rate and the time period involved. For example,

Exhibit 7.8
Mill Pond DCF Analysis

		Average		Absorption Holding and Sales Costs					Line-Item	Net	PV Factor	Present
Quarter	Lots Sold	Lot Value	Gross Sales	Sales 6.0%	Tax	Assoc. Dues	Misc. 2.0%		Profit 0.0%	Proceeds	18.000%	Value
1	6	$41,500	$249,000	$14,940	$250	$500	$4,980		$0	$228,330	0.956938	$218,498
2	6	$41,500	$249,000	$14,940	$250	$500	$4,980		$0	$228,330	0.915730	$209,089
3	12	$41,500	$498,000	$29,880	$250	$500	$9,960		$0	$457,410	0.876297	$400,827
4	10	$41,500	$415,000	$24,900	$250	$500	$8,300		$0	$381,050	0.838561	$319,534
5	8	$43,200	$345,600	$20,736	$1,000	$300	$6,912		$0	$316,652	0.802451	$254,098
6	8	$43,200	$345,600	$20,736	$1,000	$300	$6,912		$0	$316,652	0.767896	$243,156
7	10	$43,200	$432,000	$25,920	$1,000	$300	$8,640		$0	$396,140	0.734828	$291,095
8	7	$43,200	$302,400	$18,144	$1,000	$300	$6,048		$0	$276,908	0.703185	$194,718
9	5	$44,900	$224,500	$13,470	$1,000	$100	$4,490		$0	$205,440	0.672904	$138,241
10	4	$44,900	$179,600	$10,776	$1,000	$100	$3,592		$0	$164,132	0.643928	$105,689
	76		$3,240,700	$194,442	$7,000	$3,400	$64,814		$0	$2,971,044		$2,374,945

Sum of the retail values as of Time Ø on 7/1/2018

$41,500 per lot × 76 lots = $3,154,000

Indicated bulk sale value $2,374,945

Rounded $2,370,000

130 *Subdivision Valuation*

many spreadsheet programs have built-in formulas for calculating present values and *IRR*s. Typically, these formulas work well when the period used for discounting is one year. For other periods (monthly, quarterly, semi-annual, etc.), the internal formulas will often indicate the wrong answer.

All of the examples in this book calculate the discount factor based on the formula for the present value of one, which is $1 \div (1 + i)^n$, where i is the periodic interest rate and n is the time period involved. This method will ensure accurate calculation of the present value regardless of whether annual, semi-annual, quarterly, or monthly discounting is used. Obviously, the correct interest rate must be used with the associated time period. In Exhibit 7.8, the time period is quarterly, so the interest rate of 18% is divided by four. This yields the periodic interest rate, or i, and n is the quarter involved. For example, the present value factor for the fifth quarter is $1 \div (1 + 0.0450)^5$, or 0.802451 (see Exhibit 7.8).

An allocation of the DCF results are summarized in Exhibit 7.9. The sum of the retail values is always evaluated as of the *when complete* date on July 1, 2018. In this example, the sum of the retail values is 76 lots times the average starting retail lot value of $41,500 per lot, or $3,154,000. The gross proceeds are slightly higher because the analysis considers inflation in lot value prices over the absorption period. The gross proceeds reflect actual lot sales collections. Also, holding and sales costs are increasing over time based on a percentage of gross sales or specific increases for tax and association dues. The "time value"

Exhibit 7.9

Mill Pond DCF Analysis Summary

DCF Analysis Summary

Sum of the retail values—7/1/2018			$3,154,000
Add:	Lot value inflation over holding period		86,700
Gross proceeds			$3,240,700
Less:			
	Absorption holding & sales costs		
	Sales		$194,442
	Tax		7,000
	Association dues		3,400
	Miscellaneous		64,814
Profit:	Line-item profit	$0	
	Time value profit	596,099	
	Subtotal profit	$596,099	596,099
Total adjustment			$865,755
Bulk sale value			$2,374,945
		Rounded	$2,370,000
Yield rate (with zero line-item profit)			18.000%

profit is the difference between net proceeds and the present value. This is the actual dollar profit generated over time reflected in the yield rate of 18%, with no separate consideration of line-item profit (i.e., line-item profit is zero).

The results of the income capitalization approach analysis are also shown in the timeline in Exhibit 7.10, which provides an overlay of various values at the appropriate time frames. The income capitalization approach using DCF is a "top-down" process. The calculation begins with the sum of the retail values and then begins subtracting holding and sales costs over the absorption period as well as the required profit as expressed in the yield rate present value calculation to reflect the bulk sale value. Inherently all costs and profit must come out of gross proceeds from lot sales. This is distinctly different for the cost approach, which is a "bottom-up" process in which construction costs and other cost components are added to land value to reflect either bulk sale value or the sum of the retail values.

Exhibit 7.10
Value Line

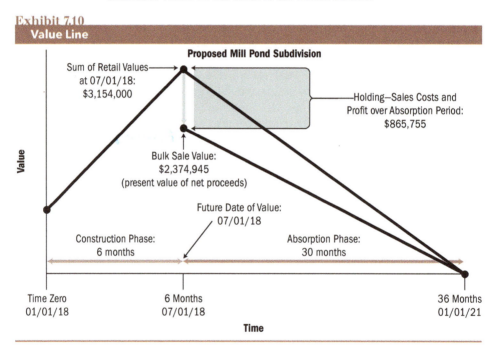

Sugarbush Case Study: Analysis with Presales of Lots

All the previous examples provided for the income capitalization approach were made from a "total inventory" perspective. In these cases, one developer typically builds the subdivision and sells the entire lot inventory at the market-supported absorption to end users either as vacant lots or as lots with a new housing unit in which the total home and lot package is sold. This section explores presales of lots to groups of separate homebuilders as part of the initial subdivision development and its effect on developer yield. The following section provides an analysis of equity returns considering mortgage financing and risk analysis.

Several methods may be employed to secure the sale of lots prior to completion of construction. Some of the more commonly used terminology includes *presale contracts, take-down agreements,* and *lot reservations.* For the purposes of this text, any agreement that is a written contract with significant non-refundable deposits that requires the buyer to purchase set amounts of lots at specific time intervals and set prices is considered to be a *presale agreement.* In most markets, these contracts are probably referred to as "presale contracts" or "take-down agreements." For the purposes of this text, any other agreements are considered to be *lot reservations* or *purchase options.* Typically, these are less secure contracts that do not have specific "hard" down payments and allow the buyer to exit the agreement with minimal recourse. They may or may not have significant purchase deposits.

Presale agreements would be preferred by subdivision developers because these agreements have less risk of nonperformance. However, no agreements are guaranteed. When presale or other agreements are considered by the appraiser, this requires a critical review in which the terms of the agreements are quantified, including the lot purchase time frames, the number and type of lots, lot pricing, and any increase in lot prices over time. The contract may require the buyer to contribute to common advertising for the project, unit owners' fees for vacant lots in inventory, or other provisions. The presale contract evaluation or analysis by the appraiser would be similar to a critical review of a proposed lease in commercial real estate appraisal.

The Sugarbush subdivision is used as a lot presales example. Four separate valuations are considered. The timing and amount of lot presales as they relate to property yield rates are studied with a sensitivity analysis considering presale timing and presale lot discount prices in which multiple groups of lots are sold to homebuilders within the same project. Presale contracts are also considered within the context of the fundamental demand forecast that is provided in the appraisal. Even when presale agreements are in place for the entire lot inventory, the market analysis and highest and best use sections of the appraisal would address the fundamental demand forecast, the proposed subdivision plan, and supported home price points.

All four of the following development scenarios are based on information presented in Exhibit 7.11. The subdivision has a total of 72 lots supporting the construction of detached residential homes, with a retail lot value of $105,000 per lot. Retail lot values are anticipated to increase by 2% per year adjusted annually throughout the absorption period. The project will have typical amenities for competing projects in the area. Holding and sales costs are estimated given the criteria in Exhibit 7.11 for real estate taxes, unit owners association fees, marketing and sales costs, and miscellaneous expenses. This structure is typical of most of the examples previously provided for the Mill Pond Subdivision.

However, this example considers lot presales to two homebuilders unrelated to the project developer. Two presale contracts were negotiated prior to the completion of the subdivision by the developer, in which Builder 1 is to purchase 12 lots immediately upon

Exhibit 7.11
Sugarbush Subdivision Lot Presales Analysis

Sugarbush Subdivision Lot Presales Analysis

General Information:	Sugarbush is a proposed single-unit subdivision currently under construction with a completion date of 1/1/2018. The project supports 76 residential lots designed for detached homes in the $400,000 to $550,000 price range.		
Lot Inventory:	Total Lots	Avg. Lot Size (Sq. Ft.)	Avg. Lot (Fr. Ft.)
	72	15,000	125
Retail Lot Values:	$105,000	2.0% per year increase	
Project Amenities:	Front entrance with signage & landscaping		
	Underground utilities (water, sewer, gas, & electricity), phone, & cable TV		
	Paved interior roads, concrete curb, public roads		
	Streetlights, water retention, & open space		
Holding and Sales Costs:	Real estate taxes	2.0%	Per year of assessed value per lot
		85.0%	Assessment ratio to retail value
			Allocated each quarter on remaining inventory
	Unit owners association fees	$75.00	per lot per quarter
	Sales costs		Estimated at 6% of gross sales
	Miscellaneous		Includes miscellaneous legal, administrative, or other costs, estimated at 2% of gross sales
Lot Presale Contracts:	Builder 1:		Contract to purchase lots at construction completion
		12	Lots @ $89,000 per lot or 84.8% of retail
	Builder 2:		Contract to purchase lots at construction completion
		12	Lots @ $89,000 per lot or 84.8% of retail
Market Absorption Forecast:		6	Lots per quarter average absorption to end users
			Equal share among home builders
		12	Quarter overall absorption period
Lot Cost:		$71,900	Average lot cost
		$5,176,800	Total cost and profit through construction phase

the completion of construction of the subdivision at a discounted price of $89,000 per lot. This reflects about a 15% discount on a regular retail value as an incentive for Builder 1 to buy the 12 lots in one transaction at a discount. Builder 2 will also be purchasing 12 lots, also at $89,000 per lot, to be closed immediately upon completion of the subdivision. The marketing forecast provides for the absorption of six lots per quarter on average within the subdivision, which is the market rate of absorption to end users. There is equal share in terms of absorption among homebuilders, and dividing 72 lots by 6 lots per quarter reflects a total holding period of 12 quarters.

Scenario 1 is shown in Exhibit 7.12. This scenario is a baseline forecast for the Sugarbush subdivision, assuming no presales. Fundamental market absorption is estimated at six lots per quarter for a total of 12 quarters, with an initial starting retail lot value of $105,000 per lot, increasing at a rate of about 2% per year. The total absorption period is three years with holding and sales costs, as shown in Exhibit 7.12. The analysis does not consider any mortgage or financing costs, and the property discount rate was estimated at 18%, reflecting a present value rounded to $5,180,000. This is the bulk sale value for the group of 72 lots based on the market absorption with a market-derived yield rate of 18% with the given developer cost of $71,900 per lot. Since there is no financing, the developer *IRR* is the same as the property yield rate of 18%, which is verified at the bottom of Exhibit 7.12. Also, the allocation of profit and expenses is provided in the DCF summary.

Under this scenario, the initial project developer will be selling all lots to end users based on the fundamental forecast either as vacant lots and/or lots improved with homes. As such, this is a single-owner developer/builder marketing inventory in the Sugarbush subdivision. This is the market value forecast ignoring presale contracts that is typically provided to a lender/client to allow for comparison and evaluation of the value conclusions with and without consideration of presales.

The Sugarbush subdivision Scenario 2 is shown in Exhibit 7.13. This analysis adds presales of lots to Builders 1 and 2. Builder 1 is purchasing a group of 12 lots at a discount of 15% of the retail price, with a builder price of $89,000 per lot. Builder 2 is also purchasing 12 lots, also at the same discount of $89,000 per lot. The gross proceeds for the builder sales occur in the first quarter of absorption, as shown in Exhibit 7.13. This provides for a good initial burst of sales when the project is initially developed. The builder sales are reflected in Time Period 1 and not time zero in the DCF to avoid the time zero profit dilemma that will be explained in Chapter 12.

Exhibit 7.12
Sugarbush Scenario 1: Market Value Analysis with No Presales of Lots

Quarter	Lot Take-Downs	Lots Sold	Remaining Lot Inventory	Builder Prices	Retail Lot Value	Gross Sales	Absorption Holding and Sales Costs Sales 6.0%	Tax	Assoc. Dues	Misc. 2.0%	Line-Item Profit 0.0%	Net Proceeds	PV Factor 18.000%	Present Value
			72											
1	6	6	66		$105,000	$630,000	$37,800	$32,130	$5,400	$12,600	$0	$542,070	0.956938	$518,727
2	6	6	60		$105,000	$630,000	$37,800	$29,453	$4,950	$12,600	$0	$545,198	0.915730	$499,254
3	6	6	54		$105,000	$630,000	$37,800	$26,775	$4,500	$12,600	$0	$548,325	0.876297	$480,495
4	6	6	48		$105,000	$630,000	$37,800	$24,098	$4,050	$12,600	$0	$551,453	0.838561	$462,427
5	6	6	42		$107,100	$642,600	$38,556	$21,848	$3,600	$12,852	$0	$565,744	0.802451	$453,982
6	6	6	36		$107,100	$642,600	$38,556	$19,117	$3,150	$12,852	$0	$568,925	0.767896	$436,875
7	6	6	30		$107,100	$642,600	$38,556	$16,386	$2,700	$12,852	$0	$572,106	0.734828	$420,400
8	6	6	24		$107,100	$642,600	$38,556	$13,655	$2,250	$12,852	$0	$575,287	0.703185	$404,533
9	6	6	18		$109,242	$655,452	$39,327	$11,143	$1,800	$13,109	$0	$590,073	0.672904	$397,063
10	6	6	12		$109,242	$655,452	$39,327	$8,357	$1,350	$13,109	$0	$593,309	0.643928	$382,048
11	6	6	6		$109,242	$655,452	$39,327	$5,571	$900	$13,109	$0	$596,545	0.616199	$367,590
12	6	6	0		$109,242	$655,452	$39,327	$2,786	$450	$13,109	$0	$599,780	0.589664	$353,669
	72					$7,712,208	$462,732	$211,319	$35,100	$154,244	$0	$6,848,813		$5,177,063
					Gross sales/lot	$107,114						Indicated Bulk Sale Value		$5,177,063
													Rounded	$5,180,000

DCF Summary

Sum of the retail values			$7,560,000
Add: Lot value inflation			152,208
			$7,712,208
Gross proceeds			
Less: Absorption holding & sales costs			
Sales			$462,732
Tax			211,319
Association dues			35,100
Miscellaneous			154,244
Profit: Line-item profit		$0	
Time value profit		1,671,750	
Subtotal profit		$1,671,750	1,671,750
Total adjustment			$2,535,145
Bulk sale value	Per lot	$71,904	$5,177,063
	Rounded		$5,180,000

Developer IRR

Indicated IRR:	Project cost	-$5,176,800
	Income Quarter 1	$542,070
	Quarter 2	$545,198
	Quarter 3	$548,325
	Quarter 4	$551,453
	Quarter 5	$565,744
	Quarter 6	$568,925
	Quarter 7	$572,106
	Quarter 8	$575,287
	Quarter 9	$590,073
	Quarter 10	$593,309
	Quarter 11	$596,545
	Quarter 12	$599,780
Indicated IRR		18.00%

Exhibit 7.13

Sugarbush Scenario 2: Analysis Considering Partial Presales of Lots

Quarter	Original Developer	Lot Take-Downs Bldr. 1	Lot Take-Downs Bldr. 2	Total Lots Sold	Remaining Lot Inventory	Builder Prices	Retail Lot Value	Gross Sales	Absorption Holding & Sales Costs: Sales 6.0%	Tax	Assoc. Dues	Misc. 2.0%	Line-Item Profit 0.0%	Net Proceeds	*PV Factor* 18.000%	Present Value
					72											
1	2	12	12	26	46	$89,000	$105,000	$2,346,000	$140,760	$32,130	$5,400	$46,920	$0	$2,120,790	0.956938	$2,029,464
2	2			2	44		$105,000	$210,000	$12,600	$20,528	$3,450	$4,200	$0	$169,223	0.915730	$154,962
3	2			2	42		$105,000	$210,000	$12,600	$19,635	$3,300	$4,200	$0	$170,265	0.876297	$149,203
4	2			2	40		$105,000	$210,000	$12,600	$18,743	$3,150	$4,200	$0	$171,308	0.838561	$143,652
5	2			2	38		$107,100	$214,200	$12,852	$18,207	$3,000	$4,284	$0	$175,857	0.802451	$141,117
6	2			2	36		$107,100	$214,200	$12,852	$17,297	$2,850	$4,284	$0	$176,917	0.767896	$135,854
7	6			6	30		$107,100	$642,600	$38,556	$16,386	$2,700	$12,852	$0	$572,106	0.734828	$420,400
8	6			6	24		$107,100	$642,600	$38,556	$13,655	$2,250	$12,852	$0	$575,287	0.703185	$404,533
9	6			6	18		$109,242	$655,452	$39,327	$11,143	$1,800	$13,109	$0	$590,073	0.672904	$397,063
10	6			6	12		$109,242	$655,452	$39,327	$8,357	$1,350	$13,109	$0	$593,309	0.643928	$382,048
11	6			6	6		$109,242	$655,452	$39,327	$5,571	$900	$13,109	$0	$596,545	0.616199	$367,590
12	6			6	0		$109,242	$655,452	$39,327	$2,786	$450	$13,109	$0	$599,780	0.589664	$353,669
	48	12	12	72				$7,311,408	$438,684	$184,437	$30,600	$146,228	$0	$6,511,459		$5,079,555
							Gross sales/lot	$101,547							**Indicated Bulk Sale Value**	**$5,079,555**
															Rounded	**$5,080,000**

DCF Summary

Sum of the retail values				$7,560,000
Add:	Lot value inflation (negative with presales)			-$248,592
	Gross proceeds			$7,311,408
Less:	Absorption holding & sales costs			
	Sales			$438,684
	Tax			$184,437
	Association dues			$30,600
	Miscellaneous			$146,228
Profit:	Line-item profit		$0	
	Time value profit		$1,431,904	
	Subtotal profit		$1,431,904	$1,431,904
Total adjustment				$2,231,853
Bulk sale value		Per lot	$70,549	$5,079,555
			Rounded	$5,080,000

Developer *IRR*

Indicated *IRR*:		
Project cost		-$5,176,800
Income	Quarter 1	$2,120,790
	Quarter 2	$169,223
	Quarter 3	$170,265
	Quarter 4	$171,308
	Quarter 5	$175,857
	Quarter 6	$176,917
	Quarter 7	$572,106
	Quarter 8	$575,287
	Quarter 9	$590,073
	Quarter 10	$593,309
	Quarter 11	$596,545
	Quarter 12	$599,780
Indicated *IRR*		16.51%

In this scenario, the builder presales do not necessarily reduce the overall holding period for the initial developer. Beginning in Quarter 1, there will be three developers in the project. All three developers will be building homes and selling completed homes and/or lots. Regardless of the number of builders, the estimated market absorption is six lots per quarter, consistent with the fundamental forecast.

The analysis is based on an equal share, in which the builders would have a pro rata allocation of any absorption allocated to the project. For example, there are three builders in the project in the first quarter: Builders 1 and 2 plus the initial developer. Each position would have an absorption allocation of two lots per quarter for a total of six lots per quarter, which is the forecast market absorption. The timeline for Scenario 2 is presented in Exhibit 7.13.

From the original developer's perspective, 24 lots have been immediately sold; however, they have been sold to two homebuilders that will be competing in the same subdivision. The original developer is still "in" the project and will also be selling lots or home and lot packages. Accordingly, the initial developer will be selling two lots per quarter until all 24 of the presale lots are absorbed. Then the full absorption of six lots per quarter will accrue to the original developer once Builders 1 and 2 are out of the project. Presales do not increase the fundamental absorption for the overall project. They do however, increase the income to the developer in Time Period 1.

Many appraisers mistakenly believe that the absorption for the project developer will be the same at six lots per month after the presales. Obviously, this is not the case. There will initially be three homebuilders in the project, all building and/or selling homes and lots, who will have equal share absorption at two lots each until Quarter 7, when Builders 1 and 2 are out of the project. This will increase the cash flow in Period 1 to the initial developer, as shown in the absorption forecast in Scenario 2 (Exhibit 7.13). Accordingly, the overall holding period is still the same at 12 quarters. Net income to the developer is summarized at the bottom of Exhibit 7.13. The presales have a reduced lot price that decreases the developer's *IRR* from the prior level of 18% to 16.5%.

In this example, the presales of 24 lots at a 15% discount in the first quarter of sales have a negative impact upon the yield achieved by the project

---

Valuations Considering Presales
Consider the following:

- Total lots in the subdivision   72 lots
- Presale contracts   24 lots in Quarter 1
- Fundamental forecast,   6 lots/quarter
  ignoring presales

What absorption should be used for the market value DCF?

The fundamental forecast Level C considers the market-supported demand and supply forecast, together with presale agreements for the subject project. Therefore, the presale agreements would be part of the market value appraisal and considered in the DCF analysis. However, the overall absorption period is the same.

developer. The indicated developer *IRR* is 16.5%, which is slightly below the overall yield rate for the entire property in Scenario 1 at 18%. This is partially explained by the 15% lot sales discount price given to the two homebuilders, and the developer maintaining an ongoing position in the project.

A second presale forecast is provided in Scenario 3, Exhibit 7.14, in which all lots are presold over time. Scenario 3 and 4 provide for complete sale of all 72 lots in the project to Builders 1 and 2. The original developer will not build homes or sell lots within the project separately, and all of the absorption will be achieved through builder sales of lots to Builders 1 and 2. This significantly reduces the holding period for the initial project developer in cases when the initial project developer is in and out of the project when the last group of lots is sold in Quarter 6, as shown in Exhibit 7.14. Also, this analysis reflects a 10% increase in the builder lot pricing in Quarter 6. The Quarter 1 purchase price is $89,000 per lot by the builders, which is a 15% discount off of the market retail value of $105,000 per lot. However, the second builder take-down in Quarter 6 has a 10% increase in the $89,000 price to the new level of $97,900 per lot in Scenario 3. Applying the same level of holding and sales costs indicates an *IRR* to the project developer of 18.45%.

This *IRR* to the developer, based on presales, is not significantly higher than the original Scenario 1 without any presales. One of the greatest determinants of return in terms of builder presales is how fast the lots are sold and, more importantly, the retail lot value discount given to builders for lot sales. The initial scenarios used a 15% discount to builders when the builder price was initially $89,000 per lot, which is 15% below the retail price level of $105,000 per lot. A sensitivity analysis can be performed to determine yield rates based on a faster required take-down by builders for lots within the project or by adjusting the lot pricing to achieve a higher yield for the initial developer.

Scenario 4 in Exhibit 7.15 provides a scenario with a significantly shorter time frame for the builder take-down of the 72 lots. Under this scenario, Builders 1 and 2 are required to purchase 36 lots in the first quarter of sales at a 15% discount, or $89,000 per lot. The second take-down has a 10% increase in the builder price to $97,900 per lot, but the required purchase is at the end of the first year of absorption in the fourth quarter. This significantly decreases the holding period for Scenario 3 and reflects a significantly higher yield rate of 27% in terms of the developer's *IRR*, as shown at the bottom of Exhibit 7.15. Accordingly, the relatively deep builder discounts (in this case a 15% discounted retail lot price) are given. It is imperative that the builder take-downs occur at a significantly reduced time frame in order to enhance yield to the developer's position in the project.

Exhibit 7414
Sugarbush Scenario 3: Analysis with Full Presales of Lots

Quarter	Lot Take-Downs	Lots Sold	Remaining Lot Inventory	Builder Prices	Retail Lot Value	Gross Sales	Absorption Holding & Sales Costs — Sales 6.0%	Tax	Assoc. Dues	Misc. 2.0%	Line-Item Profit 0.0%	Net Proceeds	PV Factor 18.000%	Present Value
			72											
1	Builders 1 & 2 36	36	36	$89,000	$105,000	$3,204,000	$192,240	$32,130	$5,400	$64,080	$0	$2,910,150	0.956938	$2,784,833
2		0	36		$105,000	$0	$0	$16,065	$2,700	$0	$0	-$18,765	0.915730	-$17,184
3		0	36		$105,000	$0	$0	$16,065	$2,700	$0	$0	-$18,765	0.876297	-$16,444
4		0	36		$105,000	$0	$0	$16,065	$2,700	$0	$0	-$18,765	0.838561	-$15,736
5		0	36		$107,100	$0	$0	$16,386	$2,700	$0	$0	-$19,086	0.802451	-$15,316
6	Builders 1 & 2 36	36	0	$97,900	$107,100	$3,524,400	$211,464	$16,386	$2,700	$70,488	$0	$3,223,362	0.767896	$2,475,206
	72					$6,728,400	$403,704	$113,098	$18,900	$134,568	$0	$6,058,130		$5,195,359

Note: 10% increase in builder lot price in Quarter 6   Gross sales/lot $93,450

Indicated bulk sale value $5,195,359
Rounded $5,200,000

DCF Summary

Sum of the retail values			$7,560,000
Add: Lot value inflation (negative with preseles)			-831,600
Gross proceeds			$6,728,400
Less: Absorption holding & sales costs			
Sales		$403,704	
Tax		113,098	
Association dues		18,900	
Miscellaneous		134,568	
Profit: Line-item profit	$0		
Time value profit	$862,771		
Subtotal profit	$862,771		862,771
Total adjustment			$1,533,041
Bulk sale value	Per lot	$72,158	$5,195,359
	Rounded		$5,200,000

Developer IRR

Indicated IRR	Project cost	-$5,176,800
	Income Quarter 1	$2,910,150
	Quarter 2	-$18,765
	Quarter 3	-$18,765
	Quarter 4	-$18,765
	Quarter 5	-$19,086
	Quarter 6	$3,223,362
	Indicated IRR	18.45%

140 *Subdivision Valuation*

Exhibit 7.15
Sugarbush Scenario 4: Analysis with Full Presales of Lots

Quarter	Lot Take-Downs	Lots Sold	Remaining Lot Inventory	Builder Prices	Retail Lot Value	Gross Sales	Absorption Holding & Sales Costs Sales 6.0%	Tax	Assoc. Dues	Misc. 2.0%	Line-Item Profit 0.0%	Net Proceeds	PV Factor 18.000%	Present Value
			72											
1	Builders 1 & 2	36	36	$89,000	$105,000	$3,204,000	$192,240	$32,130	$5,400	$64,080	$0	$2,910,150	0.956938	$2,784,833
2		0	36		$105,000	$0	$0	$16,065	$2,700	$0	$0	-$18,765	0.915730	-$17,184
3		0	36		$105,000	$0	$0	$16,065	$2,700	$0	$0	-$18,765	0.876297	-$16,444
4	Builders 1 & 2	36	0	$97,900	$105,000	$3,524,400	$211,464	$16,065	$2,700	$70,488	$0	$3,223,683	0.838561	$2,703,256
		72				$6,728,400	$403,704	$80,325	$13,500	$134,568	$0	$6,096,303		$5,454,461
												Indicated bulk sale value		$5,454,461
													Rounded	$5,450,000

Note: 10% increase in builder lot price in Quarter 6   Gross sales/lot $93,450

DCF Summary

Sum of the retail values			$7,560,000
Add: Lot value inflation (negative with presales)			-831,600
Gross proceeds			$6,728,400
Less: Absorption holding & sales costs			
Sales			$403,704
Tax			80,325
Association dues			13,500
Miscellaneous			134,568
Profit: Line-item profit		$0	
Time value profit		641,842	
Subtotal profit		$641,842	641,842
Total adjustment			$1,273,939
Bulk sale value	Per lot	$75,756	$5,454,461
	Rounded		$5,450,000

Indicated IRR:
- Project cost   -$5,176,800
- Income
  - Quarter 1 $2,910,150
  - Quarter 2   -$18,765
  - Quarter 3   -$18,765
  - Quarter 4 $3,223,683
- Indicated IRR   **Developer IRR**   27.00%

An analysis summary for the Sugarbush subdivision is provided in Exhibit 7.16. The table provides the results for all four valuation scenarios, including the initial Scenario 1 with no presales, reflecting an *IRR* to the overall project of 18% that is the same as the developer's yield. Under Scenario 1, there is one developer/builder who markets the entire lot inventory over a 12-quarter holding period. Scenario 2 introduced presales at a discount in which Builders 1 and 2 purchased initial lots in Quarter 1 with no additional presales, providing for the project developer to sell all remaining lots within the project. This only had a marginal increase to the developer yield from 18% to about 18.58% (see Exhibit 7.16). Scenario 3 provides for full presales of all lots over six quarters, also at a discount. This also had a relatively minimal increase to the developer yield at 18.45%. Scenario 4, which had the greatest yield for the entire absorption in terms of builder take-downs, occurred over a four-quarter or one-year period, resulting in an enhanced yield of about 27%. The sensitivity analysis performed for Scenarios 2 through 4 considered the timing of the builder take-downs with the same builder pricing.

Separate calculations were also made with lower builder discounts, as shown at the bottom of Exhibit 7.16. The builder take-down prices were increased from $89,000 per lot with a 15% discount to a higher price level of $94,500 per lot with a 10% builder discount. This significantly increased the yield in Scenarios 2, 3, and 4. With the lower builder lot discounts, the yield rate increased from 16.51% to 18.30% in Scenario 2, from about 18.5% to 26.3% in Scenario 3, and from about 27% to 38% in Scenario 4. Accordingly, this analysis is sensitive not only to the holding

Exhibit 7.16
Sugarbush Analysis Summary

	Scenario 1	Scenario 2	Scenario 3	Scenario 4
	Exhibit 7.12	Exhibit 7.13	Exhibit 7.14	Exhibit 7.15
	Market analysis	Partial presales	Full presales	Full presales
	No presales			
Builder lot price (15% discount)	n/a	$89,000	$89,000	$89,000
Bulk sale value	$5,180,000	$5,080,000	$5,200,000	$5,450,000
Holding period—quarters	12	12	6	4
Average sale price per lot	$107,114	$101,547	$93,450	$93,450
Market yield rate	18.0%	18.0%	18.0%	18.0%
Profit allocation	$1,671,750	$1,431,904	$862,771	$641,842
Net proceeds prior to discounting	$6,848,813	$6,511,459	$6,058,130	$6,096,303
Developer *IRR*	18.00%	16.51%	18.45%	27.00%
Analysis with Lower Initial Builder Lot Discount				
Builder lot price (10% discount)	n/a	$94,500	$94,500	$94,500
Developer *IRR*	n/a	18.30%	26.32%	37.96%

period required for the builder take-downs, but also to the actual builder pricing in terms of the discount given to builders within the project. Both the timing and price level of builder take-downs are very important in terms of the final yield generated by the project developer, as shown in the enclosed sensitivity analysis.

The appraiser must also consider the fundamental demand forecast in any valuation in which the original developer is remaining in the project and selling lots and homes in competition with other builders. The absorption to the developer's inventory must be adjusted recognizing that there is equal share among all homebuilders within the project. The absorption must consider that there is simultaneous absorption between a group of builders until the original developer is the only builder with the remaining inventory, and as such would achieve the full level of absorption as illustrated in Scenario 2. However, it is possible that multiple builders in the same project can achieve a synergy that could produce higher absorptions on a monthly or quarterly basis because of a cohesive marketing effort by several homebuilders. It would be unrealistic to anticipate that each builder would be achieving an absorption of 6 lots per quarter or 18 lots total per quarter. Any boost or benefit that may be achieved by multiple builders in a project must be tested with market performance in competing developments.

This example illustrates the impact of presale contracts on the bulk sale value conclusion and the benefits in terms of yield to the original developer. In the four presale scenarios considered, the bulk sale value conclusions did not change significantly and were in an overall range from a low of $5,180,000 in Scenario 1 to a high of $5,450,000 in Scenario 4. However, the yield to the original developer's position changed with the greatest yield for the shorter holding periods. Exhibit 7.16 also provides a summary of the profit extracted in the present value conclusions for the various scenarios. Scenario 1 had the greatest profit allocation in terms of the time value discounting and the effect of the 18% market yield rate. The longer absorption period resulted in a higher level of profit extracted. However, Scenarios 2 through 4 had lower dollar profit extracted given the shorter absorption period. The net proceeds decreased as the yield increased, especially in Scenarios 3 and 4. By far the shorter absorption time frames had the most impact on overall yield.

Many proposed subdivision developments have some level of presales that are considered in the appraisal analysis. The observation may be made that the analysis with presales is an appraisal of the developer's position in the property and is an investment value rather than a typical valuation from a "market value" perspective. Are we valuing the real estate or the developer's position considering presale contracts? For this reason, it is recommended that any appraisal considering presales should include an initial valuation with market retail lot values and the fundamental absorption forecast to establish market value ignoring presales, similar to Scenario 1. Additional values are then reported considering the presales contracts.

Sugarbush Case Study: Analysis with Mortgage Financing

Subdivision valuation almost always involves some level of mortgage financing. Given the magnitude of construction costs and the relatively long timelines involved with bringing a project from the initial conception to the point when lots are available for purchase typically requires developers with "deep pockets" for the equity component of the project and involves mortgage financing throughout the development process.

This section of the income capitalization approach provides an analysis of mortgage financing and how it can impact developer yield rates as it relates to the equity position in the property. Similar to property yield analysis in which the total property position is considered, the analysis of yield rate is calculated as the return to the initial equity investment and the cash flow attributable to the equity position in the project. When the last lot in a subdivision is sold, the value goes to $0, and as such there typically is no equity reversion.

The Sugarbush subdivision example is continued, supporting a mortgage financing example with an equity return sensitivity analysis in Exhibits 7.17 through 7.21. Summary information relating to the mortgage financing is provided in Exhibit 7.17. The Sugarbush subdivision contains 72 lots, with a retail lot value of $105,000 per lot increasing by 2% per year. The absorption period estimate is the same at 6 lots per quarter for 12 quarters, with a 3-year overall absorption period evaluated on a quarterly basis. However, the three scenarios using mortgage financing anticipate a bulk sale purchase of $5,180,000, consistent with the bulk price (indicated market value) calculated in Exhibit 7.12. However, in these examples, mortgage financing is considered stratified from a loan-to-value ratio of 70% to a high of 90% for Scenarios 5, 6, and 7. The mortgage interest rate is held level at 9%, and the lot payoff percentage is 125% of the mortgage balance per lot until the lot is paid off. This is to ensure that the lender exits the project prior to the sale of the last lots. Many lenders view this as an incentive to keep developers in the project where most of the developer return comes toward the end of the absorption period, after the mortgage is paid off.

Exhibit 7.17
Sugarbush Subdivision Analysis with Mortgage Financing

General Information

Basic lot and property information for the Sugarbush subdivision is the same. This analysis explores mortgage financing options, risk analysis, and associated equity return rates. Holding and sales costs are the same, and there are no lot presales.

Lot Inventory		Total Lots	Avg. Lot Size (Sq. Ft.)	Avg. Lot (Fr. Ft.)
		72	15,000	125

Retail Lot Values		$105,000, 2.0% per year increase	
Market Absorption Forecast		6 lots per quarter average absorption to end users	
		Equal share among homebuilders	
		12-quarter overall absorption period	
Bulk Sale Purchase Price		$5,180,000 (same as Scenario 1, Exhibit 7.12)	
Mortgage Financing:	Scenario 5	70.0%	Loan-to-value ratio, on market bulk sale value
		9.0%	Interest rate, simple interest, paid monthly
		125.0%	Payoff percentage per lot
	Scenario 6	80.0%	Loan-to-value ratio, on market bulk sale value
		9.0%	Interest rate, simple interest, paid monthly
		125.0%	Payoff percentage per lot
	Scenario 7	90.0%	Loan-to-value ratio, on market bulk sale value
		9.0%	Interest rate, simple interest, paid monthly
		125.0%	Payoff percentage per lot

The first valuation scenario is shown in Exhibit 7.18, and all of the scenarios anticipate that one developer or homebuilder is selling the entire lot inventory at the fundamental forecast rate of six lots per quarter without any presales. The initial Scenario 5 is shown in Exhibit 7.18, and two separate mortgage expense line-item categories have been provided to calculate net equity proceeds. The initial DCF analysis includes all of the same components as seen in the previous Sugarbush subdivision examples; however, mortgage interest expense has been added as the lot payoff allocations. Subtracting all holding and sales costs, together with mortgage interest expense and mortgage payoffs, provides net proceeds to the equity position in the property.

A second table is also provided with the mortgage calculations based on an initial bulk sale value of $5,180,000. For the financing examples, this is the proposed purchase of the group of 72 lots to one buyer as a bulk sale value. The buyer purchases all 72 lots and then obtains mortgage financing at a 70% loan-to-value ratio at a 9% interest rate, indicating a total loan amount under Scenario 5 of $3,626,000. This reflects total equity in the project of $1,554,000 (see Exhibit 7.18).

The mortgage accounting in terms of interest rate calculation per quarter and the loan payout is managed in the mortgage calculation tables. The initial loan proceeds are about $50,361 per lot, as shown in the table. This is the average mortgage balance per lot, which is the mortgage amount divided by 72 lots. However, it is very common in subdivision financing for the lender to require a higher payout per lot than the average loan balance per lot. In this example, the loan payout ratio is 125%. Therefore, the average loan amount per lot of $50,361 is multiplied by 1.25 to establish a payout of $62,951 per lot as the lots are sold. This is to allow the lender to "exit" the project prior to the sale of the last lot. The lender's goal is to keep the developer "vested" in the project throughout the entire marketing and selloff period, when most of the equity comes towards the end. This is in fact what is accomplished by having the higher payout ratio, as shown in Exhibit 7.18. The equity net proceeds increase substantially in the last three quarters when the loan is paid off. Over 50% of the total equity proceeds are earned by the developer in the last three quarters.

The mortgage lender views this strategy as a risk reduction measure, recognizing that subdivision development is one of the more risky commercial loans, which is reflected in higher interest rates for subdivision development as well as the mortgage loan payout ratios and other criteria.

In Scenario 5, the mortgage loan payout is estimated at about 125% of the initial mortgage amount per lot. Many of the performance measures used by the lending industry are based directly on appraisals that are completed for the proposed project. In these appraisals, the bulk sale value and the average retail value per lot are used to establish performance standards that must be met by the developer and/or determine the dollar amount of loan payouts per lot based on the continuous monitoring of absorption history within the project once subdivision infrastructure is completed and market absorption begins.

For example, the appraisal of a proposed project would have a specific forecast of market absorption in terms of the velocity of lot sales anticipated or supported by the market for the absorption forecast. All lenders monitor the absorption within financed subdivisions and may have a credit review when the absorption falls below a certain threshold. The market expected absorption is six lots per quarter. However, if the project is performing at a predetermined breakpoint, say 50% less than expected absorption, then a project review would be automatically triggered. This may involve a review of builder performance within the project and marketing efforts and could involve a lender requiring additional collateral to reduce risk as part of an ongoing loan in an existing project. Inherently, the appraisal takes on significant importance in the credit decision, and all forecasts must be supported by the market.

Exhibit 7.18
Sugarbush Scenario 5: Financing Analysis with No Presales of Lots and Mortgage Financing

Quarter	Lots Sold	Remaining Lot Inventory	Retail Lot Value	Gross Sales	Absorption Holding & Sales Costs				Mortgage Expenses		Equity Net Proceeds
					Sales 6.0%	Tax	Assoc. Dues	Misc. 2.0%	Interest Expense	Lot Payoff	
		72									
1	6	66	$105,000	$630,000	$37,800	$32,130	$5,400	$12,600	$81,585	$377,708.34	$82,776
2	6	60	$105,000	$630,000	$37,800	$29,453	$4,950	$12,600	$74,787	$377,708.34	$92,703
3	6	54	$105,000	$630,000	$37,800	$26,775	$4,500	$12,600	$67,988	$377,708.34	$102,629
4	6	48	$105,000	$630,000	$37,800	$24,098	$4,050	$12,600	$61,189	$377,708.34	$112,555
5	6	42	$107,100	$642,600	$38,556	$21,848	$3,600	$12,852	$54,390	$377,708.34	$133,645
6	6	36	$107,100	$642,600	$38,556	$19,117	$3,150	$12,852	$47,591	$377,708.34	$143,625
7	6	30	$107,100	$642,600	$38,556	$16,386	$2,700	$12,852	$40,793	$377,708.34	$153,605
8	6	24	$107,100	$642,600	$38,556	$13,655	$2,250	$12,852	$33,994	$377,708.34	$163,585
9	6	18	$109,242	$655,452	$39,327	$11,143	$1,800	$13,109	$27,195	$377,708.34	$185,170
10	6	12	$109,242	$655,452	$39,327	$8,357	$1,350	$13,109	$20,396	$226,624.94	$346,288
11	6	6	$109,242	$655,452	$39,327	$5,571	$900	$13,109	$0	$0.00	$596,545
12	6	0	$109,242	$655,452	$39,327	$2,786	$450	$13,109	$0	$0.00	$599,780
	72			$7,712,208	$462,732	$211,319	$35,100	$154,244	$509,909	$3,626,000	$2,712,904

Mortgage Calculations

Quarter	Lot Inventory	Lot Sales	Starting Mortgage Balance	Mortgage Interest & Payouts		Total Lots Paid off	Remaining Balance
				Loan Interest	Loan Payout		
0	72		$3,626,000.00				
1	66	6	$3,626,000.00	$81,585.36	$377,708.34	6.0	$3,248,291.66
2	60	6	$3,248,291.66	$74,786.58	$377,708.34	12.0	$2,870,583.32
3	54	6	$2,870,583.32	$67,987.80	$377,708.34	18.0	$2,492,874.98
4	48	6	$2,492,874.98	$61,189.02	$377,708.34	24.0	$2,115,166.64
5	42	6	$2,115,166.64	$54,390.24	$377,708.34	30.0	$1,737,458.30
6	36	6	$1,737,458.30	$47,591.46	$377,708.34	36.0	$1,359,749.96
7	30	6	$1,359,749.96	$40,792.68	$377,708.34	42.0	$982,041.62
8	24	6	$982,041.62	$33,993.90	$377,708.34	48.0	$604,333.28
9	18	6	$604,333.28	$27,195.12	$377,708.34	54.0	$226,624.94
10	12	6	$226,624.94	$20,396.34	$226,624.94	57.6	$0.00
11	6	6	$0.00	$0.00	$0.00	57.6	$0.00
12	0	6	$0.00	$0.00	$0.00	57.6	$0.00
		72		$509,908.50	$3,626,000.00		

Note: Lots are sold at the end of each quarter

DCF Summary		Developer Equity IRR		Mortgage Criteria	
Sum of the retail values—Time Ø	$7,560,000	Indicated IRR		Bulk sale value	$5,180,000
Add: Lot value inflation	152,208	Equity contribution	-$1,554,000	L/V ratio	70.0%
Gross proceeds	$7,712,208	Income Quarter 1	$82,776	Interest rate	9.00%
Less: Absorption holding & sales costs		Quarter 2	$92,703	Loan amount	$3,626,000
Sales	462,732	Quarter 3	$102,629	Equity	$1,554,000
Tax	211,319	Quarter 4	$112,555	Loan per lot	$50,361.11
Association dues	35,100	Quarter 5	$133,645	Loan payoff ratio	125.00%
Miscellaneous	154,244	Quarter 6	$143,625	Payoff per lot	$62,951.39
Mortgage interest	509,909	Quarter 7	$153,605	Monthly interest/lot	$377.71
Mortgage payoff	3,626,000	Quarter 8	$163,585	Loan burnout/quarter	19.05
Subtotal	$4,999,304	Quarter 9	$185,170	Years	4.76
Indicated equity proceeds	$2,712,904	Quarter 10	$346,288	Lenders lot exit % (% of total lots)	80%± or 57.6 lots
		Quarter 11	$596,545		
		Quarter 12	$599,780		
		Indicated equity IRR	27.39%		

Income Capitalization Approach

Other lender requirements may base the loan payouts on an overall lot sales threshold. For example, a lender may have a criterion in which the loan must be 100% paid off when the lots are 70% sold. For example, consider a project with 100 lots. When 70 lots were sold, the bank would be completely out of the project. This threshold would then be used to calculate the required mortgage loan payment per lot needed to achieve the 70% sales ratio. In Scenario 5, Exhibit 7.18, the 125% payout ratio equated to a lender lot exit ratio of 80%. Again, whether additional collateral is involved impacts the loan-to-value ratio, the interest rate, and how other performance criteria are evaluated.

In many cases, lenders will require a performance bond as part of the proposed construction of a new project. This ensures that the project will be 100% complete if for any reason the developer should default during the construction process. In many communities, performance bonds also have an added advantage. This advantage is that new home construction can commence simultaneously with site infrastructure construction when the community allows construction to begin prior to completion of the development when a performance bond has been posted. This enhances the developer's ability to bring homes online immediately after construction of the subdivision, which is common in many markets. Also, simultaneous construction of homes and site improvements can reduce the developer's and the lender's risk within a project.

Criteria 1 Two performance criteria are provided in Exhibit 7.18. Under the mortgage criterion, a loan burn-out period is provided in terms of number of quarters or total years. Under the 70% loan-to-value ratio in Scenario 5, if the developer did not sell any lots and was required to pay mortgage interest, it would take 19 quarters before no equity is left in the project. The longer the amount of time, the lower the amount of risk from both the lender's and developer's perspectives.

Criteria 2 The second performance criterion calculated is the lender's lot exit percentage. This would be the percentage of lots that must be sold before the lender is completely out of the project. Under Scenario 5, this is calculated as 80%. Accordingly, in this example with a 70% loan-to-value ratio and a 125% lot payout ratio criterion, the lender will be completely out of the project when about 80% of the lots are sold. The lower this ratio, the more secure the lender's position in the property. Also, the higher the loan burn-out time frame, the lower the stress level on an overall basis in terms of the developer defaulting on the project. Scenarios 6 and 7 were performed at the 80% and 90% loan-to-value ratios. The results are summarized in Exhibit 7.19. Under Scenario 7 (see Exhibit 7.19), the loan burn-out is in 4.9 quarters under the 90% loan-to-value ratio with the same lender exit percentage of 80%. Stated differently, if the project were to have no absorption for 4.9 quarters, the developer would have no equity in the project. Accordingly, the 90% loan-to-value ratio is a significantly higher risk from the developer's perspective with very little room for error or any dip in market performance or absorption through the initial marketing time frame. Also, it is doubtful that any lender would entertain this ratio without other security.

Under Sugarbush subdivision Scenario 5 (Exhibit 7.18) with the 70% loan-to-value ratio, the developer's equity *IRR* is about 27%. This is significantly higher than the return rates without mortgage financing and explains why almost all developments have some level of financing and provides a significant boost to the developer equity return.

Scenarios 6 and 7 are shown in Exhibit 7.19. Both examples explore the impact of increasing the loan-to-value ratio, with all remaining components of analysis staying the same. The mortgage interest rate is still 9%, and the loan payoff ratio is 125%. Under this scenario, the developer has less equity in the project. Given the spread between the mortgage interest rate of 9% and the normal *IRR* ignoring the financing of 18% in the project, the developer is receiving the benefit of the spread, reflecting an *IRR* to the equity position of about 31%, with the increase in financing with an 80% loan-to-value ratio.

The last scenario is an extreme example, in which a 90% loan-to-value ratio is used. Under this scenario, the project developer only has $518,000 equity in a project that costs $5,180,000 on a bulk sale basis, which substantially skews the return to the investor position with a 38% equity yield rate. Obviously, the equity position is more tenuous in this example given the loan burn-out statistic, which provides little or no room for any error in any portion of the development forecast. It is very doubtful that a lender could be found to allow a 90% loan-to-value ratio. If it were allowed, the interest rate would probably be significantly higher than the market loan rate of 9%. Most loan-to-value ratios are less than about 80%, However, the ratios may vary depending on individual lender criteria and whether the property is cross-collateralized with other investments, providing for a fallback position to the lender. Also, notice that equity proceeds are negative for the first four quarters. In situations like this, whether caused by the high loan-to-value ratio, lower absorption, or other causes, the lender may require that the developer maintain an interest reserve to ensure payment of all mortgage funds during the initial absorption periods.

The analysis summary under the financing scenario is shown in Exhibit 7.19. Three scenarios were investigated in which essen-

Exhibit 7.19
Sugarbush Financing Analysis Summary

	Scenario 5	Scenario 6	Scenario 7
Bulk purchase price	$5,180,000	$5,180,000	$5,180,000
Holding period—quarters	12	12	6
Average price per lot	$107,114	$107,114	$107,114
Bulk purchase—property yield rate Y_O	18.0%	18.0%	18.0%
Gross proceeds	$7,712,208	$7,712,208	$7,712,208
Total expenses, excluding financing	$863,395	$863,395	$863,395
Net proceeds, excluding financing	$6,848,813	$6,848,813	$6,848,813
Mortgage loan terms			
Interest rate	9.0%	9.0%	9.0%
Loan-to-value ratio	70.0%	80.0%	90.0%
Loan payout per lot	125.0%	125.0%	125.0%
Mortgage payoff period—quarters	10.0	10.0	10.0
Total mortgage interest payments	$509,909	$582,755	$655,601
Total mortgage payoff costs	$3,626,000	$4,144,000	$4,662,000
Dollar equity inventment	$1,554,000	$1,036,000	$518,000
Dollar equity profit	$2,712,904	$2,122,058	$1,531,212
Developer equity IRR, Y_E	27.39%	31.35%	38.18%
Financing stress points			
Loan burn-out quarters	19.0	11.1	4.9
Lender lot exit percentage	80%	80%	80%

tially all components of the analysis were the same except for the loan-to-value ratio starting at 70% in Scenario 5 and increasing to 80% in Scenario 6 and 90% in Scenario 7. The interest rate was held level, and the equity yield rates generated with the mortgage financing range from a low of about 27% with a 70% loan-to-value ratio to a high of about 38% under Scenario 7, with a 90% loan-to-value ratio. Under all three scenarios, the gross lot sales proceeds are identical, and the total expenses (excluding financing) and net proceeds are the same. The only difference is the allocation between the division of funds needed to satisfy mortgage interest and the loan payouts with the residual falling to the equity position. The highest dollar amount of profit was achieved under Scenario 5, in which the initial equity investment was $1,554,000, with total equity proceeds of $2,712,904 reflected in the 27% equity *IRR*. Accordingly, the highest dollar profit was achieved at the lower equity *IRR* of 27%, when the lowest dollar profit of $1,531,212 under Scenario 7 indicated the highest *IRR* of 38%. All three forecasts have the same holding period, and there is no difference in the mortgage interest rate or other mortgage terms.

The forecast provides a basis from which individual analysts can approach subdivision development from a property perspective as well as a mortgage equity perspective to identify areas of risk to the stakeholders in the development and the relative risk from the developer's and lender's position in a financed development. It is interesting that the lender lot exit percentage is 80% for all case scenarios. This percentage is directly tied to the loan payment per lot. Since the ratio of 125% is the same for all three scenarios, the lender lot exit percentage is also the same. Varying the payout percentage will also vary the lot exit percentage. The equity return rates are sensitive to the mortgage interest rate and loan-to-value ratio. The enclosed examples provide a basis for further study, depending on characteristics of individual projects and available mortgage financing.

8
Cost Approach

Introduction

Like the sales comparison and income capitalization approaches, the cost approach is based on market comparison and the principle of substitution. The principle of *substitution* affirms that a prudent buyer would pay no more for a property than the cost to acquire a similar site and construct subdivision improvements of equivalent desirability and utility without undue delay. Other properties can be substituted for the property being appraised, and their value is also measured in relation to the value of a new, optimal property. In short, the cost of property improvements on the effective date of appraisal plus the accompanying land value provides a measure against which prices for similar improved subdivisions may be judged.

When applying the cost approach, the appraiser must distinguish between reproduction and replacement costs and use one type of cost consistently throughout the analysis. There are three methods that may be used to estimate cost new:

- The comparative-unit method
- The unit-in-place method
- The quantity survey method

Also, three methods for estimating depreciation are available:

- The market extraction method
- The age-life method
- The breakdown method

As applied in subdivision valuation, the cost approach is unique because appraisers usually do not apply this approach to an existing group of lots. For example, consider a scenario in which an appraiser tries to apply the cost approach to a small group of lots in a large subdivision project. This situation requires a cost analysis of the entire project, in which the average value per lot is determined. Typically, the cost analysis would not directly address the characteristics of the individual lots such as size, frontage, favorable view, or other factors. When existing lots are being appraised, the income and sales comparison approaches are usually given more weight and can provide a more accurate value conclusion.

In subdivision valuation, the cost approach is most useful and beneficial for proposed projects. Comparing the results of the cost approach with the results of the income and sales comparison approaches for a new project can provide an immediate test of feasibility, which is critical for proposed developments. The cost to develop the project can be compared with the economics of the income capitalization approach and the values supported in the sales comparison. Elements of risk and obsolescence immediately come to light in such a comparison.

Cost analysis requires a keen awareness of the timing of costs and where they occur along the subdivision development timeline. As with other commercial properties, it is important to count each cost only once when dealing with subdivisions. Also, like any property type, it is possible for a new existing or proposed subdivision to have accrued depreciation. In new projects, obsolescence due to marketing externalities, superadequacies, or inadequacies may be evident.

This chapter provides an overview of the cost approach as it applies to the appraisal of the proposed Mill Pond subdivision. This chapter also introduces two additional case study examples that clarify some typical difficulties encountered when applying the cost approach to subdivision valuation. All of the examples in this chapter are for vacant lots in improved subdivisions.

Timeline Overview

The cost approach can be applied to a subdivision at the bulk sale or retail lot value level. In many appraisal reports, both levels are included as part of the cost analysis to highlight any differences between value conclusions from the cost approach versus value conclusions from the income capitalization and sales comparison approaches. The cost approach is particularly important and relevant for proposed subdivisions and can serve as a feasibility test.

The material in this chapter focuses primarily on two general cost methodologies–bulk sale level versus retail lot value level–and typical valuation issues that arise in cost approach analysis. Basic appraisal techniques such as estimating vacant land value, using the sales comparison approach, and selecting the appropriate unit of comparison (price per acre, price per unit, etc.) are not extensively covered. More complicated issues including allocating costs between phases of development and excess or surplus land valuation are considered in the examples that follow the Mill Pond analysis.

The timing of profit is very important to the cost approach for estimating the land value and the cost new. When applying the cost approach framework to subdivision appraisal, appraisers are required to consider the internal cost accounting going on in the process, where the different costs are incurred, and how these costs relate to value along the timeline. It is easy to lose track of profit and how it impacts cost and value. Depreciation must also be considered because even new projects can suffer from functional or external obsolescence.

The cost approach process is distinctly different from the income capitalization approach process. When performing the income capitalization approach, the appraiser starts with aggregate retail value and then subtracts costs and profit through the discounting process to arrive at a conclusion of bulk sale value. With the cost approach, on the other hand, the appraiser begins with raw land value and adds costs and profit to estimate a bulk sale or retail lot value.

Exhibits 8.1 and 8.2 provide timeline views of the cost approach as applied to a proposed project. As shown in these exhibits, the date of value is a future point in time as of the *when complete* date, and the appraiser is given the assignment at the point when all entitlements have been achieved and the permitting process is complete. The valuation is made when the construction period begins. The construction period is six months, and the date of value is the point when construction is 100% complete at the end of the six months. The cost approach yields a prospective value, so appropriate hypothetical or extraordinary assumptions should be considered in the analysis and included in the appraisal report.

Land value and construction costs are estimated as of the future point in time when the values are expected to occur as of the *when complete* date. In Exhibit 8.1, *as is* land value is the initial starting point and construction costs, construction profit, and any holding costs over the construction period are added to land value to reflect a bulk sale value. In this example, the only profit considered is the profit associated with the permitting

Exhibit 8.1 Timeline and Value

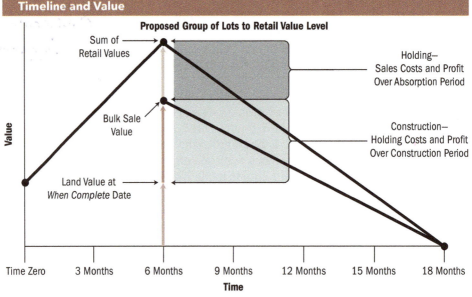

Exhibit 8.2 Timeline and Value

period, which is reflected in the *as is* land value and any profit over the construction period. Dividing the bulk sale value by the number of lots would reflect the average bulk value per lot. Also, the cost approach conclusion can be taken to the retail level, as shown in Exhibit 8.2. In this scenario, holding and sales costs together with profit over the absorption period are added to reflect the sum of the retail values. Dividing the number of lots into the indicated value by the cost approach would reflect an average retail lot value by the cost approach analysis.

The average retail lot value reached by the cost approach can be compared to a retail lot value conclusion from the income capitalization approach as a test of reasonableness or to identify any areas of depreciation or financial feasibility issues. The bulk sale value by the cost approach can also be compared directly to the bulk sale indication from the income capitalization and sales comparison approaches to identify depreciation and provide a test of reasonableness.

In subdivision valuation, there is more interaction between the income capitalization and cost approaches because the income capitalization approach requires estimates of holding and sales costs as well as the appropriate level of developer profit to use in discounting to arrive at value conclusions. Also, if the income capitalization approach is taken to the raw land value level, the cost component is directly included in the discounting process to arrive at an estimate of vacant land value. In subdivision valuation, costs tend to be considered directly in both the income capitalization and cost approaches.

For the cost approach to produce an accurate indication of value, the costs and especially the profit should be the "typical" expectation from the market and the subject-specific project criteria. If the costs and profit reflect typical expectations, the cost approach can be a true test of the conclusions generated in the income and sales comparison approaches. The appraiser should not assume that the profit and holding cost levels from the income capitalization approach can be directly input into the cost approach. This assumption can result in a cost approach that is out of balance with market value.

Applying the Cost Approach

This section provides a more detailed view of the cost approach process and the required inputs needed to arrive at a value conclusion for a proposed subdivision. The Mill Pond project is used to illustrate the application of the approach.

Relevant timeline concepts are shown in Exhibits 8.1 and 8.2. Because Mill Pond is a proposed subdivision, the cost approach requires an estimate of the time frame needed to complete construction of the lots in order to determine the *when complete* date. The construction timeline for the Mill Pond project is estimated at six months, and the completion date is six months in the future. Accordingly, a prospective value for the subdivision project will be estimated at the point in time when the lots are 100% built and the absorption period can begin. The cost approach can be taken to the bulk value level, the retail lot value level, or both levels. The bulk value and the retail lot value levels will be illustrated in this case study. The direct and indirect construction costs, holding and sales costs, and any profit are added to the current land value to reflect a bulk value by the cost approach (see Exhibit 8.1). This bulk sale value is the market value of Mill Pond as of the *when complete* date. The cost approach can also be taken to the retail lot value level by adding the appropriate holding and sales costs over the absorption period and any profit associated with the lot absorption phase.

The cost approach as applied in subdivision valuation has three required components:

- Land value at the date of valuation
- Costs and profit incentive associated with the value to be estimated (bulk level or retail level)
- Depreciation

Mill Pond Land Value

The cost approach requires a vacant land value estimate as of a specific point in time. For subdivision analysis, the date of value and the status of entitlements can have a substantial impact on the land value conclusion. The sales comparison approach is typically used to provide a land value conclusion. The Mill Pond land value is being estimated at the point when all entitlements have been achieved at the end of the permitting phase; this is an *as is* or current value conclusion. Land value as of the *when complete* date is also needed and is reflected in the analysis.

The selection of land sales involves screening recent sales of comparable subdivision land to ensure that they are as similar as possible to the subject property in terms of land use density, entitlements, size, location, and other physical characteristics. For the final land value conclusion, the most comparable sales are used and adjustments may be made for any remaining differences. For single-unit subdivision acreage, the price per unit and price per acre units of comparison are typically considered. Depending on the type of property (condominium, office, retail, etc.), other units of comparison may also be appropriate.

For vacant land value, development approvals and the development status of the land at any given time must be considered. For markets in which achieving final site plan approval is difficult, vacant land can have a substantial increase in value once approval is achieved. For markets in which site plan approval is easy to obtain, land value with "entitlements" may not be substantially higher than raw land value when ample short-term demand exists. The appraiser must understand the nuances of the market involved.

In many markets, the developer may be required to comply with certain stipulations that are placed on the development as part of the final site plan approval. Stipulations are usually site- and/or project-specific items that are required to proceed with development. For example, a developer may be required to install new traffic signals at a project entrance if the subdivision is in an area with traffic concurrency limitations along a major highway. Depending on the magnitude of the cost involved, the land may be worth less because of the required expenditure. For markets in which this is common practice, some level of "typical" required cost usually exists. Any costs above this level may result in a lower land value.

Project data for the Mill Pond subdivision is shown in Exhibit 8.3. Comparable sales data is presented in a land sales table in Exhibit 8.4. As shown in Exhibit 8.3, the project contains a total of 76 units on a 28.5-acre parcel of land. The proposed subdivision has an average density of 2.67 units per acre, and the date of value is at the end of the permitting period. As a result, the subject land is assumed to have all entitlements in place including permitting, final plat approval, and other required governmental approvals needed to build the project in the immediate future.

The sales comparison approach is used to estimate the market value of the subject vacant acreage with the available land sales shown in Exhibit 8.4. The eight land sales used for comparison purposes reflect an approximate overall size range of 18 to 45 acres of land area. The average size is about 27 acres, which is consistent with the size characteristics of the subject Mill Pond parcel. All sales have available water and sewer utilities and are located in the subject market area.

The land sales are a relatively diverse group of properties with respect to unit density. In Exhibit 8.4, the unit density ranges from 1.38 units per acre for Sale 4 to 4.5 units per acre for Sale 7. The average density is 2.61 units per acre, which compares favorably with the average density of 2.67 units per acre for the Mill Pond project. In Exhibit 8.4, a market conditions adjustment of 4% per year is applied to reflect any differences between the market sales and the subject property at the date of sale. The price per unit and price per acre units of comparison are both provided on an adjusted basis.

Next, simple grouping and sorting techniques are applied to the land sales analysis to arrive at a value conclusion for the Mill Pond acreage; this analysis is shown in Exhibit 8.5. The eight sales were divided into two groups. Land sales with full entitle-

Exhibit 8.3
Mill Pond Project Summary

General Information

Mill Pond is a proposed single-unit subdivision to be built in the immediate future. The project is located in a well-established residential area and will be marketing detached single-unit lots and/or homes with two separate price points and two lot categories.

Project Timing

Current date:	01/01/18
Construction start:	01/01/18
Construction period:	6 months
Absorption start date:	07/01/18

Site Characteristics	Units	Size (Ac.)	Units/Ac.
Site area	76	28.50	2.67

Lot Inventory by Size Category	Total Lots	Regular Lots	Cul-de-sac Lots	Avg. Lot Size (Sq. Ft.)	Avg. Lot Front Feet
Small lots	40	36	4	8,700	80
Large lots	36	32	4	11,000	100
Total	76	68	8		
%	100.0%	89.5%	10.5%		

Subdivision Site Amenities

Front entrance with signage and landscaping
Underground utilities (water, sewer, gas, and electric)
Underground phone, cable TV
Paved interior roads, concrete curb, public roads, 3,600 ln. ft. ±
Streetlights, water retention, and open space

Subdivision Common Amenities

Playground area with small parking lot, fencing, and landscaping
Unit owners association

Marketing Concept

Target Price Range for Home and Lot

			Home Price Range		
Lot Category	Lot Size Sq. Ft. ±	Home Size Sq. Ft. ±	Low	Average	High
Small lots	8,700	1,500	$140,000	$170,000	$200,000
Large lots	11,000	2,000	$180,000	$200,000	$220,000

In this market, cul-de-sac lots sell for about 10% more than typical interior or corner lots, and lot value prices are increasing by about 4% per year.

---

ments were divided from the main group of sales, which primarily represented raw land sales without entitlements at the time of sale. This division revealed a significantly different price level for land sales with entitlements as compared to sales of raw land that had not gone through a full entitlement process. Also, the sales were sorted by unit density from lowest to highest for each group.

Exhibit 8.5 reveals several trends in the comparable land sales. The sales array shows that price per acre typically increases as

Exhibit 8.4
Subdivision Land Sales

Sale No.	Date	Subdivision	Sale Price	Size (Acres)	No. Lots	Utilities*	Topography	Avg. Unit Density	Annual Time Adj. Jan. '18 4.00%	Adjusted Sale Price Per Unit	Per Acre
1	Jan-18	Strawberry Fields	$700,000	22.0	72	W & S	Wooded/open	3.27	$700,000	$9,722	$31,818
2	Oct-17	Garden Gate**	$650,000	18.5	39	W & S	Wooded/open	2.11	$654,333	$16,778	$35,369
3	Jun-17	Red Oak	$913,300	35.7	87	W & S	Wooded	2.44	$934,610	$10,743	$26,180
4	Jan-17	Pine Ridge	$387,500	21.7	30	W & S	Wooded	1.38	$403,000	$13,433	$18,571
5	Nov-16	Westside Phase III	$554,500	18.4	48	W & S	Wooded/open	2.61	$578,528	$12,053	$31,442
6	Mar-16	White Oak**	$890,000	26.3	68	W & S	Wooded	2.59	$952,300	$14,004	$36,209
7	Oct-15	Walnut Creek	$920,000	30.0	135	W & S	Wooded	4.50	$999,733	$7,405	$33,324
8	May-15	Westside Manor	$919,000	44.5	88	W & S	Wooded	1.98	$1,017,027	$11,557	$22,855
		Low	$387,500	18.4	30			1.38	$403,000	$7,405	$18,571
		High	$920,000	44.5	135			4.50	$1,017,027	$16,778	$36,209
		Average	$741,788	27.1	71			2.61	$779,942	$11,962	$29,471

* Available utilities: W = water, S = sewer
** Included full entitlements at time of sale

Exhibit 8.5
Land Sales Analysis

Sale No.	Date	Subdivision	Sale Price	Size (Acres)	No. Lots	Utilities*	Topography	Avg. Unit Density	Annual Time Adj. Jan. '18 4.00%	Adjusted Sale Price Per Unit	Per Acre
Raw Land Sales, Sorted by Density											
4	Jan-17	Pine Ridge	$387,500	21.7	30	W & S	Wooded	1.38	$403,000	$13,433	$18,571
8	May-15	Westside Manor	$919,000	44.5	88	W & S	Wooded	1.98	$1,017,027	$11,557	$22,855
3	Jun-17	Red Oak	$913,300	35.7	87	W & S	Wooded	2.44	$934,610	$10,743	$26,180
5	Nov-16	Westside Phase III	$554,500	18.4	48	W & S	Wooded/open	2.61	$578,528	$12,053	$31,442
1	Jan-18	Strawberry Fields	$700,000	22.0	72	W & S	Wooded/open	3.27	$700,000	$9,722	$31,818
7	Oct-15	Walnut Creek	$920,000	30.0	135	W & S	Wooded	4.50	$999,733	$7,405	$33,324
		Low	$387,500	18.4	30			1.38	$403,000	$7,405	$18,571
		High	$920,000	44.5	135			4.50	$1,017,027	$13,433	$33,324
		Average	$732,383	28.7	77			2.70	$772,150	$10,819	$27,365
Land Sales with Entitlements, Sorted by Density											
2	Oct-17	Garden Gate**	$650,000	18.5	39	W & S	Wooded/open	2.11	$654,333	$16,778	$35,369
6	Mar-16	White Oak**	$890,000	26.3	68	W & S	Wooded	2.59	$952,300	$14,004	$36,209
		Low	$650,000	18.5	39			2.11	$654,333	$14,004	$35,369
		High	$890,000	26.3	68			2.59	$952,300	$16,778	$36,209
		Average	$770,000	22.4	54			2.35	$803,317	$15,391	$35,789

* Available utilities: W = water, S = sewer
** Included full entitlements at time of sale

unit density per acre increases and that as the unit density per acre increases, the price per unit typically decreases. These patterns are common to most real estate markets, and these trends are considered in estimating the land value for the Mill Pond project. The "raw" land sales indicate an average price of about $27,000 per acre, while the two sales with full entitlements (Sales 2 and 6) reflect an average land value of about $36,000 per acre.

The land values for the subject property are summarized in Exhibit 8.6. Several value estimates are provided, including current *as is* land value both on a raw acreage basis and with full entitlements. Also, a future land value in six months is provided to coincide with the construction completion date. A market conditions adjustment of 2% is made for the future land value estimate. For lending clients, *as is* value would typically be reported as $1,060,000, which represents the vacant land value with entitlements as of the current date. However, the land value used in the cost analysis would be $1,080,000 as of the date of valuation when complete.

Exhibit 8.6
Mill Pond Land Value Summary

Current Land Values (1/1/2018)

Raw Land Value Estimate

Per acre	28.5 acres @	$30,000	$855,000
Per unit	76 units @	$11,000	$836,000
Rounded			$850,000

Land Value with Entitlements

Per acre	28.5 acres @	$37,000	$1,054,500
Per unit	76 units @	$14,000	$1,064,000
Rounded			$1,060,000

Future Land Values (future value, *when complete* date, 7/1/18)

Raw Land Value Estimate

Per acre	28.5 acres @	$30,000	$855,000
Per unit	76 units @	$11,000	$836,000
Rounded			$850,000
Market conditions adjustment		2.0%	17,000
Indicated value			$867,000
Rounded			$870,000

Land Value with Entitlements

Per acre	28.5 acres @	$37,000	$1,054,500
Per unit	76 units @	$14,000	$1,064,000
Rounded			$1,060,000
Market conditions adjustment		2.0%	21,200
Indicated value			$1,081,200
Rounded			$1,080,000

Improvement Value

The cost approach requires the appraiser to provide an estimate of reproduction cost new for the proposed site infrastructure. For a proposed project, the appraiser can usually assume that detailed site construction plans are available, construction cost bids have been evaluated, and actual site work contracts or cost schedules are available for comparison. These bids and/or estimates are compared with cost data from comparable subdivisions and/or sources such as CoreLogic's Marshall and Swift valuation service.

Subdivision costs can vary greatly depending on terrain, individual site characteristics, land slope, the distribution of wetlands, and other property characteristics. However, most markets will reveal a predictable level of cost components for subdivision development.

Depending on the sophistication of the project developer, the cost data provided may be just direct construction costs or a comprehensive project budget that considers all direct and indirect costs along with selling and holding costs over the absorption period. A detailed study should be made of available cost information to determine if the amounts allocated by the developer are reasonable. Proposed projects can have built-in functional obsolescence (e.g., excessive common infrastructure), and existing projects can also suffer from functional or external obsolescence.

As in most appraisal assignments, the fact that costs have been or will be incurred does not necessarily mean that value is created in an equal amount. A classic example is a proposed subdivision to be built in a suburban area where a creek must be crossed to access the main portion of the acreage. The developer was allowed to construct an earthen bridge over a large metal culvert to transverse the creek as part of the initial site planning and approval. The bridge could be built at a nominal construction cost of about $30,000. This cost was considered in the construction budget and the initial agreement to purchase the vacant land for subdivision development.

After construction was started, the local water district decided that the earthen bridge was not sufficient and the developer would have to construct a more substantial bridge of continuous poured concrete with steel supports, which would have a clear span area over a larger portion of the creek basin. The cost for the new bridge would be about $400,000. In this example, the expenditure of the additional $370,000 would not create any additional value to the subdivision lots. This cost is going to come directly out of the developer's profit and does not increase the value of the subdivision. It does, however, increase project costs and would probably be charged as a superadequacy against cost new. It may also indicate that a lower land value should have been paid for the acreage, given the unique characteristics of the acreage that require such a substantial bridge. In any case, an adjustment would be required in the cost approach.

Bulk Value vs. Retail Value Cost Analysis

The cost approach can be performed to deliver a bulk sale value. It may also be conducted to reflect a retail lot value conclusion by including holding and sales costs and profit over the absorption period. The difference between these values was illustrated in Exhibits 8.1 and 8.2.

The Mill Pond cost approach example provides a bulk sale value and gross retail conclusion. The cost analysis presentation an appraiser decides to use in an appraisal may depend on available cost data, especially information on the absorption cost, profit, and values to be reported in the appraisal. It is not uncommon to present two cost scenarios—one supporting the bulk sale conclusion and the other used to support the retail lot value conclusion—as a check on the income and sales comparison approaches.

One of the weaknesses of the cost approach with respect to the retail lot value estimate is that this approach only produces an average value per lot on a retail basis. The cost approach does not differentiate among various lot features such as creek or fairway frontage or interior, cul-de-sac, or wooded lots versus open lots. For this reason, the retail lot value estimate derived by the cost approach tends to be more accurate when the project has a relatively large number of homogeneous lots. For example, a cost approach for a group of 20 lots out of an entire subdivision of 200 lots would probably not be particularly meaningful. However, a cost approach analysis for a proposed 200-lot subdivision would probably provide a good cross-check on the retail lot value developed in the income capitalization approach portion of the appraisal. A cost paradox can be introduced into the analysis when using direct inputs from the income capitalization approach. Without appropriate tests of reasonableness, a project with poor marketability and/or an extended marketing period because of a downturn in the market would appear to have a higher value by the cost approach. This paradox is especially apparent when the subject income capitalization approach is used to provide inputs to the cost approach for holding and sales costs and profit over the absorption period.

Cost data for the Mill Pond project is shown in Exhibit 8.7. Information relating to the permitting and construction phases was provided to the appraiser by the project developer. Since the date of value is at the end of the permitting process, all the permitting expenses are historical or actual amounts spent by the developer in achieving permitting for the subject project. As shown in Exhibit 8.7, permitting expenses totaled $57,000, or about $750 per lot for the 76 lots in Mill Pond.

The construction expenses totaling $1,200,000 are based on contractors' bids for all direct construction costs for horizontal subdivision improvements (roads, water retention, storm drainage, curb and gutter, underground utilities, etc.), which is a package price for all installed site infrastructure. Remaining indirect costs include fees for surveying, engineering, final plat approval, and front entrance landscaping, as well as holding costs and taxes over the construction phase.

Exhibit 8.7
Mill Pond Cost Approach Data

Current date		01/01/2018	
Annual cost inflation rate/year		6.0%	
Construction period		6 months	
Current Cost Data		**Total Cost**	**Cost per Lot**
Permitting Phase Expenses			
Planning and conceptual drawings		$15,000	$197
Holding costs and taxes		10,000	132
Permitting fees		22,000	289
Environmental audit		2,000	26
Initial survey and topographical		8,000	105
Subtotal		$57,000	$750
Construction Phase Expenses			
Direct construction costs		$1,150,000	$15,132
Survey, engineering, and final plat		25,000	329
Front entrance with landscaping		15,000	197
Holding costs and taxes		10,000	132
Subtotal		$1,200,000	$15,789
Absorption Phase Expenses			
Sales expense:	6% gross sales or about $2,760 per lot	$209,760	$2,760
Taxes:	Year 1	5,000	
	Year 2	15,000	
	Year 3	7,000	
	Total Tax	$27,000	$355
Miscellaneous:	2% gross sales or about $920 per lot	$69,920	$920
Subtotal		$306,680	$4,035
Total cost (excluding profit)		$1,563,680	$20,574

Entrepreneurial Incentive

In this market, total incentive in the cost approach is estimated at 25% of all costs including land value. Typically, 25% of total profit is earned in the permitting phase, 10% in the construction phase, and the remainder (65%) in the absorption phase.

The absorption phase costs are estimated by the appraiser based on typical expense levels for similar projects in the area and on other available data sources. In summary, the available cost data for the Mill Pond project at the time of appraisal includes historical costs provided by the project developer, current costs in the form of site contract bids for the installation of site infrastructure, and the appraiser's estimates of future absorption and marketing costs for the lot inventory over time. Entrepreneurial incentive is 25% of total costs plus land value, as described at the bottom of Exhibit 8.7. This amount is estimated by the appraiser based on observed profit levels for similar projects in the area using market extraction techniques or primary research in the form of market surveys. A detailed example of extracting profit in a cost scenario is provided in Chapter 10.

Three general methods may be used to estimate cost new:

- Comparative-unit method
- Unit-in-place method
- Quantity survey method

The quantity survey method is the most detailed method; it is also the method most often used by contractors. This method calls for the itemization of all material involved in the project as well as labor and other costs needed to build the proposed subdivision. This level of detail is typically not required of appraisers, who usually use the comparative-unit or unit-in-place methods. The comparative-unit method is based on the overall cost per lot. The unit-in-place method requires individual estimates for utilities, storm sewer, curb and gutter, and other installed components (usually based on the price per linear foot installed).

The cost analysis for the Mill Pond project is based on the comparative-unit method, which is essentially a comparison of cost per lot. Also, a rough cost range from a national cost service is used for all subdivision infrastructure expressed as a price per linear foot of interior roadways. As shown in Exhibit 8.7, the estimated cost (excluding profit) developed by the appraiser for all three subdivision development phases is $20,574 per lot, including all direct construction costs plus indirect construction costs over the permitting, construction, and absorption phases. This estimated cost reflects a "retail" cost analysis because the costs over the absorption period are included in the cost basis and the value considered is a retail value similar to the retail lot value indication described in Exhibit 8.2.

Builder construction cost data used in the analysis must be compared with cost levels for similar projects in the area and/or costs reported by national cost data providers. Exhibit 8.8 provides comparisons with both data sources. The exhibit shows cost information from four comparable subdivisions built over the last year. This information is for direct construction costs only and as such is compared with the Mill Pond direct costs of $15,789 per lot. This cost comparison excludes most indirect costs and profit. Basic site data relating to the four comparable projects, including unit density per acre and terrain characteristics, is provided for a direct comparison with the subject project's cost estimates. The price per lot is provided along with the approximate street price per linear foot.

As shown in Exhibit 8.8, the range of costs for the comparable projects is $13,450 to $18,671 per lot. All lots have the same level of installed infrastructure with underground utilities (water, sewer, and electric), typical paved roads and street lights built to city specifications, and concrete curbs and gutters. However, Project 4 requires the installation of a sewer lift station at an additional cost of $100,000. The information provided in Exhibit 8.8 for each comparable includes total direct construction costs, tract sizes, and average lot widths in front feet, total lots, lots per acre, and linear feet of subdivision roadway. This information facilitates the comparison of cost levels in the Mill Pond project with competing projects.

As the unit density per acre increases, the cost per lot tends to decrease. Cost data from Subdivisions 1 through 3 is the most comparable for installed infrastructure, while Subdivision 4 had higher costs due to the required sewer lift station. The price per linear foot of roadway is provided for comparison with typical national cost data service information, which indicates a current adjusted cost level in the local market of about $300 to $401 per linear foot of subdivision roadway.

Information from national data providers is typically expressed on a linear foot basis for installed infrastructure. The appraiser can modify the cost data depending on the actual infrastructure installed. National cost providers do not usually include holding and sales costs over the absorption period, costs associated with permitting, profit incentive, or all types of indirect cost. Accordingly, the national data provider cost range would only be comparable to the direct construction costs for the Mill Pond project.

From the comparable cost data, a direct cost of $15,000 per lot is used for Mill Pond, given the number of units per acre for the project in comparison with the comparable data. The price per linear foot of roadway was concluded to be about $350. This conclusion brackets a direct cost range for Mill Pond, as shown in Exhibit 8.9.

The direct construction costs provided by the site contractor totaled $1,150,000, as shown in Exhibit 8.7. Results for the cost comparison support a direct cost of $1,140,000 to $1,260,000. Ac-

Exhibit 8.8
Comparable Cost Data

			Project Characteristics						Project Infrastructure						Average Cost		
									Underground								
No.	Cost Date	Project	Total Direct Costs*	Size (Acres)	Avg. Lot Size (Fr. Ft.)	Road (Ln. Ft. ±)	Total Lots	Units per Ac.	Water	Sewer	Elec.	Street Lights	Curb and Gutter		Per Lot	Ln. Ft. Road	Comments
1	Dec-17	Pine Glade	$1,067,000	24.6	87	2,800	62	2.52	Y	Y	Y	Y	Y		$17,210	$381	Typical suburban subdivision, utilities adjacent to site, mostly level terrain
2	Jun-18	Oak Hammock	$1,345,000	32.1	80	3,900	100	3.12	Y	Y	Y	Y	Y		$13,450	$345	Typical suburban subdivision, utilities adjacent to site, mostly level terrain
3	Mar-18	Meadowbrook	$2,580,000	75.0	92	6,800	150	2.00	Y	Y	Y	Y	Y		$17,200	$379	Typical suburban subdivision, utilities adjacent to site, mostly level terrain
4	Feb-17	Creekside Est.	$1,531,000	37.0	96	4,100	82	2.22	Y	Y	Y	Y	Y		$18,671	$373	Typical suburban subdivision, utilities adjacent to site, mostly level terrain, requierd installation of sewer lift station at $100,000
Analysis	Low		$1,067,000	24.6	80	2,800	62	2.00							$13,450	$345	
	High		$2,580,000	75.0	96	6,800	150	3.12							$18,671	$381	
	Average		$1,630,750	42.2	89	4,400	98.5	2.46							$16,633	$370	

National Cost Service Data

Current cost service data*   Approximate cost per linear foot: Low $300
                                                                             High $401

* Direct costs include all improvements including streets, curb and gutter, underground utilities, storm drainage, site work, and water retention.

Exhibit 8.9
Mill Pond Direct Construction Cost Summary

Per Lot Method:	76 Lots @ $15,000 =	$1,140,000
Per Unit Method:	3,600 Ln. Ft. @ $350 =	$1,260,000

cordingly, the contractor cost data appears well supported by independent confirmation from comparable data and national cost service information. The contractor information is used for the final cost estimate. When accurate data from the developer is not available, other indirect costs can be gathered from interviews with engineers, surveyors, and other professionals to conclude an approximate cost level.

Cost information on the project is presented in a traditional cost approach format in Exhibit 8.10. The entrepreneurial incentive calculation is shown in Exhibit 8.11. In this table, the current total direct and indirect construction cost of $1,563,680 is added to the current raw land value to reflect a total profit incentive of $603,400, rounded to $603,000. In this market, total profit is calculated as 25% of total cost and land value. The total profit incentive of $603,000 is allocated consistent with the information in Exhibit 8.7. Twenty-five percent is allocated toward the permitting phase, 10% toward the construction phase, and 65% over the absorption phase (see Exhibit 8.11). A detailed market extraction explaining how profit can be extracted and reapplied in a cost scenario is described in Chapter 10.

In the traditional cost presentation for the Mill Pond project (Exhibit 8.10), two separate cost levels are provided. An initial cost level with current costs as of time period zero, the current date, is provided for reference purposes. If this appraisal were for 76 recently completed existing lots, then the current cost data would be applicable for an *as is* value conclusion by the cost approach. However, the Mill Pond subdivision is a proposed project that will require a six-month construction period. The value is estimated as of the *when complete* date, which is six months in the future. Construction costs are estimated to increase at about 6% per year, which would indicate a total increase of 3% to the *when complete* date. Land values are increasing at 4% per year. Applying a 2% adjustment indicates a future raw land value rounded to $870,000. The *when complete* costs are shown in Exhibit 8.10, which reflects an average retail lot value conclusion of about $40,800 per lot as of the *when complete* date.

Notice that raw land value is used in the cost analysis because all of the permitting costs and profit are included as part of cost new. If *as is* land value with full entitlements was used for the land value component, the cost associated with the permitting period and permitting profit would be excluded from the cost new analysis to avoid any double-counting of cost and profit over the permitting phase. In Exhibit 8.11, raw land value is used because the profit es-

Exhibit 8.10
Mill Pond Traditional Cost Approach Format

Reproduction Cost New, Less Depreciation

Direct Construction Costs	Current Costs	Per Lot 76 Lots	%	When Complete Date 3.0%
Horizontal improvements (streets, utilities, site work, etc.)	$1,150,000	$15,132	38.1%	$1,184,500
Front entrance sign and landscaping	15,000	197	0.5%	15,450
Common Amenities				
None	–	–	0.0%	–
Indirect Construction Costs				
Planning and conceptual drawings	15,000	197	0.5%	15,450
Holding costs and taxes—permitting phase	10,000	132	0.3%	10,300
Permitting fees	22,000	289	0.7%	22,660
Environmental audit	2,000	26	0.1%	2,060
Initial survey and topographical	8,000	105	0.3%	8,240
Survey, engineering, and final plat	25,000	329	0.8%	25,750
Holding costs and taxes—construction phase	10,000	132	0.3%	10,300
Holding and Sales Costs Absorption Period				
Sales expense	209,760	2,760	7.0%	216,053
Tax expense	27,000	355	0.9%	27,810
Miscellaneous	69,920	920	2.3%	72,018
Subtotal: All Direct and Indirect Costs	$1,563,680	$20,574	51.8%	$1,610,591
Entrepreneurial Incentive—Profit				
(25% ± of all costs, plus land value)	603,000	7,934	20.0%	620,000
Reproduction Cost New (Current Date)	$2,166,680	$28,509	71.8%	$2,230,591
Less: Depreciation				
Physical none noted	–	–	0.0%	–
Functional none noted	–	–	0.0%	–
External none noted	–	–	0.0%	–
Depreciated Improvement Value	$2,166,680	$28,509	71.8%	$2,230,591
Add: Raw Land Value	850,000	–	28.2%	870,000
Indicated Value by Cost Approach	$3,016,680		100.0%	$3,100,591
Rounded	$3,020,000			$3,100,000
Indicated Retail Value per Lot	$39,700			$40,800

Exhibit 8.11
Profit Allocation

Mill Pond Profit Incentive Calculation		Current Costs	When Complete Costs
Direct and indirect construction costs		$1,563,680	$1,610,591
Land value		850,000	870,000
Subtotal		$2,413,680	$2,480,591
Total profit allocation	25.0%	$603,420	$620,148
Rounded		$603,000	$620,000
Mill Pond Profit Allocation by Phase			
Permitting phase	25.0%	$150,750	$155,000
Construction phase	10.0%	60,300	62,000
Absorption phase	65.0%	391,950	403,000
	100.0%	$603,000	$620,000

timate of 25% is applied to raw land value and all direct and indirect construction costs. Profit and costs would be overestimated if the 25% profit criteria were applied to the land value with entitlements.

It is entirely appropriate to use raw land value in the traditional cost approach example in Exhibit 8.10. However, the appraiser should be aware that raw land value is not representative of *as is* land value at the time of appraisal. If this appraisal was being performed for a lending client, the appraiser must report the raw land value with entitlements. This effect is also shown in Exhibit 8.12, which provides bulk and retail cost indications for the Mill Pond project. The cost approach in Exhibit 8.12 uses *as is* land value with full entitlements. The cost new excludes the costs associated with achieving the entitlements over the permitting phase and the permitting phase profit because all of these amounts are inherently included in the *as is* land value with all entitlements. As a result, the higher land value with entitlements is used in Exhibit 8.12, and any costs and profit associated with achieving the entitlements are eliminated from the cost new.

The cost approach for the Mill Pond project indicates an approximate bulk sale value of $2,380,000, or about $31,300 per lot. The sum of the retail values by the cost analysis is $3,100,000, or about $40,800 per lot. This conclusion is the average retail lot value, and it can be compared directly with the retail lot value from the income capitalization approach or sales comparison approach as a test of feasibility.

Exhibit 8.13 summarizes the initial analysis results for the Mill Pond project as derived from the income capitalization and cost approaches. The bulk value conclusion and gross retail indication developed by the cost approach are higher than those reached in the income capitalization approach. However, the results are within a reasonable range. The Mill Pond Case Study continues in Chapter 9 with the sales comparison approach and the final value conclusion.

In this case study application, no depreciation is indicated in the cost approach because Mill Pond is a new, proposed project and does not have any physical depreciation. However, new projects can have functional or external obsolescence, which should be considered directly in the cost approach to value. In this example, no functional or external obsolescence was observed.

Depreciation

Depreciation is a measure of loss in value in the cost approach. In appraisal methodology, depreciation is measured or examined in three separate categories:

- Physical deterioration

Exhibit 8.12
Cost Approach Comparison: Bulk and Retail Values *When Complete*

Reproduction Cost New, Less Depreciation		Bulk Sale Estimate	Gross Retail Estimate
Permitting Phase			
Planning and conceptual drawings		-	-
Holding costs and taxes--permitting phase		-	-
Permitting fees -		-	-
Environmental audit		-	-
Initial survey and topographical		-	-
Permitting profit		-	-
Construction Phase			
Direct construction costs			
Horizontal improvements (streets, utilities, site work, etc.)		$1,184,500	$1,184,500
Survey, engineering, and final plat		25,750	25,750
Front entrance sign and landscaping		15,450	15,450
Holding and sales costs		10,300	10,300
Common area amenities: none		-	-
Construction phase profit		62,000	62,000
Holding and Sales Costs Absorption Period			
Sales expense		n/a	$216,053
Tax		n/a	$27,810
Miscellaneous		n/a	$72,018
Absorption period profit		n/a	$403,000
Reproduction Cost New		$1,298,000	$2,016,881
Less: Depreciation			
Physical none noted		-	-
Functional none noted		-	-
External none noted		-	-
Depreciated Improvement Value		$1,298,000	$2,016,881
Add: Land value with full entitlements		1,080,000	1,080,000
Indicated Value by Cost Approach	Rounded	$2,378,000	$3,096,881
Rounded		$2,380,000	$3,100,000
Indicated Bulk Sale Value/Lot		$31,316	
Rounded		$31,300	
Indicated Retail Value/Lot			$40,789
Rounded			$40,800

Exhibit 8.13
Initial Analysis Results from Income Capitalization and Cost Approaches

	Bulk Sale Value	Gross Retail Indication
Mill Pond Project (*when complete* date)		
Value by income capitalization approach	$2,370,000	$3,240,000
Value by cost approach	$2,380,000	$3,100,000

172   *Subdivision Valuation*

- Functional obsolescence
- External obsolescence

Physical deterioration relates to physical wear and tear over time. Functional obsolescence is related to a deficiency or superadequacy in a property that causes a loss in value. Functional obsolescence can be measured as a loss in income or the difference in cost between an appropriate item and a deficient or superadequate item. External obsolescence relates to conditions outside a property and is one of the most common forms of depreciation found in subdivision valuation.

Physical deterioration is usually measured with an age/life calculation. This type of depreciation is mostly found in existing subdivision projects rather than proposed projects. Appraisers usually must value a subset of lots within an existing project rather than an entire subdivision, and in these cases the cost approach is not applicable. A retail lot value estimate is typically made using the sales comparison approach. The bulk sale scenario is considered, and the value estimate will also be made using the income capitalization or sales comparison approach. Valuing a small group of lots in a larger project by the cost approach is not particularly accurate and seldom done. Accordingly, there are relatively few situations in which appraisers actually encounter physical deterioration in a subdivision when using the cost approach. The cost approach is almost always employed for a new proposed project, and proposed projects do not usually have physical deterioration. As with all elements of depreciation, physical deterioration should be considered, but actual adjustments for physical deterioration are rarely applied for proposed projects.

Functional obsolescence typically occurs in subdivisions when the scale of the amenities and/or project design does not match the marketing concept. In most cases, superadequate common amenities are installed in a project but do not produce a dollar-for-dollar increase in value or quicker absorption in the local marketplace.

The process for measuring functional obsolescence is similar to the process for measuring external obsolescence. A typical DCF analysis is employed in the income capitalization approach to estimate a bulk sale value. The bulk sale value is then compared with costs including the superadequate item to ascertain the magnitude of the adjustment for functional obsolescence. It is sometimes difficult to determine if the full effect of the functional obsolescence has been considered in this process. For example, lots may have a lower value because of an external influence, which may not necessarily be directly related to or fully explained by the functional obsolescence.

Changes in employment opportunities in an area can cause a general reduction in price levels for homes and lots. A subdivision design and amenity package that may have been well received and supported at the time of the initial construction may be superadequate or deficient under a different set of circumstances or after a change in the economic environment.

External obsolescence in subdivision development typically has two effects:

- A slowdown in lot sales (market absorption)
- A reduction in retail lot values

These effects are most accurately measured by a DCF analysis using the income capitalization approach in a before-and-after scenario or by comparing a typical economic application versus the actual situation. The difference in the two value estimates would indicate the adjustment that would be applied in a cost analysis under a "financially feasible" scenario. The financially feasible scenario would have typical market-oriented profit and holding costs within the cost approach. When the holding costs increase and profit decreases due to functional or external obsolescence, the difference in cash flows and the present value conclusions from income capitalization analysis are measured to arrive at a lump-sum adjustment.

Other Cost Approach Issues

This section provides a brief overview of common issues that arise in subdivision valuation problems such as allocating land value and/or common infrastructure between phases. Examples are introduced to illustrate how the cost approach can be used to address these issues.

Allocating Land Value Between Phases

Allocating land value among the various phases of a larger planned development or subdivision project can be difficult because the process involves several different scenarios and because values can vary depending on the frame of reference used for the value conclusion and whether the appraiser is performing a valuation for the entire project or subcomponents of the larger subdivision. Also, the effective date of the land value estimate for both the parent parcel and the various phases along with remaining excess land has an impact on the various land value conclusions. The land value estimate for the larger parent parcel may be different from the sum of the values of smaller subcomponents of the parent parcel. Smaller parcels usually sell for a higher price per acre or per unit than large tracts of land.

When the various subcomponents of a land parcel do not exactly add up to the value of the whole, the appraiser must address the individual issues of land value for the various phases as well as timeline and size dynamics within the overall valuation. Also, different phases or pods within the development may have different densities, home price points, or other characteristics that would impact the value estimates for the various phases within the overall project. Density and/or price-point differentials between various phases can be extremely complicated, especially when allocating overall land value among various phases or providing independent values for either the phase being appraised or the excess land value for future phases.

Common infrastructure may be installed as part of the initial phases, which adds incremental value to the excess or surplus land reserved for future phases. The incremental value increase would assume that future phases have implied "development rights" and can make use of common infrastructure installed as part of the initial phases within the project, which may require an extraordinary assumption in the valuation of a relatively complicated mixed-use project. Adjustments to land value can be made for price points and/or building density by developing hypothetical bulk sale estimates for future phases to ascertain the general magnitude of the land value supported for the independent pod. However, this type of analysis can be very complicated and is beyond the scope of this book.

Exhibit 8.14 provides land value data for the Sacramento Hills project, a proposed single-unit subdivision of 638 lots or units that will support three separate building phases on 232 acres. Exhibit 8.15 shows how land value can be allocated between the current and future phases of the development.

As shown in Exhibit 8.14, the price per unit comparison method is given the most weight because the phases have different unit densities. For example, Phase 1 supports an average density of 2.5 units per acre, while Phase 2 supports an average density of 3.0 units per acre. Typically, larger tracts of land of 150 to 250 acres reflect a price level of about $20,000 per unit. Smaller tracts of 60 to 100 acres reflect a value level of about $24,000 per unit. The market conditions adjustment is 5% per year. Vacant land that may make use of common infrastructure built as part of the initial phase will experience a land value increase of about 15% after Phase 1 is built. In this case, the appraiser assumes that the land developed in future phases can utilize common infrastructure installed as part of the initial phase. The appraiser must ascertain whether future phases have development rights to infrastructure built in the initial phase and explain how the "property rights" impact land value conclusions for future phases.

Exhibit 8.15 summarizes the land values estimated for the Sacramento Hills project. The larger parent parcel has a value of

Exhibit 8.14
Sacramento Hills Data

Sacramento Hills:

Proposed single-unit subdivision development located in a well-established and expanding suburban market. The site recently received final site plan approval and the necessary permits to allow immediate construction. The project was approved for 638 lots or units on a 232-acre tract. The marketing concept is for single-unit detached homes in the $360,000 to $525,000 price range. The project is divided into three phases. All common infrastructure will be built in Phase 1 and the construction period is 12 months.

Site Characteristics:

	Units	Size (Ac.)	Units/Ac.
Phase 1	150	60.00	2.50
Phase 2	225	75.00	3.00
Phase 3	263	97.00	2.71
Total	638	232.00	2.75

Land Sales:

Recent land sales for tracts with full entitlements reflect the following market values:

Large tracts: (150 to 250 acres)
    Price per unit: $20,000

Small tracts: (60 to 100 acres)
    Price per unit: $24,000

Market conditions adjustment: 5.0% yr.

Common infrastructure:
    Installed common infrastructure in the initial phase adds 15% to remaining excess land value.

Exhibit 8.15
Sacramento Hills Land Value Summary

Current Land Values

Parent parcel (232 ac. or 638 units)	638 units @ $20,000 =	$12,760,000
Rounded		$12,760,000
Phase 1 only (60 ac. or 150 units)	150 units @ $24,000 =	$3,600,000
Rounded		$3,600,000

Future Land Values (in 12 months)

Phase 2 only (75 ac. or 225 units)	225 units @ $24,000 =		$5,400,000
Adjustments			
Market conditions		5.0%	$270,000
Infrastructure		15.0%	$810,000
Total			$6,480,000
Rounded			$6,480,000
Phases 2 and 3 (172 ac. or 488 units)	488 units @ $20,000 =		$9,760,000
Adjustments			
Market conditions		5.0%	$488,000
Infrastructure		15.0%	$1,464,000
Total			$11,712,000
Rounded			$11,710,000

$20,000 per unit; this amount would reflect the *as is* land value for the entire ownership prior to any development. If Phase 1 were being valued separately, then the value estimate for Phase 1 (land only) would be $24,000 per unit. The remaining land area, excluding Phase 1 (prior to the construction of Phase 1), would be valued at $20,000 per unit. Exhibit 8.15 shows how component parts may not add up to the value of the whole.

Subdivision valuation typically requires the appraiser to estimate future land values for any remaining excess land that is reserved for future phases when Phase 1 is complete. Exhibit 8.15 provides a value estimate for Phases 2 and 3 twelve months in the future. The Phase 2 land, if it were valued separately, would have a value estimate starting at $24,000 per unit with a market conditions adjustment of 5% and an infrastructure adjustment of 15%. Typically, common infrastructure (utility backbone systems, sewer lift stations, main entrance boulevard, etc.) that is installed as part of the initial phase adds contributory value to excess land reserved for future building construction. The incremental increase in this example is 15%.

The incremental increase may be the result of a pro rata distribution of common costs over all lots in the project or may be a market-derived adjustment based on the observed difference between vacant land with entitlements and common infrastructure and land sales with entitlements but no infrastructure. Care must be taken when using a pro rata cost allocation because it assumes that cost contributes 100% to an increase in value. Some level of profit may be earned as part of the installation of common infrastructure. The appraiser should recognize that the cost incurred, especially with common amenities, may not yield a dollar-for-dollar increase in the land value of the vacant land or finished lots.

The future land values in Exhibit 8.15 demonstrate how land values can differ depending on the client's request. For example, if only Phase 2 land were being appraised, the value estimate would start at $24,000 per unit, with the appropriate adjustments for market conditions and infrastructure. If Phases 2 and 3 were valued as one parcel, the land would be valued at $20,000 per unit, with appropriate adjustments for market conditions and infrastructure. This example shows that component parts do not always add up to the value of the whole. If the Phase 2 and Phase 3 land parcels were appraised separately, the value would be higher than the value of the combined parcel as a result of differences in tract size. The appraiser and client typically consider the different scenarios and the appropriate methods as part of the scope of work decision.

Valuing Large Planned Development Acreage

Subdivision development valuation methodology may be used to estimate the value of a large tract of land when the highest and best use is to market component parts to individual buyers. For example, a property may have just been re-zoned to support a large project consisting of eight individual pods developed with a combination of professional offices, multiple-unit apartments, and single-unit homes. The overall project contains 760 acres, and the individual pods range from 40 to 100 acres in size. The development also supports a small commercial area, which would allow for neighborhood-oriented retail sales within the project.

An appraiser would estimate the land value for the larger parent parcel in this example by

1. Providing independent component land values for the various pods within the project, and
2. Performing a time discounting valuation analysis with a typical sell-out for the individual pods to developers, who would then subdivide each pod and market individual lots

This process would result in an *as is* land value for the larger planned development vacant acreage. This land value would be appropriate in situations when sales of similar large planned development acreage are not available, or when the size of the project would require the marketing of component parts.

Valuation of "Common" Land

Another valuation problem typically encountered by appraisers is the valuation of "common" land within a larger planned development. This type of valuation could be a separate appraisal of common area or a valuation of conservation land after a project has been developed. Some developers donate common land to conservation groups. These conservation groups are typically non-profit organizations, and developers can receive IRS tax deductions for donating common land.

Usually, common land will not have any specific economic use other than acting as a natural buffer or common area supporting the surrounding residential project. A difficult problem arises when the appraiser must identify an economic use or benefit that can be made of the common land in order for it to have value and an identified market. In this case, the appraiser must analyze the rights available to the common land as specified in the subdivision development documents and/or master plan to determine any uses that may be made of the common acreage.

For example, if the common acreage could support remote water retention for subdivision development land, then the common land area would have a component value in support of other elements in the planned development. As long as this right is marketable and could be used for other pods within the project, the common land may support an independent value. Also, common land may be used to support golf courses, recreational facilities, and/or other common amenities for the overall project.

Land designed to support golf courses would be valued based on a typical highest and best use identified by the appraiser. For the land to have value, it must have an identifiable economic use and a market in which it could be sold separately. Also, there may be a market in which common land is regularly purchased for conservation purposes.

Future Infrastructure Costs

Subdivision development often involves the construction of substantial common area improvements that are used in all phases of the project. This infrastructure may include a clubhouse, swimming pool, tennis courts, riding trails, and a wide variety of other common amenities.

Most or all of a project's common amenities are usually installed as part of the initial Phase I construction. However, some developers delay the actual construction of common amenities until future phases are built. It is common for project zoning approvals to have a phasing schedule that defines when each component of the common elements must be installed and may even have specific dates when future phase construction must commence. The requirement for specific common infrastructure to be installed in the future introduces several problems within the appraisal analysis.

The first problem is deciding whether these common amenities contribute value to the Phase I lots if they are not yet built. Generally, Phase I lots are appraised as if the infrastructure is in place, which would give full benefit to future infrastructure that is yet to be constructed. Obviously, this issue would be addressed as a hypothetical condition or extraordinary assumption in the appraisal report.

The second problem arises when infrastructure is not built as part of Phase 1 but is instead required to be built as part of Phase 2 or over multiple future phases. This may result in a reduced land value for the Phase 2 vacant site. Any prospective purchaser of the Phase 2 land would consider the required cost to install all of the common amenities or other required infrastructure, so this issue should be considered in the underlying land value estimate for the Phase 2 acreage. The land may have a lower value because of the requirement to construct common amenities that serve the whole project and not just Phase 2. Because of this aspect of land value analysis within the subdivision valuation framework, the appraiser must be aware of the cost of infrastructure, how the infrastructure is allocated within a larger planned development or multi-phase subdivision, and when the infrastructure is to be installed.

Allocation of Common Infrastructure

Another issue that usually surfaces in the cost approach is how to allocate costs for common infrastructure among the various phases of a project. This cost allocation is a relatively simple calculation as long as the cost of the common infrastructure is evenly allocated on a per-unit basis throughout the project. The issue can be complicated if different phases in the project have different densities, price points, and contributions of common improvements.

For example, a large multi-phase project may provide a common clubhouse, swimming pool, tennis courts, or other amenities as part of the overall amenity package shared by all phases within the development. However, the common amenities may have the greatest contributory value to the lower-priced homes.

The lower-priced homes would typically be located on smaller lots that would not support private swimming pools, so a typical purchaser of a lower-priced home would recognize the desirability of the common area swimming pool and other amenities. Homeowners at the lower and lower-middle price ranges may make greater use of common amenities. As a result, these common amenities would generate a higher contributory value to homes in the lower price range.

Homes at the upper end of the price range in the same development may have larger lots, and a high percentage of these homes may include private swimming pools. Owners of these higher-priced homes may be indifferent to the inclusion of common amenities as part of the overall development. In this case, common amenities may not contribute any value to the higher-priced homes, result in a faster absorption, or produce any other perceived benefits. The appraiser must consider multiple price points within the project, how the common amenities contribute to each price point, and how to allocate common infrastructure "value" within the project.

To illustrate how costs of common infrastructure are allocated within a subdivision, consider the Gator Pond subdivision described in Exhibits 8.16, 8.17, and 8.18. The Gator Pond project is a proposed multi-phase, detached, single-unit subdivision that will be built in the immediate future. Phase 1 has 106 lots and a targeted marketing concept for three price points. Common infrastructure is estimated to produce contributory value equal to its pro rata cost for all price points. The future phases will include 242 units for a total project size of 348 units on a parcel of about 129 acres.

The cost approach analysis has been completed for the Phase 1 construction. All common infrastructure, including utility backbone systems and project amenities, is to be installed as part of the initial Phase 1 construction. The total cost is $1,245,000, as shown in Exhibit 8.17. Dividing the total common infrastructure and amenity package cost by all 348 lots indicates an average allocation of $3,578 per lot. The contributory value for Phase 1 is 106 lots at the average infrastructure cost of $3,578, or $379,268

Exhibit 8.16
Gator Pond Subdivision

General Information

Gator Pond is a proposed, multi-phase, detached single-unit subdivision that will be built in the immediate future. The project has a definite site plan layout for Phase 1 with 106 lots supporting 106 units. The marketing concept is to support three separate price points coinciding with the three lot size categories described below.

The main entrance boulevard with utility "back bone," front brick wall, and entrance signage and landscaping will be built as part of Phase 1. The pool complex will be built during Phase 2 at a cost of about $300,000. Land value is constant over the construction period.

Definite site plan layouts for future phases are not available, but the full allowed density of 242 lots supporting 242 residential units will be used in the future phases.

Site Characteristics

Phase	Units	Size (Ac.)	Units/Ac.
Phase 1	106	45.7	2.32
Future phases	242	83.0	2.92
Total project	348	128.7	2.70

Lot Characteristics—Phase 1

		Lot Size Sq. Ft.		
Lot Category	Lots	Low	Average	High
Sixty foot	55	6,600	7,343	9,462
Eighty foot	26	8,328	9,946	12,164
Hundred foot	25	14,760	16,160	29,027
	106			

Subdivision Site Amenities

Brick screen wall along main road, front entrance signage, and landscaping
Underground utilities (water, sewer, gas, and electric)
Underground phone, cable TV
Paved interior roads, concrete curb, public roads
Streetlights, streetscaping, water retention, and open space

Subdivision Common Amenities

Clubhouse building with two restrooms and kitchen area, in-ground commercial swimming pool with concrete deck, parking area, playground area, fencing, and landscaping
Unit owners association

Exhibit 8.17
Cost Approach Summary–Gator Pond Subdivision

Reproduction Cost New, Less Depreciation

			$	Per Lot (106 Total)	%
Direct Construction Costs					
Horizontal improvements (streets, utilities, site work, etc.)			$1,966,300	$18,550	31.7%
Front entrance sign—Phase 1 only			20,000	189	0.3%
Landscaping			10,000	94	0.2%
Other direct costs			5,000	47	0.1%
Construction overhead allocation			10,000	94	0.2%
Indirect Construction Costs					
Indirect costs during permitting phase			100,000	943	1.6%
Closing and legal costs			50,000	472	0.8%
Engineering, design, and surveying			130,000	1,226	2.1%
Permits			130,000	1,226	2.1%
Contingency and misc.			100,000	943	1.6%
Common Improvements	348 units				
Front entrance, walls, and signage	$300,000				
Front entry boulevard and utility backbone	520,000				
Clubhouse and pool (will be built in future phase)	300,000				
Street trees	75,000				
Screen fencing	50,000				
Subtotal common	$1,245,000				
Common per unit	$3,578				
Phase 1 allocation			379,268	3,578	6.1%
Holding and Sales Costs					
Tax			59,000	557	1.0%
Sales expense			242,000	2,283	3.9%
Miscellaneous			60,000	566	1.0%
Profit incentive			1,550,000	14,623	25.1%
Reproduction Cost New			$4,811,568	$45,391	77.8%
Less: Depreciation					
Physical	none noted		0	0	0.0%
Functional	none noted		0	0	0.0%
External	none noted		0	0	0.0%
Depreciated Improvement Value			$4,811,568	$45,391	77.8%
Add: Land Value	45.7 acres @ $30,000 =	$1,371,000			
(raw land basis)	106 units @ $13,000 =	$1,378,000			
Rounded		$1,375,000	1,375,000	12,972	22.2%
Indicated Value by Cost Approach			$6,186,568	$58,363	100.0%
Rounded			$6,187,000		
Indicated Value per Lot				$58,400	rounded

(see Exhibit 8.17). This allocation assumes that the improvements contribute pro rata to every lot in the project, and 100% of cost will be returned on a pro rata basis. Common infrastructure may have an allocation greater or less than cost, depending on the market's acceptance and reaction to the proposed amenity package. Any diminution from the actual cost would be a depreciation issue to consider.

Assuming a typical pro rata allocation, land values for future phases can be estimated for the subject project. Exhibit 8.18 provides a land value allocation for the *as is* land value and the future value after Phase 1 is built with the full amenity package and other common infrastructure. The *as is* value estimates reflect a site and the contributory value of zoning entitlements, as shown in Exhibit 8.18. In this example, the price per unit comparison used is the same for both parcel sizes, and there is no market conditions adjustment.

Future value estimates for the Gator Pond project include excess land area. The excess land area supports 242 units and has entitlements in place as part of the project permitting and contributory value for the common infrastructure. As shown in Exhibit 8.18, applying the average allocation per lot of $3,578 to the remaining excess land indicates that common infrastructure contributes $865,876 to future phases. However, the developer of

Exhibit 8.18
Land Value Summary–Gator Pond Subdivision

As Is Value Estimates		
Phase 1 Only		
Phase 1 raw land value	106 units @ $13,000	$1,378,000
Add: contributory value zoning entitlements	15.00%	$206,700
Total		$1,584,700
Rounded		$1,585,000
Parent Parcel		
Entire subdivision acreage	348 units @ $13,000	$4,524,000
Add: contributory value zoning entitlements	15.00%	$678,600
Total		$5,202,600
Rounded		$5,200,000
Future Value Estimates		
Remaining Land Area--Future Single-Unit Phases		
Excess land area	242 units @ $13,000	$3,146,000
Add: contributory value zoning entitlements	15.00%	$471,900
Add: contributory value common infrastructure	242 units @ $3,578	$865,876
Less: obligation to build clubhouse and pool		
Estimated cost		($300,000)
Total		$4,183,776
Rounded		$4,180,000

the future phases must install the clubhouse and swimming pool complex. Stated differently, the obligation to build the clubhouse and swimming pool must occur simultaneously with the construction on the excess land area. Whether the excess land supports one phase or multiple phases, this entire cost component will be incurred as part of the future development. The contributory value of the excess land must consider this cost, and the cost is subtracted to reflect an *as is* land value considering the obligation to expend capital as part of the Phase 2 construction for common improvements. The actual contribution of common improvements for the remaining excess land after Phase 1 is built is $865,876 less $300,000 for the cost of the pool complex.

Project size is also a consideration in determining the economic feasibility of common amenities. For example, appropriate infrastructure to support the targeted marketing concept for a subdivision may not be financially feasible for a relatively small group of lots. The same infrastructure installed in a larger subdivision with a greater number of lots would have a lower overall cost per lot and may be well supported in terms of the cost/benefit relationship.

Moreover, the actual cost of the infrastructure is not necessarily returned by an increase in retail lot value. In many markets, amenity packages contribute to faster market absorption, resulting in a shorter holding period. Ultimately, the amenities may contribute to increased lot value and/or enhanced market absorption.

9
Sales Comparison Approach

Introduction

The sales comparison approach is a primary valuation method for most commercial properties, including subdivisions. This approach has already been used to estimate the retail lot value in the income capitalization approach and the vacant land value in the cost approach for the Mill Pond project. This chapter will investigate how the sales comparison approach is used to directly compare a group of comparable bulk lot sales with the proposed Mill Pond subdivision.

The sales comparison approach makes use of comparable sales to estimate the market value of a proposed project or existing group of lots. This approach assumes a market in which current bulk sales are readily available. Unfortunately, this is not always possible. Appraisers often experience difficulty in applying a direct sales comparison approach in estimating a bulk sale value for an existing group of lots or a proposed subdivision.

In markets with available sales, appraisers can use the sales comparison approach as a direct measure of market value and compare its results with those of the cost and income capitalization approaches. When limited data is available, evidence from available bulk sales may be compared to results from the cost or income capitalization approaches as a general test of reasonableness. In many cases, the greatest benefit of the sales comparison approach is that it can act as a check on other approaches. Another significant benefit of the sales comparison approach is its ability to reveal micromarket supply and demand trends as well as applicable discounts for bulk lot purchases. For example, the application of the income capitalization approach may support a bulk sale value that is 15% less than the sum of the retail values. Stated differently, the flat discount reflected in the income capitalization approach is 15%. A review of market sales in the same market may reveal a significantly lower or higher discount, revealing current supply and demand trends in a macromarket that are not readily evident from inferred or fundamental demand analysis.

Another benefit of the sales comparison approach is that it is easily understood by clients and provides strong market evidence as part of a rate extraction analysis or bulk value conclusion. Rate extraction can be applied to historical bulk sales as well as a prospective analysis of income and expenses provided by interviews with project developers. Rate extraction is the only method that can be used to support matched pairs when using discounting methodology that includes line-item profit as a subdivision expense. This methodology relies heavily on a market-extracted yield analysis to support the split rates used in the DCF analysis.

Applying a sales comparison approach that employs a flat discount methodology to check the reasonableness of the income capitalization and cost approaches often provides market confirmation of the results and increases the client's confidence in those results. Even if truly comparable sales are not available for comparison purposes, the results of the sales comparison approach often bracket a market-supportable flat discount that confirms the premise behind the bulk sale methodology used.

Applying the Sales Comparison Approach

The flat discount method and bulk value price per lot method are most commonly used to compare recent sales to a subject property. These methods can be used for a group of existing lots or a proposed subdivision.

The first step in the sales comparison approach is to conduct a search for comparable bulk sales transactions. It is important to compare bulk sales that have a similar marketing concept as the subject project and a similar timeline for the absorption of lot inventory. The timeline for future absorption has a significant impact on the bulk sale flat discount. Physical units of comparison including the amenities offered within the project, lot sizes, locations, and other factors are also considered during the comparable sales selection process.

Most markets have relatively few bulk sales transactions, which may hinder the appraiser. In this case, the appraiser must determine if there is sufficient information to adequately apply the sales comparison approach and whether the available comparable sales are consistent with the characteristics of the subject property and can result in a meaningful analysis.

Basic project information for the Mill Pond subdivision is shown in Exhibit 9.1. This same information was used in the income capitalization and cost approaches. This chapter covers the final approach to value, and a reconciliation will be completed to determine the final value indications for the Mill Pond project.

After comparable sale information has been gathered, the market sales are compared with the property being appraised. Exhibit 9.2 presents four comparable market sales of groups of lots in existing projects. The flat discount and the bulk sale price per lot are both provided for comparison purposes. All projects are new or recently built and currently experiencing initial sell-out. The table provides the bulk sale purchase prices as well as the average prices per lot on a bulk sale basis. For example, Project 1(the River View subdivision) has a group of 62 lots that sold for $2,074,000, or about $33,452 per lot. The average or typical retail price level for a finished lot in this market is $45,500. Dividing the actual purchase price per lot of $33,452 by $45,500 would indicate that the bulk lot purchase price is about 74.36% of the typical retail value. Conversely, the flat discount when calculated from the retail value level is about 26.5%.

In Exhibit 9.2, the bulk sale discount is calculated for all four comparable sales, and the resulting range is from a low of 10.0% (as indicated by Sale 4) to a high of 32.3% (as indicated by Sale 3). The targeted marketing price range for the home and lot package in each project and the estimated market absorption for each group purchased are included in the table. The absorption forecasts range from six to ten lots per quarter, and most of the absorptions range from 1 to 1½ years for each group of lots. However, Sale 3 had a longer absorption time period of three years with a significantly higher discount, which partially explains why subdivision projects are often phased over time. The cost to carry inventory over time is significant, and many developers target each phase size to achieve sell-out within one to three years. Timelines of more than three years can significantly reduce profit, especially for financed projects.

Sale 4 is different from the first three sales because the buyer agreed to sell groups of 15 lots over time with no lot price increases and a minimal down payment. Accordingly, the builder would be able to purchase groups of 15 lots over an approximate 1.41-year period. This sale indicates the lowest bulk sale discount because of the favorable purchase agreement that allows for purchases of small groups of lots over time.

Exhibit 9.1
Mill Pond Project Summary

General Information

Mill Pond is a proposed single-unit subdivision to be built in the immediate future. The project is located in a well-established residential area and will be marketing detached single-unit lots and/or homes with two separate price points and two lot categories.

Project Timing

Current date:	01/01/18
Construction start:	01/01/18
Construction period:	6 months
Absorption start date:	07/01/18
Absorption time frame:	30 months

Site Characteristics	Units	Size (Ac.)	Units/Ac.
Site area	76	28.50	2.67

Lot Inventory by Size Category

	Total Lots	Regular Lots	Cul-de-sac Lots	Avg. Lot Size (Sq. Ft.)	Avg. Lot Front Feet
Small lots	40	36	4	8,700	80
Large lots	36	32	4	11,000	100
Total	76	68	8		
%	100.0%	89.5%	10.5%		

Subdivision Site Amenities

Front entrance with signage and landscaping
Underground utilities (water, sewer, gas, and electric)
Underground phone, cable TV
Paved interior roads, concrete curb, public roads, 3,600 ln. ft.±
Streetlights, water retention, and open space

Subdivision Common Amenities

Playground area with small parking lot, fencing, and landscaping
Unit owners association

Marketing Concept

Target Price Range for Home and Lot

Lot Category	Lot Size Sq. Ft. ±	Home Size Sq. Ft. ±	Home Price Range		
			Low	Average	High
Small lots	8,700	1,500	$140,000	$170,000	$200,000
Large lots	11,000	2,000	$180,000	$200,000	$220,000

In this market, cul-de-sac lots sell for about 10% more than typical interior or corner lots, and lot value prices are increasing by about 4% per year.

Exhibit 9.2 also provides developer information gathered from a recent interview about a project that will enter the market soon. This project will contain 60 lots to be built in the immediate future, and the developer has indicated a willingness to sell the entire 60-lot inventory at a 20% discount to a local builder. The exact purchase price has not been established, but the developer anticipates that it will be somewhere between $31,000 and $36,000 per lot on a bulk sale basis. While this information is not a concluded market sale, it is relevant market information

Exhibit 9.2
Comparable Bulk Sales Data

No.	Sale Date	Project	Bulk Lot Purchase				Indicated Bulk Sale Discount	Project Price Points (price range: home and lot package)		Estimated Market Absorption		Comments
			Sale Price	Lots	Price per Lot	Average Retail Value per Lot		Low	High	Lots per Qtr.	Years	
1	Dec-17	River View	$2,074,000	62	$33,452	$45,500	-26.5%	$185,000 to	$210,000	10	1.55	Typical detached home lots, includes all site infrastructure, minimal project amenities
2	Jul-17	Lake View	$827,000	24	$34,458	$44,000	-21.7%	$170,000 to	$200,000	6	1.00	Typical detached home lots, includes all site infrastructure, minimal project amenities
3	Mar-17	Mountain View	$2,833,000	96	$29,510	$43,600	-32.3%	$175,000 to	$205,000	8	3.00	Typical detached home lots, includes all site infrastructure, clubhouse with pool
4	Feb-17	Valley View	$2,025,000	45	$45,000	$50,000	-10.0%	$215,000 to	$250,000	8	1.41	Typical detached home lots, includes all site infrastructure, minimal project amenities. Purchased in groups of 15 lots over time, with no lot price increase and minimal down payment.
5	Current (developer interview)	DCB Development	n/a	60	n/a	n/a	-20.0%	$200,000 to	$250,000	8	1.00	Proposed subdivision, includes all site infrastructure, minimal project amenities. Developer will be offering the entire 60 lots for sale to one home builder.

because it helps to confirm that historical trends are consistent with current price levels.

When applying the sales comparison approach, it is imperative to compare projects that have a similar lot absorption time horizon as well as a similar total number of lots being sold in comparison to the subject. A criterion for the bulk sale scenario is a sale of all the lots to one purchaser as well as an absorption period that considers the absorption rate or time frame of the market absorption to typical end users. In the Mill Pond Case Study, an inventory of 76 lots with an absorption time frame of about 2½ years was being appraised. Accordingly, sales to one purchaser in one bulk transaction with a similar number of lots must be used and reflect a similar absorption time horizon as the subject property. Sale 4 was not a good comparable because groups of only 15 lots with relatively short absorption time frames were being sold. This sale might be a good comparison for an appraisal of a group of 10 to 20 lots, but it has significantly different characteristics from the subject property and would make a poor comparison.

In estimating the bulk sale value for the Mill Pond project, the most weight is given to Sales 1 and 3. These projects are marketing homes in an overall price range similar to the subject's, their purchase terms are more indicative of a typical bulk sale of an entire lot inventory, and they have a similar absorption timeline (Mill Pond's absorption time period is 2½ years). As a result, the bracketed bulk discount range for the subject project would be 26% to 32%. Because the subject project contains 76 lots and the appraiser's goal is to estimate the bulk sale value for all 76 lots as one transaction, the most weight is given to Sale 1. Sale 1 is more comparable to the subject with respect to project size, price points, and absorption, which are all considered in the estimation of a bulk discount using the flat discount method. Longer timelines typically require greater discounts for bulk sales. The Mill Pond bulk sale flat discount is about 28%.

The final step of the sales comparison approach is to calculate the actual bulk sale value for the subject subdivision, which can be done by either

1. Concluding a bulk price per lot and multiplying this amount directly by the number of lots in the subject project, or
2. Using the retail lot estimate as part of the income capitalization or cost approach to reconcile an appropriate retail lot value for the subject project and then applying the bulk sale discount to the average retail lot value

The first method reflects a bulk sale value per lot derived directly from the sales comparison approach and is completely independent from the other approaches to value. The second method introduces the retail lot value conclusion from the income capitalization approach to assist in calculating the bulk sale value. Both methods are summarized in Exhibit 9.3.

When the bulk lot value method is applied, the subject bulk lot value is estimated at about $31,000 per lot, with the most weight given to Comparable Sales 1 and 3. Applying this amount to the 76 lots in the Mill Pond project indicates a bulk sale value of approximately $2,360,000. When the flat discount is used to estimate the bulk sale value, a retail lot value is needed for the calculation. For the Mill Pond project, the income capitalization approach reflects an average retail lot value of $41,500 per lot as of the *when complete* date. Applying a flat discount of 28% to the retail value indicates a bulk sale value of $29,888 per lot. Applying this amount to the 76 lots in the project reflects a bulk sale conclusion of $2,270,000.

The first method has the benefit of being totally independent, but would require a second level of analysis in which the bulk sale value per lot is established in the sales comparison approach. The second method has the disadvantage of introducing information from another approach into the bulk sale discount conclusion by the sales comparison approach, but may reflect a more accurate number because a more accurate retail lot value is available for comparison purposes. Both methods are shown in Exhibit 9.3 and reflect a relatively consistent value range for the Mill Pond project.

Exhibit 9.3

Sales Comparison Approach Bulk Sale Conclusions		
Mill Pond Bulk Sale Value		
Bulk Lot Value Method		
Indicated bulk lot value from market sales		$31,000
	76 lots @ $31,000	$2,356,000
	Rounded	$2,360,000
Retail Lot Value Method		
Subject retail lot value estimate (from retail lot value conclusion in income capitalization approach)		$41,500
Less: bulk sale discount of	28.0%	(11,620)
Indicated bulk value per lot		$29,880
Indicated bulk sale value subject project	76 lots @ $29,880	$2,270,880
	Rounded	$2,270,000
Flat Discount Comparison		
Indicated flat discount from market sales		28.0%
Flat discount reflected in subject income capitalization approach analysis		26.9%
Flat discount reflected in subject cost approach analysis		23.2%

Depending on the level of accuracy and the available comparable sales information, the appraiser may want to compare the bulk sale discount estimated with those reached via the income capitalization or cost approach to value. This method uses the sales comparison approach to check the value conclusions from the previous two approaches. In markets with limited bulk sale information, the sales comparison approach is typically used for this purpose.

The flat discount comparison is also shown at the bottom of Exhibit 9.3. The flat discount chosen for the subject property is 28%, based on a comparison with market sales. This flat discount is compared to the indicated flat discounts from both the income capitalization and cost approaches. The income capitalization approach indicated a bulk sale value of $2,370,000, and the sum of the retail values is $3,240,000. Dividing the bulk sale value by the gross retail number reveals that the bulk sale value is about 73.15% less than the retail value conclusion, which would indicate a 26.85% flat discount, rounded to 26.9%. This same calculation is applied to the two values derived in the cost approach, which indicates a flat discount of 23.2%. It appears that information from the sales comparison approach reflects a flat discount that is very close to the results from the income capitalization approach. Both the sales comparison and income capitalization approaches reflect higher flat discounts than the cost approach conclusion. In estimating the final value conclusion by the sales comparison approach, the most weight is given to the bulk value per lot method, concluding a value of $2,360,000.

Exhibit 9.4

Mill Pond Reconciliation and Final Value Conclusion

Mill Pond Proposed Project (*when complete* date)	Market Value Bulk Sale Scenario
Value by income capitalization approach	$2,370,000
Value by cost approach	$2,380,000
Value by sales comparison approach	$2,360,000
Estimated market value (prospective value, *when complete* date)	$2,375,000
Mill Pond Current Value	
Current vacant land value (*as is* value, current date)	$1,060,000

Mill Pond Value Conclusion

As shown in Exhibit 9.4, the three approaches to value applied to the proposed Mill Pond project reflect an overall value range from a low of $2,360,000 (as indicated by the sales comparison approach) to a high of $2,380,000 (as indicated by the cost approach). The income capitalization approach reflects a bulk sale conclusion of $2,370,000. The three approaches to value indicate a relatively narrow value range for the bulk sale conclusion, and equal weight was given to each approach in reflecting a final value conclusion of $2,375,000. This final value conclusion is a prospective value as of the *when complete* date, which for the Mill Pond project is six months in the future as of July 2018. The reconciliation and final conclusion of value also provide a current *as is* value for the vacant land, including all entitlements as of the current date. This indicated value from the cost approach analysis is $1,060,000.

This chapter explored the two primary techniques applied to analyze market sales in a subdivision valuation appraisal. When making a direct comparison using sales, the flat discount method or bulk price per lot method is used in comparing the sales with the subject. The sales comparison approach is applied in most appraisals as a test of reasonableness to support conclusions from the cost and income capitalization approaches. The main difficulty with the sales comparison approach is finding sales with absorption timelines, price points, locations, and other physical characteristics that are similar to the subject property. The sales comparison approach can be an effective valuation tool because it generates data and analysis results from completely different data sets than the data typically employed in the income capitalization and cost approaches.

The income capitalization and cost approaches tend to be interrelated because many of the inputs needed in the income capitalization approach rely on the cost estimates provided in the cost approach. The sales comparison approach provides a separate market conclusion and often verifies or validates the information from the other approaches. This verification increases the comfort level of the users of the appraisal analysis, even in cases when conclusive market data is not available.

The second primary application of the sales comparison approach is rate extraction. To perform a rate extraction, the same general information needed for a bulk sale flat discount is used. Retail lot values and holding costs over the anticipated absorption period are added to the analysis, and matched pairs of line-item profit and discount rates can be estimated from each market sale. When future builder forecasts are known, current sales data can be used to calculate yield and profit expectations to apply to a subject property. Even though it is based on future forecasts, this information is related to current purchase prices and tends to be more relevant than historical data. A detailed market extraction example is provided in Chapter 10.

10
Yield, Line-Item Profit, and Discounting

Profit Concepts and the Subdivision Timeline

The allocation of profit throughout the three phases of subdivision development is one of the most difficult concepts to understand when analyzing and appraising subdivision developments. A good understanding of where costs and profit occur along the timeline and how to measure profit is essential to the proper application of all three approaches to value. One of the best ways to understand the dynamics of profit along the timeline is to study the history of a subdivision project throughout the three phases of development. In the following Madison Square Case Study, a subdivision project is analyzed over the entire timeline to measure the profit earned at each stage of development.

Madison Square Case Study: Yield Rate Extraction

Exhibit 10.1 provides data on the Madison Square subdivision project, including an itemized list of the length of time for each phase, the costs associated with development, and the lot sales history over the absorption period. The permitting phase expenses and holding costs were $20,000 per quarter, and the construction expenses and holding costs over the construction phase were $378,000 per quarter. All 60 lots were sold over a two-year period, and Exhibit 10.1 shows the indicated values and timing of the sales. Absorption period costs and holding expenses are

Exhibit 10.1
Madison Square Subdivision Purchase and Sale History

Raw Land Purchase Price:		$600,000
Raw Land Sale Date:	3 years ago	
Time Periods:	Permitting process	6 months
	Construction period	6 months
	Absorption period	24 months
Land:	Raw land acquisition cost	$600,000.00
Purchase Offers:	Land with entitlements	$740,000.00
	Bulk sale purchase offer	$1,650,000.00
Income and Expenses:	**Permitting Phase Expenses**	
	Planning and conceptual drawings	$20,000
	Holding costs and taxes	2,000
	Permitting fees	3,000
	Environmental audit	5,000
	Survey and topographical	10,000
	Total	$40,000
	Avg./qtr.	$20,000
	Construction Phase Expenses	
	Direct construction costs	$720,000
	Survey, engineering, and final plat	20,000
	Front entrance with landscaping	15,000
	Holding costs and taxes	1,000
	Total	$756,000
	Avg./qtr.	$378,000
	Absorption Phase Income	

Lot sales:

Quarter	Lot Sales	Average Sale Price
1	10	$34,900
2	7	$34,900
3	8	$35,500
4	6	$35,500
5	9	$37,000
6	7	$37,000
7	7	$37,000
8	6	$37,000
	60	

	Absorption Phase Expenses	
	Sales expense:	6% gross sales
	Taxes:	Minimal Year 1: $1,000
		Year 2: $4,000
	Miscellaneous:	2% gross sales
Other:	All construction costs are evenly distributed over each phase on a quarterly basis.	
Description:	Sixty patio home lots ranging from 9,000 to 12,000 sq. ft. in size, supporting a single-unit price range from $150,000 to $175,000 for home and lot package. This is a typical detached home project on a 22-acre site with a density of 2.73 units per acre.	

summarized at the bottom of the table, and many of the costs associated with lot sales are expressed as a percentage of gross sales; this is common in most real estate markets. Some expenses such as taxes are reported on a lump-sum basis, while other expenses such as marketing costs are typically set at a percentage of gross sales. Costs can vary depending on the size of the project, property characteristics, and common elements within the subdivision. From the developer's perspective, faster-selling lots mean less holding and sales costs as well as higher profit. Keep in mind that subdivision valuation is very time-sensitive.

In the Madison Square subdivision development, raw land was purchased at an initial price of $600,000 to begin the permitting process. As shown in Exhibit 10.2, the overall timeline was three years from the initial purchase of the raw land through the eventual sale of the last lot. The permitting and construction phases each lasted six months, and the marketing phase required a 24-month absorption period. The subdivision is a 60-lot patio home development with lots ranging from about 9,000 square feet to 12,000 square feet in size. Typical single-unit home and lot package prices range from approximately $150,000 to $175,000. The subdivision is located in a relatively high-demand residential suburb of a major metropolitan area where supply and demand were in balance at the time of the initial project absorption. Site construction included installation of all interior roads, underground utilities (water, sewer, and electric), and phone and cable television. No

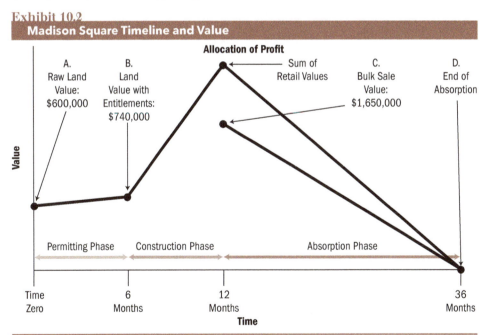

Exhibit 10.2 Madison Square Timeline and Value

homes were built as part of the original site construction. Also, the project has relatively minimal amenities, which mostly consist of open areas, water retention, a main front entrance with landscaping, and other miscellaneous site improvements.

One developer took the Madison Square project through all three phases of development. However, during the permitting and construction of the project, two offers were received. At the end of the permitting process, the developer received an offer to purchase the vacant site after the entitlements were achieved for $740,000. The offer was rejected, and the subdivision improvements were installed by the initial developer. Later, when all subdivision improvements were 100% built but before the sale of any lots, a second offer was made by a different party for $1,650,000. The developer decided to reject the second offer and continued with the eventual sell-out of all 60 lots over a 24-month absorption period. Both offers were fair and consistent with the value of the project at each respective point in time.

The profit for the overall development from time period zero through the eventual sale of all lots at the end of 36 months can be calculated using DCF analysis. Both dollar profit and the internal rate of return (yield rate) are calculated using DCF analysis, as shown in Exhibit 10.3. The time period covers all three subdivision phases and includes the actual lot sales and their timing throughout the historic absorption period. The present value calculation considers all permitting, construction, and absorption costs for the eventual sell-out of all 60 lots within the project.

The internal rate of return (*IRR*) or yield rate from the development is about 22.922%, as shown in Exhibit 10.3. Because no line-item profit is included in subdivision expenses, this rate is a "true" *IRR*. All of the net proceeds were discounted at an appropriate yield rate in order to exactly equal the initial land investment of $600,000. In this case, the interest or discount rate needed to deliver a present value of $600,000 is 22.922%. All of the remaining examples in this section use the "true" *IRR* model with $0 line-item profit. The significance of line-item profit as it relates to the yield rate chosen for the discounting is discussed in more detail in the next section of this chapter. The total dollar profit is $589,236. As shown in Exhibit 10.3, this profit is received over the last 24 months during the absorption phase of the development, with the developer taking the entire project from time period zero through the eventual sell-out of all the lots (from Points A to D). The yield rate throughout the entire development period is 22.922%, as shown in Exhibits 10.3 and 10.4.

Subdivision development is unique in that raw land is often not purchased unless the developer is certain that the land will achieve a final site plan approval for subdivision development

Exhibit 10.5
Madison Square DCF Analysis

Quarter	Phase	Lots Sold	Average Lot Sale Price	Gross Sales	Permitting Costs	Cons. Costs	Absorption Holding and Sales Costs			Line-Item Profit 0.0%	Net Proceeds	PV Factor 22.922%	Present Value
							Sales 6.0%	Tax	Misc. 2.0%				
1	Permitting	0			$20,000		$0	$0	$0	$0	-$20,000	0.945802	-$18,916
2	Permitting	0			$20,000		$0	$0	$0	$0	-$20,000	0.894541	-$17,891
3	Construction	0				$378,000	$0	$0	$0	$0	-$378,000	0.846059	-$319,810
4	Construction	0				$378,000	$0	$0	$0	$0	-$378,000	0.800204	-$302,477
5	Absorption	10	$34,900	$349,000			$20,940	$250	$6,980	$0	$320,830	0.756835	$242,815
6	Absorption	7	$34,900	$244,300			$14,658	$250	$4,886	$0	$224,506	0.715816	$160,705
7	Absorption	8	$35,500	$284,000			$17,040	$250	$5,680	$0	$261,030	0.677020	$176,723
8	Absorption	6	$35,500	$213,000			$12,780	$250	$4,260	$0	$195,710	0.640327	$125,318
9	Absorption	9	$37,000	$333,000			$19,980	$1,000	$6,660	$0	$305,360	0.605622	$184,933
10	Absorption	7	$37,000	$259,000			$15,540	$1,000	$5,180	$0	$237,280	0.572799	$135,914
11	Absorption	7	$37,000	$259,000			$15,540	$1,000	$5,180	$0	$237,280	0.541754	$128,547
12	Absorption	6	$37,000	$222,000			$13,320	$1,000	$4,440	$0	$203,240	0.512392	$104,139
		60		$2,163,300	$40,000	$756,000	$129,798	$5,000	$43,266	$0	$1,189,236		$600,000
													$600,000

Note: actual land purchase price =

Summary

Sum of the retail lot values	$2,094,000
Add: Lot value inflation over the holding period	69,300
Gross sales	$2,163,300
Less: Absorption holding and sales costs	
Sales	$129,798
Tax	5,000
Miscellaneous	43,266
Construction costs	756,000
Permitting costs	40,000
Land purchase price	600,000
Total direct and indirect costs	$1,574,064
Total dollar profit	$589,236

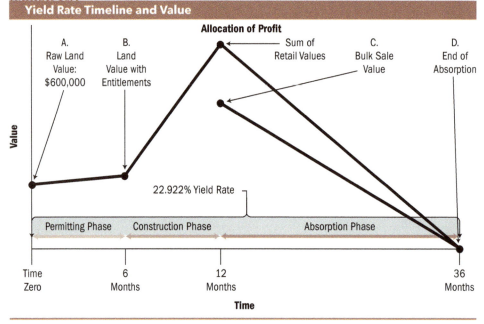

Exhibit 10.4 Yield Rate Timeline and Value

with an appropriate density and configuration. Usually, a developer will place a contract on vacant land with a down payment on a sales contract with the rights to take the property through the permitting process to achieve site plan approval. Typically, the property is not actually purchased until all entitlements are achieved. This is relatively unique to subdivision development, and yield rates actually used by developers are usually based on the "entitlement point of purchase" rather than the point when the initial deposit is made on the sales contract for raw land. For convenience purposes, this point in time is referred to as the *entitlement point of purchase*, as shown in Exhibits 10.5 and 10.6.

Exhibit 10.5 illustrates how the DCF analysis is modified to solve for the *IRR* or yield rate for the project under the entitlement point of purchase scenario. In this case, the actual acquisition costs as of Point B on the timeline are $600,000 for the raw land plus the $40,000 that was spent in the preceding six months to achieve entitlements. As shown in Exhibit 10.6, the contract will be closed when the developer achieves the entitlements, and the point of purchase is at the end of the permitting phase. Typically, the developer starts the "time clock" for the DCF analysis at Point B, which is the actual point of purchase. Recalculating the yield rate from Points B through D indicates a yield rate of 27.182%.

Since no line-item profit is included, the yield rate shown is a "true" yield rate or *IRR* in which the present value of the net proceeds exactly equals the initial acquisition price or cost. This

Exhibit 10.5
Madison Square Analysis: Yield at Entitlement Purchase Date

Quarter	Phase	Lots Sold	Average Lot Sale Price	Gross Sales	Permitting Costs	Cons. Costs	Absorption Holding and Sales Costs					Net Proceeds	PV Factor 27.182%	Present Value
							Sales 6.0%	Tax	Misc. 2.0%	Line-Item Profit 0.0%			
1	Construction			0	$0	$378,000	$0	$0	$0	$0	-$378,000	0.936368	-$353,947
2	Construction			0	$0	$378,000	$0	$0	$0	$0	-$378,000	0.876785	-$331,425
3	Absorption	10	$34,900	$349,000			$20,940	$250	$6,980	$0	$320,830	0.820994	$263,399
4	Absorption	7	$34,900	$244,300			$14,658	$250	$4,886	$0	$224,506	0.768753	$172,590
5	Absorption	8	$35,500	$284,000			$17,040	$250	$5,680	$0	$261,030	0.719835	$187,899
6	Absorption	6	$35,500	$213,000			$12,780	$250	$4,260	$0	$195,710	0.674031	$131,915
7	Absorption	9	$37,000	$333,000			$19,980	$1,000	$6,660	$0	$305,360	0.631141	$192,725
8	Absorption	7	$37,000	$259,000			$15,540	$1,000	$5,180	$0	$237,280	0.590980	$140,228
9	Absorption	7	$37,000	$259,000			$15,540	$1,000	$5,180	$0	$237,280	0.553375	$131,305
10	Absorption	6	$37,000	$222,000			$13,320	$1,000	$4,440	$0	$203,240	0.518163	$105,311
		60		$2,163,300	$0	$756,000	$129,798	$5,000	$43,266	$0	$1,229,236		$640,000
													$600,000
													40,000
													$640,000

Note: actual land purchase price = + costs

Summary

Sum of the retail lot values	$2,094,000
Add: Lot value inflation over the holding period	69,300
Gross sales	$2,163,300
Less: Absorption holding and sales costs	
Sales	$129,798
Tax	5,000
Miscellaneous	43,266
Less: Construction costs	756,000
Permitting costs	0
Land purchase price	640,000
Total direct and indirect costs	$1,574,064
Total dollar profit	$589,236

Note: The land purchase price in this scenario is $600,000 plus $40,000 in permitting costs, or $640,000.

Exhibit 10.6
Entitlement Point of Purchase Timeline and Value

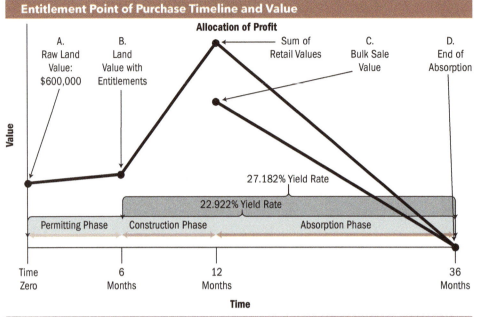

scenario is typically employed for real estate developments, especially for single-unit subdivision development purposes, and results in a higher *IRR* to the ownership position because the time frame has been shortened and some of the risk has been removed. The total dollar profit is the same in both scenarios.

In the entitlement point of purchase scenario, the developer would lose the $40,000 in permitting costs plus the deposit that was placed on the initial sales contract if the local authorities do not approve the project. It is not uncommon for this to happen. If, after an initial investigation and due diligence process, it becomes clear that the project cannot be permitted, the developer cuts the losses and moves onto another parcel. This partially explains why subdivision development must achieve relatively high yield rates as compared to other real estate investments.

The only major difference between the DCF analyses shown in Exhibits 10.3 and 10.5 is the time frame. The time frame in Exhibit 10.5 has been shortened by two quarters in estimating the point of purchase yield rate. Notice that the actual dollar profit of $589,236 earned in each scenario is the same. This amount, which is the dollar difference between the present value of $640,000 and the net proceeds of $1,229,236, is calculated at the bottom of Exhibit 10.5. All the profit has been considered in the yield rate used for the analysis and is referred to as the *time-value profit* for the sake of convenience. Time-value profit will be compared to line-item profit in the next section of this chapter.

Yield, Profit, and the Three Subdivision Phases

The Madison Square Case Study can also be used to illustrate the estimation of yield and profit for all three phases of development—the permitting phase, the construction phase, and the absorption phase. All three scenarios use the original time frame and consider the entire 36-month period (Points A through D).

The initial input for the Madison Square project in Exhibit 10.1 indicates that the developer received an offer to purchase the land for $740,000 after entitlements were achieved. If the developer accepted that offer and sold the property at Point B for $740,000, the yield rate would be 31.562%, as shown in Exhibit 10.7. This yield rate is relatively high because the time period is only six months and interest rates are expressed on an annual basis. Since this income was earned over a relatively short six-month period, the annual yield rate appears high. The *IRR* or yield rate for the permitting period is 31.562%.

Profit and yield over the construction phase can also be calculated in this example. If the purchaser bought the land with entitlements for $740,000 and then accepted the second offer to sell the property after lot construction was 100% complete (Point C in Exhibit 10.2), then the yield rate achieved over the construction period would be about 32.126%, as shown in Exhibit 10.8.

The purchase price of the Madison Square project was $740,000, and the buyer spent an additional $756,000 in construction costs and holding expenses over the construction period. The total investment is $1,496,000 over six months, with a sale price of $1,650,000. In this case, about $154,000 in profit is earned over a six-month period.

The last scenario considered is the extraction of profit and yield over the absorption period, from Points C through D in Exhibit 10.2. Using the bulk purchase of $1,650,000 and considering the actual sell-out scenario over the 24-month absorption period with associated holding and sales costs indicates a yield rate of 17.998%. The summary in Exhibit 10.9 shows that the sum of the retail values less holding and sales costs together with the absorption profit is the dollar difference between the net proceeds of $1,985,236 and the bulk sale purchase price of $1,650,000, or $335,236. Since there is no line-item profit, the total profit is the difference between the net proceeds and the present value calculation and is referred to as the *time-value profit*. This is the total dollar profit earned on the initial investment of $1,650,000.

As described in the initial valuation of the entire project from Point A through Point D, total profit was $589,236, as shown at the bottom of Exhibit 10.10. Performing separate yield and profit calculations for each phase of the subdivision project allocates total dollar profit between the permitting, construction, and

Exhibit 10.7
Madison Square Analysis: Permitting Yield DCF Analysis

Quarter	Phase	Lots Sold	Average Lot Sale Price	Gross Sales	Permitting Costs	Cons. Costs	Absorption Holding and Sales Costs			Line-Item Profit 0.0%	Net Proceeds	PV Factor 31.562%	Present Value
							Sales 6.0%	Tax	Misc. 2.0%				
1	Permitting	0		$0	$20,000	$0	$0	$0	$0	$0	-$20,000	0.926865	-$18,537
2	Permitting	0		$740,000	$20,000	$0	$0	$0	$0	$0	$720,000	0.859080	$618,537
		0		$740,000	$40,000	$0					$700,000		$600,000

Summary:
Land sales price $740,000
Less: Permitting costs 40,000
Land purchase price 600,000
Profit allocated to permitting phase $100,000

Note: actual land purchase price = $600,000

Exhibit 10.8
Madison Square Analysis: Construction Yield DCF Analysis

Quarter	Phase	Lots Sold	Average Lot Sale Price	Gross Sales	Permitting Costs	Cons. Costs	Absorption Holding and Sales Costs			Line-Item Profit 0.0%	Net Proceeds	PV Factor 32.126%	Present Value
							Sales 6.0%	Tax	Misc. 2.0%				
1	Construction	0		$0	$0	$378,000	$0	$0	$0	$0	-$378,000	0.925655	-$349,898
2	Construction	0		$1,650,000	$0	$378,000	$0	$0	$0	$0	$1,272,000	0.856838	$1,089,898
		0		$1,650,000	$0	$756,000					$894,000		$740,000

Summary:
Bulk value sale price $1,650,000
Less: Construction costs 756,000
Permitting costs 0
Land purchase price with entitlements 740,000
Total profit $154,000

Note: actual land purchase price = $740,000

Exhibit 10.9
Madison Square Analysis: Bulk Sale Yield DCF Analysis

Quarter	Phase	Lots Sold	Average Lot Sale Price	Gross Sales	Permitting Costs	Cons. Costs	Absorption Holding and Sales Costs				Line-Item Profit 0.0%	Net Proceeds	PV Factor 17.998%	Present Value
							Sales 6.0%	Tax	Misc. 2.0%				
1	Absorption	10	$34,900	$349,000	$0	$0	$20,940	$250	$6,980	$0	$320,830	0.956941	$307,016
2	Absorption	7	$34,900	$244,300	$0	$0	$14,658	$250	$4,886	$0	$224,506	0.915737	$205,588
3	Absorption	8	$35,500	$284,000	$0	$0	$17,040	$250	$5,680	$0	$261,030	0.876307	$228,742
4	Absorption	6	$35,500	$213,000	$0	$0	$12,780	$250	$4,260	$0	$195,710	0.838574	$164,117
5	Absorption	9	$37,000	$333,000	$0	$0	$19,980	$1,000	$6,660	$0	$305,360	0.802466	$245,041
6	Absorption	7	$37,000	$259,000	$0	$0	$15,540	$1,000	$5,180	$0	$237,280	0.767913	$182,211
7	Absorption	7	$37,000	$259,000	$0	$0	$15,540	$1,000	$5,180	$0	$237,280	0.734848	$174,365
8	Absorption	6	$37,000	$222,000	$0	$0	$13,320	$1,000	$4,440	$0	$203,240	0.703207	$142,920
		60		$2,163,300	$0	$0	$129,798	$5,000	$43,266	$0	$1,985,236		$1,650,000

Note: actual bulk sale purchase price = $1,650,000

Summary:

Sum of the retail values		$2,094,000
Add: Lot value inflation over the holding period		69,300
Gross sales		$2,163,300
Less: Absorption holding and sales costs		
Sales	129,798	
Tax	5,000	
Miscellaneous	43,266	
Bulk sale purchase price	1,650,000	
Total profit	$335,236	

absorption phases. Total dollar profit for the permitting phase was $100,000, and the construction phase indicated a total profit of $154,000. Adding the dollar profit earned over the absorption phase ($335,236) results in the same total dollar profit for the entire investment scenario.

Depending on the purchase price at each point in time, the actual dollar profit and yield may be allocated differently between the various phases. The important point to consider is that the total dollar profit is the same within the overall development process. This example provides a means for allocating profit among all three phases of a typical subdivision development. This is an extremely powerful analytical tool, especially when reapplying yield rates to an appropriate position in a subdivision development consistent with the profit expectation for each development phase and associated timeline.

It may be difficult at first to understand why separate DCF analyses are performed for each investment scenario at different points along the timeline. The answer is that each DCF analysis is as of the point in time of the initial purchase or acquisition at Point A, B, or C. The time clock is reset for each DCF analysis as if it were a separate investment opportunity. The yield rate over the entire development period, assuming purchase at time period zero, was previously calculated to be 22.922%. This rate could be viewed as the average yield over the entire development period for the subdivision project.

Yield rates from a market extraction scenario similar to the Madison Square Case Study should always be compared to yield rates from other sources to determine the appropriate yield rate for a specific valuation problem. Yield rates for subdivision development are typically published in a variety of investment reports or bulletins for use by appraisers and other professionals. These yield rates are typically based on an entitlement point

Exhibit 10.10
Madison Square Yield and Profit Summary

Description	Timeline Period Start	Timeline Period Finish	Profit Earned	Yield Rate	Reference Exhibit
Subdivision Phase					
Permitting phase	Point A to	Point B	$100,000	31.562%	10.7
Construction phase	Point B to	Point C	$154,000	32.126%	10.8
Absorption phase	Point C to	Point D	$335,236	17.998%	10.9
			$589,236		
Overall Timeline					
Entire holding period	Point A to	Point D	$589,236	22.922%	10.3 and 10.4
Entitlement point of purchase	Point B to	Point D	$589,236	27.182%	10.5 and 10.6

Exhibit 10.11
Yield Graph, All Yield Rates

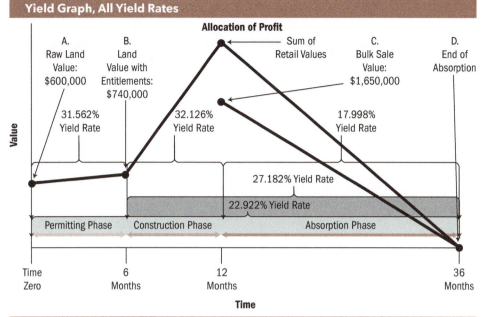

of purchase scenario in which the subdivision development is taken through the entire process of permitting, construction, and eventual absorption. The Madison Square example should make it very clear that the so-called "average" yield rate over the entire time frame may or may not be indicative of individual yield rates associated with each development phase. Each development phase is studied on its own merits and may or may not have a yield rate equivalent to the average for the overall development.

For example, when appraising a proposed subdivision to estimate the *when complete* bulk sale value, a novice appraiser might research a national survey data source and find that yield rates range from about 22% to 35%. This range would coincide with the yield rate for the entire holding period of 22.922%, or the entitlement point of purchase yield rate of 27.182%. However, if the Madison Square rate distribution were applicable in a particular market, it would only be appropriate to use a lower yield rate in the 18% range consistent with the Madison Square rate extraction. The notion that a "one rate fits all" conclusion for subdivision analysis can be gleaned from national published data is incorrect. The rate chosen for the absorption period analysis to reflect a *when complete* bulk sale value must recognize the individual risk and profit relationships of the absorption phase only. The published rates are not specific to the absorption period only, and the average yield rate over the entire development may not be appropriate.

In summary, the Madison Square Case Study demonstrates how profit and yield can be calculated at any point along the timeline for each phase of development or the entire development holding period from the point in which the initial raw land was purchased until the sale of the last lot. The time period zero yield rate is 22.922%, as shown in Exhibit 10.10.

A corollary analysis was conducted immediately after the initial calculation to consider a scenario based on the entitlement point of purchase, when a developer typically purchases vacant land. This analysis illustrates that the developer can achieve a higher yield rate by delaying the initial purchase until all permitting and/or entitlements have been achieved. This is the scenario followed by most developers. In this case, the time clock for the DCF process is started at the initial closing of the vacant land sale, rather than the contract date. Most reporting services that regularly report yield rates by developers for subdivision or other development projects employ the time frames used by developers. Although the entitlement point of purchase date is not always used, it should be kept in mind when a reporting service is used to estimate the yield rate to apply in a subdivision appraisal.

In the Madison Square example, higher yield rates were generated during the permitting and construction phases as compared to the absorption phase. Comparing these results with the discussion of profit and markets in Chapter 6, the Madison Square example is consistent with the characteristics of Market B in Exhibit 6.1. In this market, there was difficulty in achieving permitting and/or construction and relative ease in marketing and absorption. If the data was more consistent with the Market A profile shown in Exhibit 6.1, the permitting and construction phases would be expected to have relatively low component yield rates as compared to the absorption phase. Dissecting a bulk sale like the one in this example can provide clues to market behavior and assist in the selection of an appropriate yield rate. The rate should be consistent with the property being appraised and the applicable time frames.

The analysis may also explain market behavior in the area under study. For example, in the Madison Square project, if higher yield rates are generated from the permitting and construction phases, it may be common to find projects in which the initial developer achieves permitting and entitlements, constructs the subdivision, and then regularly sells the entire group of lots in a bulk sale scenario. If there is greater yield in the absorption phase, then developers may stay involved in projects throughout the entire marketing period to achieve higher yields.

Timeline and profit concepts can be difficult to understand. Many examples have been provided in this book to help the reader visualize the different points along the timeline and establish the point of reference for each discounting or valuation problem. While the math may seem daunting, it is relatively simple once the appropriate inputs have been determined within the framework of the appropriate timelines.

Yield and Line-Item Profit

All of the examples presented up to this point have used zero line-item profit and the true yield rate or *IRR* as discounting conventions in the income capitalization approach. This section will explore both methods and how they are applied in more detail.

The easiest way to understand the interaction of profit and yield within the discounting process is to examine a historical bulk sale and extract the indicated market yield rate from the market sales transaction. In the previous section, the Madison Square Case Study was used to discuss timeline concepts and investigate profit throughout the three subdivision phases. This section will continue the case study to consider the yield and profit associated with bulk sale value and the absorption time period from points C to D in Exhibits 10.10 and 10.11. Accordingly, the rate analysis will only cover the absorption period and isolate the appropriate yield and line-item profit amounts to reapply to a subdivision valuation for a bulk sale of a group of lots. The analysis process is the same for proposed and existing lot inventory.

The Madison Square project had a bulk sale price of $1,650,000 for all 60 lots prior to any absorption. This is the point in time when the lots are 100% built but before any lots are sold.

Scenario 1 provides an analysis of the sale price to extract the *IRR* or yield rate associated with the market sale. Since the Madison Square project was a historical sale, the exact pattern of lot sales for each quarter and the average sale price for the various lots sold in each quarter are known. This information could be ascertained from public records or sale-reporting services. Gross sales are calculated for each quarter over the eight-quarter (two-year) absorption period for the Madison Square subdivision. Holding and sales costs include sales expenses, real estate taxes, and any miscellaneous expenses. Both sales costs and miscellaneous expenses are a ratio of gross sales. Sales costs are 6% of gross sales over time, and miscellaneous costs are 2% of gross sales. Real estate tax is a fixed amount estimated at $250 per quarter for the first year, and $1,000 per quarter for the last year. Exhibit 10.12 has an expense category for line-item profit, but there is no profit reported in this category in Scenario 1. Line-item profit equals zero in this analysis. As described in Chapter 7, the sum of the retail values is based on the initial retail lot value per lot times the number of lots. In examples with inflation or expected increases in lot value over time, a separate inflation adjustment is made to reflect gross sales. (See the summary at the bottom of Exhibit 10.12). This facilitates an accurate indication for the sum of the retail values.

The present value factor is estimated using a yield rate of 17.998%. This yield rate was determined by changing the rate until the present value of the sell-out exactly equaled the initial purchase price of $1,650,000. Accordingly, the *IRR* is 17.998%, with zero line-item profit. Since there is no line-item profit in the expenses in Scenario 1, the *IRR* is the "true" yield rate for the project because all of the profit was allowed to flow through into the calculation of the *IRR*.

The analysis summary in Exhibit 10.12 indicates a total dollar profit of $335,236. This amount is the difference between the net proceeds and the present value. For the sake of convenience, this profit is labeled as *time-value profit*. There is zero line-item profit. As a result, all profit in this scenario is considered in the yield rate of 17.998%. The developer who purchased this group of lots sold 60 lots over eight quarters, generated gross sales of $2,163,300, paid the holding sales costs over the absorption period, and made a profit of $335,236 with a purchase price of $1,650,000. Thus, the *IRR* to the investor with zero line-item profit is 17.998%.

Exhibit 10.13 provides a second DCF scenario for the Madison Square bulk sale. Under Scenario 2, line-item profit is included as an expense. This scenario illustrates the second method that may be used to estimate the present value of a subdivision. Line-item profit is essentially a deduction that is included as part of expenses in the DCF analysis. In Exhibit 10.13, line-item profit is estimated at 8%, which is 8% of gross sales and not an interest rate. Like all of the other expenses, line-item profit is calculated as a percentage of gross sales. Net proceeds would be gross sales less typical holding and sales costs and line-item profit. Accordingly, the net proceeds have a lower value in Scenario 2 than in Scenario 1 (Exhibit 10.12), which has zero line-item profit. Again, the discount rate needed to equate the sale price of $1,650,000 with net proceeds is solved through iteration. With 8% line-item profit (8% of gross sales), the discount rate is 8.9%.

The terminology was changed from *yield rate* to *discount rate* in Scenario 2 to reinforce the notion that this rate of return is not a true *IRR* or yield rate because line-item profit has been included in the expense allocation. The discount rate used in this scenario is a "hybrid" rate, which is not a true *IRR* or yield rate. Mathematically, it is calculated in the same way as an *IRR*. However, because the inputs do not allow all of the profit to flow through into the calculation of the interest rate, this "hybrid" rate

Exhibit 10.12
Madison Square Analysis: Scenario 1, Zero Line-Item Profit

Quarter	Lots Sold	Average Lot Sale Price	Gross Sales	Absorption Holding and Sales Costs			Line-Item Profit 0.0%	Net Proceeds	PV Factor 17.998%	Present Value
				Sales 6.0%	Tax	Misc. 2.0%				
1	10	$34,900	$349,000	$20,940	$250	$6,980	$0	$320,830	0.956941	$307,016
2	7	$34,900	$244,300	$14,658	$250	$4,886	$0	$224,506	0.915737	$205,588
3	8	$35,500	$284,000	$17,040	$250	$5,680	$0	$261,030	0.876307	$228,742
4	6	$35,500	$213,000	$12,780	$250	$4,260	$0	$195,710	0.838574	$164,117
5	9	$37,000	$333,000	$19,980	$1,000	$6,660	$0	$305,360	0.802466	$245,041
6	7	$37,000	$259,000	$15,540	$1,000	$5,180	$0	$237,280	0.767913	$182,211
7	7	$37,000	$259,000	$15,540	$1,000	$5,180	$0	$237,280	0.734848	$174,365
8	6	$37,000	$222,000	$13,320	$1,000	$4,440	$0	$203,240	0.703207	$142,920
	60		$2,163,300	$129,798	$5,000	$43,266	$0	$1,985,236		$1,650,000

Note: actual bulk sale purchase price = $1,650,000

Summary:

Sum of the retail lot values			$2,094,000
Add: Lot value inflation over holding period			69,300
Gross sales			$2,163,300
Less: Absorption holding and sales costs			
	Sales		$129,798
	Tax		5,000
	Miscellaneous		43,266
Profit: Line-item profit		$0	
Time value profit		335,236	
		$335,236	$335,236
Bulk sale value			$1,580,700

Exhibit 10.15
Madison Square Analysis: Scenario 2, Considering Line-Item Profit

Quarter	Lots Sold	Average Lot Sale Price	Gross Sales	Absorption Holding and Sales Costs				Line-Item Profit 8.0%	Net Proceeds	PV Factor 8.900%	Present Value
				Sales 6.0%	Tax	Misc. 2.0%					
1	10	$34,900	$349,000	$20,940	$250	$6,980		$27,920	$292,910	0.978234	$286,535
2	7	$34,900	$244,300	$14,658	$250	$4,886		$19,544	$204,962	0.956942	$196,137
3	8	$35,500	$284,000	$17,040	$250	$5,680		$22,720	$238,310	0.936114	$223,085
4	6	$35,500	$213,000	$12,780	$250	$4,260		$17,040	$178,670	0.915739	$163,615
5	9	$37,000	$333,000	$19,980	$1,000	$6,660		$26,640	$278,720	0.895807	$249,679
6	7	$37,000	$259,000	$15,540	$1,000	$5,180		$20,720	$216,560	0.876309	$189,773
7	7	$37,000	$259,000	$15,540	$1,000	$5,180		$20,720	$216,560	0.857236	$185,643
8	6	$37,000	$222,000	$13,320	$1,000	$4,440		$17,760	$185,480	0.838577	$155,539
	60		$2,163,300	$129,798	$5,000	$43,266		$173,064	$1,812,172		$1,650,006

Note: actual bulk sale purchase price = $1,650,000

Summary:

Sum of the retail values		$2,094,000
Less: Lot value inflation over holding period		69,300
Gross sales		$2,163,300
Less: Absorption holding and sales costs		
Sales	$129,798	
Tax	5,000	
Miscellaneous	43,266	
Profit: Line-item profit	$173,064	
Time-value profit	162,166	
	335,230	335,230
Bulk sale value		$1,650,006

Matched Pairs: Line-Item Profit and Discount Rate

Line-Item Profit	Discount Rate	
0.00%	17.998%	← "True" yield rate or IRR
4.00%	13.497%	
6.00%	11.210%	
8.00%	8.900%	
10.00%	6.564%	
12.00%	4.201%	

is labeled as a *generic discount rate*, not a *yield rate*. Both yield rates and internal rates of return require that all income, expenses, and profit be allowed to flow through into the calculation. This is not the case for Scenario 2.

The market extraction in Scenario 2 paired an 8% line-item profit with a discount rate of 8.9%. The question typically asked at this point is, "Where does the 8% line-item profit come from?" This number is selected in conjunction with the discount rate used for the present value calculation. Exhibit 10.13 provides a list of "matched pairs" of discount rates and related line-item profit. Under Scenario 2, an 8% line-item profit indicated a discount rate of 8.9%. An infinite number of scenarios could be run with different levels of line-item profit.

Line-item profit and the discount rate are selected together as a "matched pair." For example, the analysis could be run with a 4% line-item profit (4% of gross sales) and a 13.497% discount rate, a 6% line-item profit and an 11.210% discount rate, or a 12% line-item profit and a 4.200% discount rate. In each case, the present value would be the same–$1,650,000.

The purpose of this exercise is to understand that when line-item profit is employed in a subdivision discounting problem, the discount rate must be selected in conjunction with line-item profit. Since this information comes from a market sale, it could be reapplied to a subject property for a valuation scenario in which line-item profit is considered in the DCF analysis. If a line-item profit of 8% were to be used, the appropriate discount rate would be 8.9%.

Alternatively, the true yield rate could be used with zero line-item profit. In this case, the yield rate would be 17.998%, and either method would give the same results using a discounting calculation. Recognize that if the line-item profit method is used, the discount rate must be selected in conjunction with the line-item profit. A sensitivity analysis similar to the analysis performed in Scenarios 1 and 2 should be made in the subject market to determine the appropriate relationship between the matched pairs of line-item profit and the discount rate.

Essentially, the process of using line-item profit in conjunction with an appropriate discount rate is simply allocating total profit between the line-item profit as an expense category and the time-value profit considered in the discount rate. The total dollar profit is the same for any matched pair calculation. For example, total profit was $335,236 in Scenario 1. Scenario 2 essentially split the profit between a line-item allocation and expenses and the time-value profit through the discounting process. In Scenario 2 (see Exhibit 10.13), line-item profit is $173,064 and time-value profit (the difference between net proceeds and present value) is $162,166. Total profit is almost identical to the profit indicated in Scenario 1, or $335,230; the only difference is in the rounding of the discount rate number. This example demonstrates that using the line-item profit method or discounting with the "true" yield rate would equal the same results. The obvious question then becomes, "If both methods generally result in the same answer, which method should be used and under what circumstances?" The answer depends on many considerations–some that are client-based preferences and others that relate to the observed pattern of market behavior in the area of the property being appraised. In some cases, the decision is influenced by the time period associated with the absorption forecast. This is discussed in more detail in the Time Zero Profit Dilemma section in Chapter 12.

A subdivision appraisal assignment may involve different methods depending on the intended use of the appraisal and the actual appraisal problem and property under investigation. The line-item profit technique may be used when a client specifically wants to see the dollar profit earned as line-item profit with an appropriate matched pair yield rate. The advantage of the line-item technique is that it specifically treats profit as a deduction, and some lenders interpret lending regulations as requiring line-item profit within the DCF analysis. Obviously, if the correct matched pair of line-item profit and discount rate is used, the analysis would be exactly the same as employing the *IRR* with zero line-item profit.

Line-item profit can also be employed when absorption periods are extremely short and the yield-rate–only method of measuring profit would not generate sufficient dollar profit to attract capital to a bulk sale. For example, a bulk sale with an absorption period of four months would generate relatively minimal dollar profits if an *IRR* calculation was used for calculation purposes. When using line-item profit over the short holding period, a sufficient level of dollar profit would be extracted because the line-item profit is a function of a percentage factor applied to gross sales, which would ensure some minimal level of profit for extremely short absorption periods. Accordingly, method selection may be influenced by the time period associated with the absorption analysis. In fact, discount rates can vary widely depending on the time frames associated with absorption periods for the project under study.

The true property yield rate method is straightforward, easy to understand, and typically generates rates of 15% to 30% for subdivision development. These rates can be compared directly with yield rates from reporting services and are typically employed when market activity is relatively stable and typical absorption periods are within a predictable range. However, as described in the previous section, be careful when applying published results for yield rates for an overall development project (all three phases) to only the absorption phase. A rate extraction sensitivity analysis should be made to ensure that the appropriate rate is selected.

If the methodologies for either the line-item profit method or the true yield rate method are employed correctly, the analysis should generate the same or similar results. If not, the appraiser is probably making an error in the application of the methodology.

Once the appraiser selects the methodology to use for the discounting process, the next step is to estimate the appropriate yield rate or discount rate in conjunction with the line-item profit selected. Rate selection is derived from market extraction or surveys and interviews with knowledgeable market participants. The next section explores how market extraction is used in the sales comparison approach.

Extracting Yield Rates in the Sales Comparison Approach

In the sales comparison approach application in Chapter 9, three comparable sales of competing subdivisions were used for comparison purposes. These same comparable sales can be used to demonstrate how appropriate yield or discount rates with line-item profit can be extracted for a valuation problem. This comparable sales information can also be used to extract market rates for indicated yield or to apply the split-rate method for matched pairs of discount rates and line-item profit. Historical sales information can be used when a property has already gone through the absorption period, similar to the examples previously presented in this chapter. Alternatively, information relating to a recent sale can be used to extract indicated market yield for a bulk sale transaction. In this case, the developer's forecast for absorption and typical expenses can be used to indicate current yield rate expectations from the market sales.

For example, when the retail lot value level is known, Sale 1 (the River View subdivision) can be analyzed to determine typical holding and sales costs over the estimated absorption period. This analysis is shown in Exhibit 10.14. The bulk sale price is $2,074,000, and at the time of sale the retail lot value price is $45,500. Applying typical 8% sales costs, a tax allocation, and miscellaneous expenses of 2% per year indicates the net proceeds shown in Exhibit 10.14. In this example, an 8% line-item profit was included in the expenses, and the discount rate needed to equate the present value of the net proceeds with the bulk sale price is 12.248%. When using a split-rate method, a discount rate of 12.248% would be used with an 8% line-item profit. The true

IRR is also calculated in Exhibit 10.14, and this rate comes out to be 23.470%. These amounts are summarized in Exhibit 10.15. A similar analysis was also performed for the Lake View and Mountain View bulk sales. Thus, a pattern of extracted yield rates is developed from the three market sales for which adequate information is available. The results are shown in Exhibit 10.15.

The last three columns of the table in Exhibit 10.15 provide information relating to the rate extraction analysis. Two methods may be used in discounting net proceeds over time when using the income capitalization approach and DCF analysis. The true yield rate with zero line-item profit or a related group of matched pairs may be used for the analysis. When using a true yield rate, there is no line-item profit. Stated differently, the line-item profit is zero. Exhibit 10.15 reflects *IRR*s ranging from 21.0% for Sale 3 to 28.7% for Sale 2. When applying an *IRR* in estimating the yield rate for a project with zero line-item profit, the range would be expected to lie between about 21% and 29%, based on available market sales.

The second method of using matched pairs requires the appraiser to choose a specific line-item profit and calculate the indicated discount rate or choose a selected discount rate and then calculate the indicated line-item profit. In this example, line-item profit was held constant at 8% for each comparable sale and the indicated discount rate was calculated. The line-item profit dollar amount is based on 8% of gross sales and is not an interest rate. The discount rates associated with an 8% line-item profit range from 12.3% for Sale 1 to 14.71% for Sale 3. When using the split-rate method and selecting an 8% line-item profit, the market-derived discount rate should be between about 12% and 15%. In Chapter 9, the most weight was given to Sale 1, which would indicate a 12.25% discount rate when using an 8% line-item profit.

For comparison purposes, Exhibit 10.15 also provides the yield rate associated only with the absorption phase with zero line-item profit. This rate would be applicable when applied to a similar problem for a bulk sale valuation. If applied correctly, the analysis results should be similar to those derived from the line-item profit method.

When applying the information gathered in the sales comparison approach, one of the greatest difficulties is finding sales with absorption time horizons, price points, locations, and other physical characteristics that are similar to the subject property. The sales comparison approach can be an effective valuation tool because it entails generating data and analysis results from a completely different data set than that typically employed in the income capitalization and cost approaches.

Exhibit 10.14
River View Rate Extraction

Quarter	Lots Sold	Average Lot Sale Price	Gross Sales	Absorption Holding and Sales Costs				Line-Item Profit 8.0%	Net Proceeds	PV Factor 12.248%	Present Value
				Sales 8.0%	Tax	Misc. 2.0%					
1	10	$45,500	$455,000	$36,400	$250	$9,100		$36,400	$372,850	0.970290	$361,773
2	10	$45,500	$455,000	$36,400	$250	$9,100		$36,400	$372,850	0.941462	$351,024
3	10	$45,500	$455,000	$36,400	$250	$9,100		$36,400	$372,850	0.913491	$340,595
4	10	$45,500	$455,000	$36,400	$250	$9,100		$36,400	$372,850	0.886351	$330,476
5	10	$45,500	$455,000	$36,400	$1,000	$9,100		$36,400	$372,100	0.860017	$320,012
6	10	$45,500	$455,000	$36,400	$1,000	$9,100		$36,400	$372,100	0.834466	$310,505
7	2	$45,500	$91,000	$7,280	$1,000	$1,820		$7,280	$73,620	0.809674	$59,608
	62		$2,821,000	$225,680	$4,000	$56,420		$225,680	$2,309,220		$2,073,993

Note: actual bulk sale purchase price = $2,074,000

Analysis Summary:

Sum of the retail values		$2,821,000
Add: Lot value inflation over holding period		0
Gross Sales		$2,821,000
Less: Absorption holding and sales costs		
Sales	$225,680	
Tax	$4,000	
Miscellaneous	$56,420	
Profit:		
Line-item profit	$225,680	
Time-value profit	$235,227	
		$460,907
Subtotal profit		$460,907
Bulk sale value		$2,073,993
Line-item profit (as a percent of gross sales)		8.000%
Discount rate (considering line-item profit)		12.248%

Matched Pairs

Discount Rate	
23.470%	IRR
20.708%	
17.918%	
15.098%	
12.248%	
9.365%	
6.449%	

Line-Item Profit
0.000%
2.000%
4.000%
6.000%
8.000%
10.000%
12.000%

Exhibit 10.15
Comparable Bulk Sales–Rate Extraction

			Bulk Lot Purchase							Market Rate Extraction		
											Matched Pairs	
No.	Sale Date	Project	Sale Price	Lots	Price per Lot	Average Retail Value per Lot	Indicated Flat Bulk Sale Discount	Absorption Time Horizon Yrs.	Indicated IRR	Given Line-Item %	Indicated Discount Rate
1	Dec-17	River View	$2,074,000	62	$33,452	$45,500	−26.5%	1.6	23.47%	8.00%	12.25%
2	Jul-17	Lake View	$827,000	24	$34,458	$44,000	−21.7%	1.0	28.67%	8.00%	13.11%
3	Mar-17	Mountain View	$2,755,000	96	$28,698	$43,600	−34.2%	3.0	21.00%	8.00%	14.71%

Extracting Profit in the Cost Approach

One of the best ways to study the allocation of cost and profit in the cost approach is to review the results of a bulk sale transaction from a cost perspective. Information on the Madison Square subdivision can also be used to study the allocation of profit in the cost approach. This same example is used to explain how costs are allocated when performing a cost approach either to the bulk sale or the retail lot value level.

Exhibit 10.16 provides a summary of Madison Square project information. This project is a 60-lot subdivision with a known historical sales pattern. The entire time frame of the development was considered, from the initial purchase of vacant raw land at time period zero to the eventual sale of the last lot. All costs and profit associated with the process of permitting and achieving entitlements, construction, and the absorption of the lots are included. The profit allocated to each phase is shown at the bottom of Exhibit 10.16. The permitting phase had a total profit of $100,000, the construction phase had a total profit of $154,000, and profit from the absorption phase totaled $335,236. The total profit for all three phases is $589,236.

Exhibit 10.17 provides a copy of the DCF analysis that was performed on the Madison Square project over the entire time frame. This project generated a true yield rate of 22.922%. The analysis is taken to the raw land value level to exactly equal the initial land purchase price. Accordingly, all costs and value are accounted for in the system of numbers given in the Madison Square example. A summary of the cost and profit appears at the bottom of Exhibit 10.17. The total profit is the difference between the gross sell-out and all costs associated with the project, including the initial purchase of the vacant site for $600,000.

Exhibit 10.18 provides a summary of costs for each point in time along the timeline. The easiest way to visualize these costs is to start from the bottom and work up to the top. This is a "bottom-up" process, like the graphic representation of cost taken to the retail lot value level in Exhibit 10.19. Starting with an initial vacant land value of $600,000, taking the land through the permitting process, and then spending $40,000 to earn a profit of $100,000 provides a land value with entitlements of $740,000. Taking land value with entitlements of $740,000 and adding construction costs, any holding costs over the construction period, and the construction phase profit of $154,000 indicates a bulk value conclusion of $1,650,000. Taking the bulk sale value of $1,650,000 and adding absorption costs and profit over the absorption period indicates the sum of the retail values, plus a lot value inflation of $2,163,300, which is the actual gross sales income from the Madison Square project over the absorption period.

Exhibit 10.16
Madison Square Subdivision Purchase and Sale History

Raw Land Purchase Price:				$600,000
Raw Land Sale Date:	3 years ago			
Time Periods:	Permitting process			6 months
	Construction period			6 months
	Absorption period			24 months
Land:	Raw land acquisition cost			$600,000
Purchase Offers:	Land with entitlements			$740,000
	Bulk sale purchase offer			$1,650,000
Income and Expenses:	**Permitting Phase Expenses**			
	Planning and conceptual drawings			$20,000
	Holding costs and taxes			2,000
	Permitting fees			3,000
	Environmental audit			5,000
	Survey and topographical			10,000
	Total			$40,000
	Avg./qtr.			$20,000
	Construction Phase Expenses			
	Direct construction costs			$720,000
	Survey, engineering, and final plat			20,000
	Front entrance with landscaping			15,000
	Holding costs and taxes			1,000
	Total			$756,000
	Avg./qtr.			$378,000
	Absorption Phase Income			

		Quarter	Lot Sales	Average Sale Price
	Lot sales:	1	10	$34,900
		2	7	$34,900
		3	8	$35,500
		4	6	$35,500
		5	9	$37,000
		6	7	$37,000
		7	7	$37,000
		8	6	$37,000
			60	

Absorption Phase Expenses			
Sales Expense:	6% gross sales		
Taxes:	Minimal Year 1:		$1,000
	Year 2:		$4,000
Miscellaneous:	2% gross sales		
Profit Summary (See Exhibit 10.10):			
Permitting phase			$100,000
Construction phase			154,000
Absorption phase			335,236
Total profit			$589,236

Yield, Line-Item Profit, and Discounting

Exhibit 10.17
Madison Square DCF Analysis

Quarter	Phase	Lots Sold	Average Lot Sale Price	Gross Sales	Permitting Costs	Cons. Costs	Absorption Holding and Sales Costs					Net Proceeds	PV Factor 22.922%	Present Value
							Sales 6.0%	Tax	Misc. 2.0%	Line-Item Profit 0.0%				
1	Permitting	0			$20,000		$0	$0	$0	$0	-$20,000	0.945802	-$18,916
2	Permitting	0			$20,000		$0	$0	$0	$0	-$20,000	0.894541	-$17,891
3	Construction	0				$378,000	$0	$0	$0	$0	-$378,000	0.846059	-$319,810
4	Construction	0				$378,000	$0	$0	$0	$0	-$378,000	0.800204	-$302,477
5	Absorption	10	$34,900	$349,000			$20,940	$250	$6,980	$0	$320,830	0.756835	$242,815
6	Absorption	7	$34,900	$244,300			$14,658	$250	$4,886	$0	$224,506	0.715816	$160,705
7	Absorption	8	$35,500	$284,000			$17,040	$250	$5,680	$0	$261,030	0.677020	$176,723
8	Absorption	6	$35,500	$213,000			$12,780	$250	$4,260	$0	$195,710	0.640327	$125,318
9	Absorption	9	$37,000	$333,000			$19,980	$1,000	$6,660	$0	$305,360	0.605622	$184,933
10	Absorption	7	$37,000	$259,000			$15,540	$1,000	$5,180	$0	$237,280	0.572799	$135,914
11	Absorption	7	$37,000	$259,000			$15,540	$1,000	$5,180	$0	$237,280	0.541754	$128,547
12	Absorption	6	$37,000	$222,000			$13,320	$1,000	$4,440	$0	$203,240	0.512392	$104,139
		60		$2,163,300	$40,000	$756,000	$129,798	$5,000	$43,266	$0	$1,189,236		$600,000

Note: actual land purchase price = $600,000

Summary:

Sum of the retail values		$2,094,000
Add: Lot value inflation over holding period		69,300
Gross sales		$2,163,300
Less: Absorption holding and sales costs		
Sales	129,798	
Tax	5,000	
Miscellaneous	43,266	
Construction costs	756,000	
Permitting costs	40,000	
Land purchase price	600,000	
Total costs		$1,574,064
Total dollar profit		$589,236

Exhibit 10.18
Madison Square Summary

Analysis Results

Sum of the retail values	$2,094,000
Add: Lot value inflation over holding period	69,300
Gross sales	$2,163,300
Less: Absorption phase costs and profit	
Sales	129,798
Tax	5,000
Miscellaneous	43,266
Absorption profit (See Exhibit 10.10)	335,236
Bulk sale value	$1,650,000
Less: Construction phase costs and profit	
Construction phase costs	756,000
Construction phase profit (See Exhibit 10.10)	154,000
Land value with entitlements	$740,000
Less: Permitting phase costs and profit	
Permitting phase costs	40,000
Permitting phase profit (See Exhibit 10.10)	100,000
Raw land value	$600,000

Exhibit 10.19
Timeline and Value

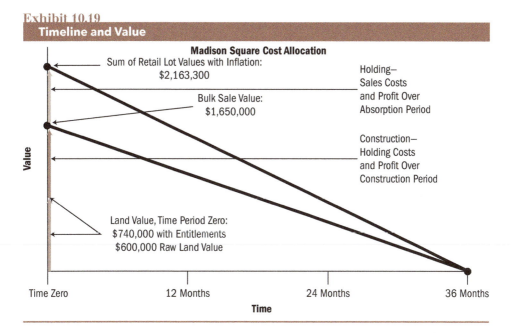

Madison Square Cost Allocation

If the cost approach were taken to the bulk sale level, the only profit included would be that associated with the permitting and construction phases. If the cost approach were taken to the retail lot value level, then the profit earned over the absorption phase would also be included. In the cost approach, the profit is allocated to the appropriate phase and the appropriate costs are shown for each phase of development.

Exhibit 10.20 presents Madison Square project information in a traditional cost format. Notice that raw land value is used for the land value estimate. Because raw land value is used, all costs incurred during the permitting process and the profit over the permitting process are included as part of reproduction cost new. The subdivision was new at the time of development, and no physical depreciation is indicated. Also, no functional or external obsolescence is evident. The traditional cost format in Exhibit 10.20 typically groups costs into the following categories:

- Direct construction costs
- Common infrastructure
- Indirect construction costs
- Holding and sales costs over the absorption period
- Entrepreneurial incentive

The traditional cost format also includes a line-item allocation for total profit incentive. In this case, since the cost approach is reflecting retail lot value and starts with raw land value, profit over all three phases ($589,236) is included. The cost approach reflects a total cost rounded to $2,160,000 over all three development phases, which when divided by the number of lots indicates an average retail lot value conclusion of about $36,000 per lot. This amount includes lot value inflation over the holding period. The initial starting retail lot value was $34,900, and the sum of the retail values as of the initial starting date is $2,094,000.

Since the Madison Square project is a historical sale, the information derived from it is used in allocating profit in the cost approach. However, unlike the income capitalization approach, profit in the cost approach is usually calculated as some percentage of overall costs. This calculation is shown at the bottom of Exhibit 10.20, where profit is a percentage of various cost levels. For example, a profit of $589,236 divided by the indirect and direct construction costs would indicate a profit level of 74%. Profit as a percentage of all costs plus land value is 37.4%. Profit as a component of the overall project costs (including profit) is 27.2%. How profit is calculated and allocated is based on a study of the local marketplace and may vary depending on local developers' preferences. Most developers run profit as a straight percentage of all costs plus land value (37.4% in this case) or view profit as a component of overall gross sell-out (27.2% in this case). If the Madison Square project was used as a comparable sale for a proposed project and cost was taken to the retail lot value level, then profit could be estimated at about 27% as a component of total project cost.

The future expectations of developers can also be considered and may provide even more relevant information to apply in both the income capitalization and cost approaches for a proposed project. Typical developer expectations with respect to retail lot value level, absorption time frame, and construction cost can be analyzed to form market-oriented conclusions about

Exhibit 10.20
Traditional Cost Approach Summary—Madison Square

	$	Per Lot (106 Total)	%
Reproduction Cost New, Less Depreciation			
Direct Construction Costs			
Horizontal improvements	$720,000	$12,000	33.28%
(streets, utilities, site work, etc.)			
Front entrance sign and landscaping	$15,000	$250	0.69%
Other direct costs	-	-	0.00%
Common Amenities			
None	-	-	0.00%
Indirect Construction Costs			
Planning and conceptual drawings	20,000	333	0.92%
Engineering design, topo., and surveying	30,000	500	1.39%
Environmental	5,000	83	0.23%
Permitting fees	3,000	50	0.14%
Holding costs, taxes, and misc.	3,000	50	0.14%
Holding and Sales Costs Absorption Period			
Sales expense	129,798	2,163	6.00%
Tax expense	5,000	83	0.23%
Miscellaneous	43,266	721	2.00%
Entrepreneurial Incentive—Profit	589,236	9,821	27.24%
Reproduction Cost New	$1,563,300	$26,054	72.26%
Less: Depreciation			
Physical none noted	-	-	0.00%
Functional none noted	-	-	0.00%
External none noted	-	-	0.00%
Depreciated Improvement Value	$1,563,300	$26,054	72.26%
Add: Raw Land Value	600,000	10,000	27.74%
Indicated Value by Cost Approach	$2,163,300	$36,054	100.0%
Rounded	$2,160,000	$36,000	
Indicated Retail Value per Lot (including inflation)		$36,000	
Initial Starting Retail Lot Value		$34,900	

Total Profit vs. Cost	Cost	Profit	Profit/Cost
Direct and indirect construction costs	$796,000	$589,236	74.0%
Direct and indirect construction costs and absorption expenses	$974,064	$589,236	60.5%
All costs plus land value	$1,574,064	$589,236	37.4%
Profit as a component of total project cost	$2,163,300	$589,236	27.2%

yield and profit in an *IRR* calculation and a total dollar profit calculation in a cost approach application.

Exhibits 10.21 and 10.22 provide a cost approach summary in which the cost approach is sorted by phase. The cost and profit associated with each phase are included in the cost tabulation. Exhibit 10.21 provides a cost estimate that is taken to the retail lot value level. The information from the Madison Square project is summarized, and the average retail lot value indicated by the cost approach is $36,000 per lot. Exhibit 10.22 provides a bulk value estimate by the cost approach. Accordingly, the value re-

Exhibit 10.21
Sorted Cost Approach Summary, Retail Lot Value Level–Madison Square

	$	60 Per Lot	%
Reproduction Cost New, Less Depreciation			
Permitting Phase			
Planning and conceptual drawings	$20,000	$333	0.92%
Holding costs and taxes	2,000	33	0.09%
Permitting fees	3,000	50	0.14%
Environmental audit	5,000	83	0.23%
Survey and topographical	10,000	167	0.46%
Permitting profit	100,000	1,667	4.62%
Construction Phase			
Direct construction costs			
Horizontal improvements (Streets, utilities, site work, etc.)	720,000	12,000	33.28%
Front entrance landscaping	15,000	250	0.69%
Indirect construction costs			
Survey, engineering, and final plat	20,000	333	0.92%
Holding costs and taxes	1,000	17	0.05%
Construction phase profit	104,000	1,733	4.81%
Absorption Phase			
Sales and promotional	129,798	2,163	6.00%
Tax expense	5,000	83	0.23%
Miscellaneous	43,266	721	2.00%
Absorption phase profit	385,236	6,421	17.81%
Reproduction Cost New	$1,563,300	$26,054	72.25%
Less: **Depreciation**			
Physical none noted	-	-	0.00%
Functional none noted	-	-	0.00%
External none noted	-	-	0.00%
Depreciated Improvement Value	$1,563,300	$26,054	72.25%
Add: **Raw Land Value**	$600,000	$10,000	27.74%
Indicated Value by Cost Approach	$2,163,300	$36,054	99.99%
Rounded	$2,160,000	$36,000	
Indicated Retail Value per Lot		$36,000	

(Note: Includes lot value inflation relating to gross sales)

Exhibit 10.22
Sorted Cost Approach Summary, Bulk Lot Value Level–Madison Square

Reproduction Cost New, Less Depreciation			
Permitting Phase	**$**	**60 Per Lot**	**%**
Planning and conceptual drawings	$20,000	$333	1.25%
Holding costs and taxes	2,000	33	0.13%
Permitting fees	3,000	50	0.19%
Environmental audit	5,000	83	0.31%
Survey and topographical	10,000	167	0.63%
Permitting profit	100,000	1,667	6.25%
Construction Phase			
Direct construction costs			
Horizontal improvements (streets, utilities, site work, etc.)	720,000	12,000	45.00%
Front entrance landscaping	15,000	250	0.94%
Indirect construction costs			
Survey, engineering, and final plat	20,000	333	1.25%
Holding costs and taxes	1,000	17	0.06%
Construction phase profit	104,000	1,733	6.50%
Absorption Phase			
Sales and promotional	n/a	-	0.00%
Tax expense	n/a	-	0.00%
Miscellaneous	n/a	-	0.00%
Absorption phase profit	n/a	-	0.00%
Reproduction Cost New	$1,000,000	$16,666	62.51%
Less: Depreciation			
Physical none noted	-	-	0.00%
Functional none noted	-	-	0.00%
External none noted	-	-	0.00%
Depreciated Improvement Value	1,000,000	16,666	62.51%
Add: Raw Land Value	600,000	10,000	37.50%
Indicated Value by Cost Approach	$1,600,000	$26,666	100.01%
Rounded	$1,600,000	$27,000	
Indicated Bulk Value per Lot		$27,000	

flected is divided by the number of lots to derive an average bulk lot value. In this scenario, the cost and profit associated with the absorption phase are excluded from the cost approach. Again, the only profit is that which occurs over the permitting and construction phases. Since the cost and profit associated with the construction phase are included in cost new, raw land value is used.

Examples using raw land value or land value with entitlements are explained in more detail in Chapter 11. The purpose of this case study is to show how comparable sales information can be used to extract profit in the cost approach and to calculate the appropriate ratio of profit that can be applied in a cost approach to solve a valuation problem. A similar extraction can be made on a group of market sales from which a range of supportable profit levels can be extracted; the resulting ratios can be stratified similarly to the results that appear at the bottom of Exhibit 10.20.

11
Land Value Using the Subdivision Development Method

Overview

One of the original applications of the subdivision development method was to provide an estimate of land value. In this application, the appraiser values a vacant tract of land with immediate development potential. This analysis can be used to estimate raw land value or land value with some or all entitlements. This valuation scenario is typically employed for vacant parcels of land that are located in "in-fill" locations with very few, if any, available vacant land sales. The development method may be used for comparison purposes and to check the results of the sales comparison approach. The analysis concludes land value as a residual after all costs, profit, and other elements over the three phases of development have been considered in the income capitalization approach. An appraiser using this technique is often required to provide alternative conceptual subdivision site plan layouts for the vacant site and/or to consider realistic unit densities per acre that the property can achieve. Through the use of DCF analysis, present value estimates for each concept are calculated and the most probable concept or development scenario is given the most weight in arriving at a supportable *as is* land value. This technique can be subject to a great deal of variability depending on the inputs used in the analysis and the time frames needed to achieve permitting, construction, and market absorption. When calculated as a residual, land value can vary widely depending on the analysis inputs.

The sales comparison approach is always the preferred method for estimating *as is* vacant land value, but in some cases land sales are not available. When limited or no land sales are available, the development approach can be used to check the results of the sales comparison approach, particularly in volatile or depressed/limited sales markets. The subdivision development method can be used in these situations. However, the land as vacant must be suitable for economically feasible development and have a highest and best use for immediate or near-term subdivision development. The highest and best use determination is critical. Just because a property can be developed does not necessarily mean that there is immediate market demand for the project. The appraiser performs market analysis consistent with the inferred and fundamental supply and demand methods described in Chapter 2. The time horizon for the subject site development as well as current market demand must be determined as part of the highest and best use analysis. Once the site qualifies under the four tests of highest and best use for development, the subdivision development method may be used to estimate land value.

The property in its *as is* condition must have appropriate land zoning in place for subdivision development. Accordingly, the legally permissible use section of the highest and best use analysis would consider the current zoning category and the ability of the market to support financially feasible development on the site. If the property does not have appropriate zoning, any values delivered by the subdivision development method would be hypothetical. Under this circumstance, the appraiser should not label the value as current *as is* market value.

Hypothetical value estimates are often provided to assist the property owner in determining a future course of action with respect to the rezoning of a parcel of land. For example, the appraiser could provide hypothetical value estimates based on a single-unit residence, office, or commercial rezoning for a tract of land, which would provide valuable input for a developer who must consider the costs and/or time frames for achieving specific zoning and the economic benefit that may be achieved by a favorable rezoning. For the subdivision development method to conclude an *as is* land value, the underlying zoning must be in place for the use under consideration. Otherwise, the analysis is completely hypothetical.

When appraising a property that has zoning for future development in place, the appraiser then considers any remaining "entitlements" that would be necessary to develop the property under a typical maximally productive financially feasible scenario. Various conservative, typical, and optimistic value estimates may also be provided to allow the appraiser to bracket typical value levels for the property development.

A site may essentially be raw land and have zoning in place for future development but no other entitlements. Entitlements are all the items required to achieve permitting for immediate development. Typically, achieving entitlements entails a site plan review process in which the following data is considered:

- Topographical surveys
- Perimeter site surveys
- The placement of trees and any existing buildings
- Wetland surveys
- Environmental audits
- Preliminary subdivision plan layouts
- Other required criteria for the local project review board (which may involve neighborhood meetings)

This review process may be extensive. Once final site plan approval has been achieved and all other governmental approvals have been obtained, building permits can be pulled and construction can commence. The land now has full entitlements.

At the time of the appraisal, the property owner has hopefully already taken the property through some level of permitting in order to obtain site plan approval. If this is not the case, the appraiser would be required to suggest a suitable subdivision site plan layout and value the proposed subdivision plan via the subdivision development method. This process may be beyond the capabilities of most appraisers. Rather than consider hypothetical layouts for the property, the appraiser concludes an appropriate unit density per acre for the subject property based on comparable projects. Essentially, the appraiser would conclude a reasonable or typical development scenario and associated density for the vacant land, identify the appropriate price points and marketing concept, and then apply income capitalization analysis to deliver a current land value estimate.

Timeline Concepts

Exhibits 11.1 and 11.2 show typical timelines in which raw land value is being estimated. As shown in Exhibit 11.1, the discounting period covers the entire time frame from current land status through all three subdivision phases until the last lot is sold. The appraiser is required to estimate the following:

- The necessary time period and costs for achieving permitting
- Any permitting profit
- Holding and construction costs over the construction phase

- The construction time frame
- Any construction profit
- Typical holding and sales costs associated with the absorption period
- The absorption period time frame
- Any absorption period profit

The value line in Exhibit 11.2 should be familiar from previous chapters. Using this typical timeline, the income capitalization approach is used to estimate value. The income capitalization approach starts with the sum of the retail values; costs and profit are then subtracted over the various phases of development to reflect a bulk sale or vacant land value.

Exhibit 11.1
Income Capitalization Approach Timeline

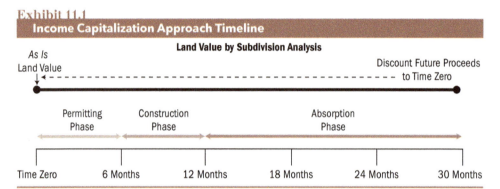

Exhibit 11.2
Value Line

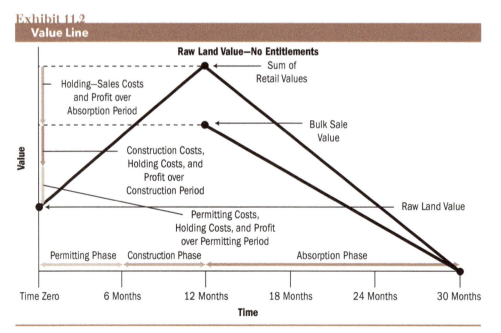

Under the land value scenario, all costs and profit associated with the absorption and construction periods are subtracted to consider the time value elements in the DCF analysis. The land value used may be raw land value for the subject property or some level of land value with entitlements. Entitlements can be partial or full–i.e., at the point when construction can begin immediately.

Exhibit 11.2 provides a scenario in which raw land value is the objective of the analysis. Under this scenario, permitting costs and profit would also be subtracted to reflect raw land value as of time period zero. Also, the required permitting time period must be considered, which would match a scenario in which the *as is* status of the land has no entitlements in place other than the underlying zoning and land use designation.

Exhibit 11.3 shows a second scenario reflecting land value with entitlements. Accordingly, the cost of entitlements and any associated profit are not subtracted in the discounting process to allow the higher land value with entitlements to be concluded. A keen awareness is required on the part of the appraiser to discern the exact status of the property's permitting and entitlements as of the date of valuation.

Exhibit 11.3

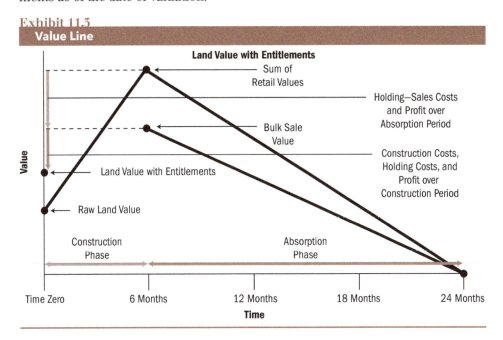

Park View Case Study: Applying the Income Capitalization Approach

The next section of this chapter is concerned with the Park View Case Study, which illustrates the calculation of raw land value for vacant acreage. Since raw land value is the objective of this analysis, the timeline used for this case study would match the one in Exhibit 11.2.

Exhibit 11.4 provides data for the Park View site. Vacant land is being valued as of the current date, and the site has single-unit residential zoning in place, supporting a density of one to four units per acre. Typical time periods for the permitting, construction, and absorption phases are provided, along with utility and physical status. Single-unit marketability data for the subject acreage is also presented. The market currently supports immediate development for single-unit homes at the lower price point, ranging from $160,000 to $200,000. Marketability information was developed from a separate inferred and fundamental demand analysis for the subject property in which property productivity was analyzed in light of future determinants of single-unit residential development in the property's immediate area. This process was explained in Chapter 2.

The highest and best use conclusion is summarized in Exhibit 11.5. Currently, the development of typical, detached single-unit residences with a density of one to four units per acre is legally permissible on the site. The physically possible criteria indicates that the site would support an overall density of 2.5 to 3.0 units per acre with a most likely density of about 2.75 units per acre,

Exhibit 11.4
Park View Land Development Status

Current Date:	1/1/2018	
Current Land Zoning:	R-1a, single-unit residential, 1-4 units per acre	
	Minimum lot size: 10,000 sq. ft.	
	Minimum lot width: 50 fr. ft.	
Land Use Designation:	Low-density residential, 1-4 units per acre	
	Detached single-unit residences	
Typical Time Periods:	Permitting process	6 months
	Construction period	6 months
	Absorption period	12 months
Utility Status:	Available central city water, sewer, and electric utilities adjacent to property along main road frontage. Adequate capacity for immediate development.	
Physical Status:	30.26 acres, 800 fr. ft. along main road frontage, irregular in shape, mostly level, wooded with some open areas, and well drained. Good appeal for single-unit residential development.	
Single-Unit Marketability:	Situated in a suburban growth area with good demand characteristics and demonstrated residential demand for home and lot package in the $160,000 to $360,000 price range. Demand and supply are in balance. This area supports new demand in the near future of 275 to 300 units per year in this overall price range, with one to five subdivisions competing in the area at any given time. Two projects recently completed their absorption in the lower price point range ($160,000 to $200,000), with only one project marketing inventory at the current time and one new project to come online in 1.5 years.	

which is typical for similar projects in the area. This stratification is used by the appraiser to provide conservative, most likely, and optimistic value estimates for the vacant land. The financially feasible uses include a current overall approximate price range of $160,000 to $360,000 for homes in this area. However, the time horizon for competing projects in the area supports a maximally productive use at lower price points in the $160,000 to $200,000 range.

Exhibit 11.5

Park View Highest and Best Use

Highest and Best Use as Vacant:	
Legally Permissible:	Detached single-unit development, 1-4 units per acre
Physically Possible:	Given site characteristics and zoning criteria, the typical density that may be achieved within the maximally productive price range is 2.5 to 3.0 units per acre. The most likely density is 2.75 units per acre.
Financially Feasible:	Detached single-unit residential development supporting homes in the $160,000 to $360,000 price range with typical densities of 2.5 to 3.0 units per acre. Current demand and supply conditions support immediate development.
Maximally Productive:	The maximally productive use is supported for homes in the lower price point range, $160,000 to $200,000, in the area at the current time. The density supported is from 2.5 to 3.0 units per acre, with a most likely estimate based on comprable projects of about 2.75 units per acre.
Highest and Best Use as Improved:	Not applicable, this is a vacant tract of land and has no existing building improvements.

The property must have a current highest and best use for immediate development in order for the value from this approach to be representative of an appropriate *as is* land value conclusion. The Park View site has met the highest and best use test for immediate development, and the next step is to estimate the following:

- Typical expenses associated with obtaining final site plan approval
- Permitting costs and profit over the permitting phase
- Construction costs and profit (if any) over the construction phase
- Initial starting retail lot value and pattern of increase
- The time period needed to absorb the lot inventory
- Typical holding and sales costs over the absorption phase
- Absorption phase profit
- Time period associated with each phase of development

The Park View development costs are presented in Exhibit 11.6. With a density of three units per acre, the 30.26-acre parcel would support about 91 lots. Seventy-six lots could be developed on the subject site, with a minimum density of 2.5 units per acre. The most likely density is about 2.75 units per acre, or about 83 lots on the Park View parcel. Three separate scenarios are used for the Park View land value estimate based on each density calculation. Also, the permitting and construction costs would be

Exhibit 11.6
Park View DCF Development Data

Subdivision Density:

			Lots
(30.26 acres)	Maximum density: 3.0 units/acre		91
	Minimum density: 2.5 units/acre		76
	Most likely density: 2.75 units/acre		83

Income and Expenses:

	Number of Lots		
Permitting Phase Expenses (6 months)	76	83	91
Planning and conceptual drawings	$15,000	$15,000	$18,000
Holding costs and taxes	$2,000	$2,000	$2,000
Permitting fees	$7,600	$8,300	$9,100
Environmental audit	$1,500	$1,500	$1,500
Survey and topographical	$4,000	$4,000	$4,000
Total	$30,100	$30,800	$34,600
Avg./qtr.	$15,050	$15,400	$17,300
Construction Phase Expenses (6 months)			
Direct construction costs			
Cost per lot: $17,500	$1,330,000	$1,452,500	$1,592,500
Survey, engineering, and final plat	$20,000	$20,000	$20,000
Front entrance with landscaping	$15,000	$15,000	$15,000
Holding costs and taxes	$1,000	$1,000	$1,000
Total	$1,366,000	$1,488,500	$1,628,500
Avg./qtr.	$683,000	$744,250	$814,250

Retail Lot Value

			Lot Value Allocation
Home Price Point		Home and Lot	Ratio 25%
Low		$160,000	$40,000
Average		$180,000	$45,000
High		$200,000	$50,000
Estimated lot value (increasing at 5%/yr.):			$45,000

Market Absorption

Lots per quarter	12

Absorption Phase Expenses

Sales expense: (as % of gross sales)		8%
Taxes:	Year 1	$1,000
	Year 2	$3,000
Miscellaneous: (as % of gross sales)		4%
Yield Rate (with zero line-item profit)		21.50%

different depending on the density and number of lots delivered under each scenario. Exhibit 11.6 shows the relevant costs. Retail lot value is estimated at about $45,000 per lot on average for all three density levels. Market absorption is estimated at about 12 lots per quarter with absorption phase expenses. A yield rate of 21.5% with zero line-item profit is used for the DCF analysis.

Applying all of these inputs to the three development scenarios reflects the *as is* land values shown in Exhibits 11.7, 11.8, and 11.9. The absorption period for 76 lots and 83 lots is about the same at seven quarters. The 91-lot scenario would require eight quarters for complete absorption. A summary of all three scenarios for the Park View vacant acreage is provided in Exhibit 11.10. A reasonable value range of $890,000 to $1,010,000 appears to be supported. The most likely scenario estimated by the appraiser is 2.75 units per acre, which would indicate a mid-range land value of $950,000. Overall land value was concluded at $950,000, which is consistent with the most likely valuation scenario.

The Park View example provides a typical valuation under various scenarios for a vacant tract of land. The property had a highest and best use of immediate subdivision development, which is required in order for the analysis to be representative of *as is* land value. This example introduced acreage unit density as a sensitivity test in estimating land value for the subject property. Variability can be encountered in other areas of a vacant land valuation scenario. In fact, there could be a wide range of variables and complicated scenarios under which ranges of value could be developed; to some extent, this adds variability to the value conclusion, especially if the site has not gone through a site plan review process that includes a subdivision plan with defined unit densities. When a final site plan is not available, the appraiser must anticipate typical densities that may be achieved for the proposed subdivision. This process reduces the accuracy of the value and reinforces the need to provide a supportable value range with a most likely value estimate under subdivision land use. When detailed plans are available and final site plan approval has been achieved at the time of analysis, income capitalization approach results may be more accurate.

Exhibit 11.7
Park View Acreage Land Value (83-Lot Scenario)

Quarter	Phase	Lots Sold	Average Lot Value	Gross Sales	Permitting Costs	Cons. Costs	Absorption Holding and Sales Costs			Net Proceeds	PV Factor 21.500%	Present Value
							Sales 8.0%	Tax	Misc. 4.0%			
1	Permitting	0			$15,400		$0	$0	$0	-$15,400	0.948992	-$14,614
2	Permitting	0			$15,400		$0	$0	$0	-$15,400	0.900585	-$13,869
3	Construction	0				$744,250	$0	$0	$0	-$744,250	0.854648	-$636,072
4	Construction	0				$744,250	$0	$0	$0	-$744,250	0.811054	-$603,627
5	Absorption	12	$45,000	$540,000			$43,200	$250	$21,600	$474,950	0.769683	$365,561
6	Absorption	12	$45,000	$540,000			$43,200	$250	$21,600	$474,950	0.730423	$346,914
7	Absorption	12	$45,000	$540,000			$43,200	$250	$21,600	$474,950	0.693165	$329,219
8	Absorption	12	$45,000	$540,000			$43,200	$250	$21,600	$474,950	0.657808	$312,426
9	Absorption	12	$47,250	$567,000			$45,360	$1,000	$22,680	$497,960	0.624255	$310,854
10	Absorption	12	$47,250	$567,000			$45,360	$1,000	$22,680	$497,960	0.592412	$294,998
11	Absorption	11	$47,250	$519,750			$41,580	$1,000	$20,790	$456,380	0.562194	$256,574
Totals		83		$3,813,750	$30,800	$1,488,500	$305,100	$4,000	$152,550	$1,832,800		$948,364
											Indicated land value	$948,364
											Rounded	$950,000

Exhibit 11.8
Park View Acreage Land Value (91-Lot Scenario)

Quarter	Phase	Lots Sold	Average Lot Value	Gross Sales	Permitting Costs	Cons. Costs	Absorption Holding and Sales Costs			Net Proceeds	PV Factor 21.500%	Present Value
							Sales 8.0%	Tax	Misc. 4.0%			
1	Permitting	0			$17,300		$0	$0	$0	-$17,300	0.948992	-$16,418
2	Permitting	0			$17,300		$0	$0	$0	-$17,300	0.900585	-$15,580
3	Construction	0				$814,250	$0	$0	$0	-$814,250	0.854648	-$695,897
4	Construction	0				$814,250	$0	$0	$0	-$814,250	0.811054	-$660,401
5	Absorption	12	$45,000	$540,000			$43,200	$250	$21,600	$474,950	0.769683	$365,561
6	Absorption	12	$45,000	$540,000			$43,200	$250	$21,600	$474,950	0.730423	$346,914
7	Absorption	12	$45,000	$540,000			$43,200	$250	$21,600	$474,950	0.693165	$329,219
8	Absorption	12	$45,000	$540,000			$43,200	$250	$21,600	$474,950	0.657808	$312,426
9	Absorption	12	$47,250	$567,000			$45,360	$1,000	$22,680	$497,960	0.624255	$310,854
10	Absorption	12	$47,250	$567,000			$45,360	$1,000	$22,680	$497,960	0.592412	$294,998
11	Absorption	12	$47,250	$567,000			$45,360	$1,000	$22,680	$497,960	0.562194	$279,950
12	Absorption	7	$47,250	$330,750			$26,460	$1,000	$13,230	$290,060	0.533518	$154,752
Totals		91		$4,191,750	$34,600	$1,628,500	$335,340	$5,000	$167,670	$2,020,640		$1,006,378
											Indicated land value	$1,006,378
											Rounded	$1,010,000

Land Value Using the Subdivision Development Method

Exhibit 11.9
Park View Acreage Land Value (76-Lot Scenario)

Quarter	Phase	Lots Sold	Average Lot Value	Gross Sales	Permitting Costs	Cons. Costs	Absorption Holding and Sales Costs				Net Proceeds	PV Factor 21.500%	Present Value
							Sales 8.0%	Tax	Misc. 4.0%				
1	Permitting	0			$15,050		$0	$0	$0		-$15,050	0.948992	-$14,282
2	Permitting	0			$15,050		$0	$0	$0		-$15,050	0.900585	-$13,554
3	Construction	0				$683,000	$0	$0	$0		-$683,000	0.854648	-$583,725
4	Construction	0				$683,000	$0	$0	$0		-$683,000	0.811054	-$553,950
5	Absorption	12	$45,000	$540,000			$43,200	$250	$21,600		$474,950	0.769683	$365,561
6	Absorption	12	$45,000	$540,000			$43,200	$250	$21,600		$474,950	0.730423	$346,914
7	Absorption	12	$45,000	$540,000			$43,200	$250	$21,600		$474,950	0.693165	$329,219
8	Absorption	12	$45,000	$540,000			$43,200	$250	$21,600		$474,950	0.657808	$312,426
9	Absorption	12	$47,250	$567,000			$45,360	$250	$22,680		$498,710	0.624255	$311,322
10	Absorption	12	$47,250	$567,000			$45,360	$250	$22,680		$498,710	0.592412	$295,442
11	Absorption	4	$47,250	$189,000			$15,120	$250	$7,560		$166,070	0.562194	$93,364
Totals		76		$3,483,000	$30,100	$1,366,000	$278,640	$1,750	$139,320		$1,667,190		$888,737
										Indicated land value			$888,737
										Rounded			$890,000

238 *Subdivision Valuation*

Exhibit 11.10
Land Value Summary and Conclusion

Results from subdivision development analysis:	
Optimistic density of 3.0 units per acre	$1,010,000
Most likely density of 2.75 units per acre	$950,000
Conservative density of 2.5 units per acre	$890,000
Estimated land value	$950,000

12
Special Topics

This chapter provides an overview of special topics relating to subdivision valuation. The first section discusses common deficiencies found in subdivision valuation that appraisers should be aware of when appraising subdivisions or other property types for which a bulk sale valuation scenario is considered. Other topics explored in this chapter include dollar profit, yield, timeline concepts, and a subdivision absorption example. The effect on yield and profit is explored for very short marketing time frames with the time zero profit dilemma example. This discussion delves into the issues involved to ensure that sufficient profit is considered when discounting present value for short marketing time frames. A contrast is made between the two discounting methods (split-rate method vs. single yield rate method) and selecting an appropriate rate. Developer risk reduction startegies, lot sales to potential homeowners, proposed construction performance bonds, and super pad sites are also discussed.

Common Deficiencies Found in Subdivision Appraisals

This section addresses common deficiencies and problems typically found in subdivision appraisals as well as common misconceptions regarding subdivision analysis. This discussion will help appraisers focus on areas of weakness typically found by review appraisers who regularly review subdivision appraisals and clients who lend on subdivision projects.

Highest and Best Use Analysis

Some appraisals lack a detailed highest and best use analysis that provides a supportable conclusion for financially feasible development. Typically, this deficiency is found in appraisals of proposed subdivisions or highest and best use conclusions for vacant tracts of land for which subdivision valuation methodology is used to estimate *as is* vacant land value.

The highest and best use section of the appraisal should define a group of financially feasible development alternatives that are physically possible, legally permissible, and financially feasible. For a proposed project to be financially feasible, it must have a bulk sale value that supports cost with a reasonable market-supported level of developer profit. Cost, retail lot values, and absorption are the primary areas of interest. The maximally productive subdivision development scenario would include information on the individual marketing concept and the price points that could be supported in the proposed project in light of current market demand characteristics. Of particular importance to financially feasible development are current supply and demand characteristics and their ability to support sustained absorption.

This book provides an introductory discussion and examples of how to perform a market-supported fundamental demand analysis and highest and best use conclusion. A more comprehensive overview of marketability analysis and highest and best use applications can be found in *Market Analysis for Real Estate: Concepts and Applications in Valuation and Highest and Best Use*, second edition.[1]

Lack of an Appropriate Marketability Study

Another common deficiency is an incomplete or deficient marketability study in the appraisal report. Since subdivision market value is entirely dependent on the absorption of lots over time, market analysis is critical to the appraisal. Market analysis techniques are described and explained in detail in Chapter 2 of this book. This discussion includes an overview of the inferred and fundamental demand analysis methods, in which the project marketing concept and related home price points are analyzed in comparison to the market determinants of supply and demand and future supply and demand characteristics over time. Chapter 2 includes a Level C market analysis illustrating the estimation of market absorption for the Mill Pond subdivision. A Level C market analysis incorporates future-oriented forecasting techniques, makes extensive use of primary data, and provides

---

1. Stephen F. Fanning, *Market Analysis for Real Estate: Concepts and Applications in Valuation and Highest and Best Use*, 2nd ed. (Chicago: Appraisal Institute, 2014).

detailed submarket data on which to base absorption and net operating income projections as well as a competitive ranking of the subject property.

This book provides a basic overview of marketability concepts. More comprehensive treatment is available in *Market Analysis for Real Estate*, second edition.

Support for Absorption Rates

The appraisal must provide support for the market absorption estimated for a proposed or existing group of lots. Apparently, many appraisals performed for lenders and other clients include little or no direct market evidence or analysis to support the absorption estimate. The appraisal must provide an explanation of the subdivision marketing concept and price points associated with the subject lot inventory and the determinants for future demand over time. All of the estimates are made consistent with the point in time that the lots will be placed on the market. For a proposed project, this would be as of the date when site infrastructure is complete and the lots are made ready to accept residential dwelling units. The absorption analysis is supported through application of the six-step market analysis process, in which inferred and fundamental supply and demand analysis is considered.

Problems in this area also relate to the consideration of presales and how they are handled in the market value conclusion. The appraisal process requires appropriate market analysis and project evaluation, and a fundamental demand forecast is required for both highest and best use analysis as well as the value conclusion based on absorption to end users. When presales are involved, it may be advisable to provide two appraisal value conclusions. The first is a value conclusion ignoring presales based on the fundamental forecast and retail lot values, with associated market-oriented holding and sales costs and required yield. This is the market value ignoring presales. A second value may be provided that directly considers presales like the examples provided in Chapter 7. This is a separate value opinion that may be different from the market scenario considering the fundamental forecast, and it is contingent upon the performance under the presales contracts. The difficulty arises when the appraisal does not have a fundamental demand analysis and relies entirely on the presale contracts or builder estimates for the absorption forecast and resulting conclusions. The appraisal must provide a market-oriented fundamental analysis and absorption forecast to conclude the highest and best use, regardless of whether there are presales to be considered in the analysis.

Any appraisal using the subdivision methodology must specifically address and provide market-derived support for the absorption forecast. This material provides an explanation of the six-step market analysis procedure and a Level C market analysis example. Again, more comprehensive treatment is available in *Market Analysis for Real Estate*, second edition.

Lack of Support for Discount Rates

Some appraisals do not provide support for the yield rate or discount rate used in the income capitalization approach. The discount rate used in the DCF analysis can be supported through comparisons with market sales from recent bulk sale transactions, market studies conducted by the appraiser, or third-party published surveys. When a third-party survey is used, it is imperative to compare the inputs and criteria used to produce the survey results with the actual characteristics of the subject project and the property component being appraised.

The appraisal should include discussion of yield rates and equity yield rates as appropriate, depending on the methods used for the bulk-sale market value conclusion. This is a common criticism from users in the industry, especially lending clients.

This book provides full coverage of how discount rates are extracted from the market and applied in an appraisal for the "true" yield rate method and the split-rate method. Comprehensive examples and explanations are provided in Chapters 7, 9, and 10. Appraisers must understand how to apply proper rate analysis. Also, the discussion of the time zero profit dilemma that appears later in this chapter provides more insight into the selection of yield rates.

Consideration of Cost vs. Feasibility

One very common deficiency mentioned by reviewers relates to the cost new of a proposed project versus the financially feasible or market-supported value generated by the sell-out of the individual lots. The use of feasibility analysis and the general use of the term *financial feasibility* requires a study to support a specific "accept or reject" decision. The decision criteria would typically be provided by the client. There may be a specific criterion that the project is feasible if it supports a particular *IRR* within a specified absorption period.

When this area of inquiry is mentioned by a lender, the lending client is usually looking for a cost/value feasibility determination to ensure that the economics of the project as indicated by the income capitalization and sales comparison approaches support the cost. Stated differently, the cost plus a reasonable market profit is in line with the value conclusions derived from the income capitalization and sales comparison approaches (i.e., the project is economically feasible). This problem is magnified in the analysis when the appraisal does not include a cost approach analysis.

The feasibility issue also relates to the previously mentioned highest and best use deficiency. Again, the lack of support for a financially feasible development is a concern. A proposed subdivision's financial success is entirely dependent on the future absorption of lots over time. All subdivision appraisals that involve a group of lots to be sold over time must have a thorough study of cost (especially for proposed projects), market absorption, and ultimately the feasibility of the proposed development. However, in the valuation of an existing group of lots or units, the feasibility issue is not particularly relevant. For existing inventory, historical costs may or may not have any influence on current values.

Understanding Profit Concepts

Profit concepts relate to the interpretation of the term *profit* in subdivision valuation. This predicament is explained by a simple question that is posed to appraisal students in the author's appraisal seminars. In the seminars, information is presented for two development scenarios similar to Scenarios 1 and 2 involving the Ridgewood subdivision, as shown in Exhibits 12.1 and 12.2. These two bulk sale scenarios illustrate the question posed to the students. Exhibit 12.3 provides a summary of the two bulk sale forecasts.

Scenario 1 in Exhibit 12.1 provides for a four-quarter absorption period with a present value calculation based on a yield rate of 40.0% with no line-item developer profit, reflecting a bulk sale value conclusion rounded to $920,000. The summary at the bottom of the DCF indicates that Scenario 1 generated $242,802 in total profit. This is the difference between the present value of $918,028 and the net proceeds of $1,160,830. Since there is no line-item profit, all the profit is reflected in the present value calculation with the yield rate of 40.0%. Scenario 2 involves the same subdivision but presents the DCF with a longer holding period. The holding period is increased from 4 quarters to 12 quarters, with a yield rate of 17.25%. The yield rate was chosen to reflect the same bulk sale value of $918,028, rounded to $920,000. Scenario 1 reflects a yield rate of 40.0%, and Scenario 2 is lower at 17.25%. The example was engineered to have a higher dollar profit for the longer holding period by increasing lot value with inflation over time.

After reviewing the two sales scenarios, the following question is posed: "Which scenario generates the greatest profit to the developer?" Surprisingly, about half of the students typically choose Scenario 2 as generating the greatest profit, probably because the dollar profit of $289,348 in Scenario 2 exceeds the profit of $242,802 in Scenario 1. This conclusion totally contradicts the primary goal of the developer, which is to sell lots or units as quickly as possible

Exhibit 19.1
Ridgewood Scenario 1: Shorter Absorption Period

Quarter	Lots Sold	Remaining Lots	Retail Lot Value	Gross Sales	Absorption Holding & Sales Costs					Line-Item Profit 0.0%	Net Proceeds	PV Factor 41.5%	Present Value
					Sales 6.0%	Tax	Assoc. Dues	Misc. 2.0%				
		36										
1	9	27	$35,000	$315,000	$18,900	$5,355	$900	$6,300	$0	$283,545	0.909091	$257,768
2	9	18	$35,000	$315,000	$18,900	$4,016	$675	$6,300	$0	$285,109	0.826446	$235,627
3	9	9	$36,050	$324,450	$19,467	$2,758	$450	$6,489	$0	$295,286	0.751315	$221,853
4	9	0	$36,050	$324,450	$19,467	$1,379	$225	$6,489	$0	$296,890	0.683013	$202,780
	36			$1,278,900	$76,734	$13,508	$2,250	$25,578	$0	$1,160,830		$918,028
										Indicated Bulk Sale Value		$918,028
										Rounded		$920,000
										Time Value Profit		$242,802

Exhibit 12.2
Ridgewood Scenario 2: Longer Absorption Period

| Quarter | Lots Sold | Remaining Lots | Retail Lot Value | Gross Sales | Absorption Holding & Sales Costs ||||| Line-Item Profit 0.0% | Net Proceeds | PV Factor 17.25% | Present Value |
					Sales 6.0%	Tax	Assoc. Dues	Misc. 2.0%					
		36.0										
1	3	33.0	$35,000	$105,000	$6,300	$5,355	$900	$2,100	$0	$90,345	0.958647	$86,609
2	3	30.0	$35,000	$105,000	$6,300	$4,909	$825	$2,100	$0	$90,866	0.919003	$83,506
3	3	27.0	$36,050	$108,150	$6,489	$4,596	$750	$2,163	$0	$94,152	0.881000	$82,948
4	3	24.0	$36,050	$108,150	$6,489	$4,137	$675	$2,163	$0	$94,686	0.844567	$79,969
5	3	21.0	$37,132	$111,396	$6,684	$3,787	$600	$2,228	$0	$98,097	0.809642	$79,423
6	3	18.0	$37,132	$111,396	$6,684	$3,314	$525	$2,228	$0	$98,645	0.776160	$76,565
7	3	15.0	$38,246	$114,738	$6,884	$2,926	$450	$2,295	$0	$102,183	0.744063	$76,031
8	3	12.0	$38,246	$114,738	$6,884	$2,438	$375	$2,295	$0	$102,746	0.713294	$73,288
9	3	9.0	$39,393	$118,179	$7,091	$2,009	$300	$2,364	$0	$106,416	0.683797	$72,767
10	3	6.0	$39,393	$118,179	$7,091	$1,507	$225	$2,364	$0	$106,993	0.655520	$70,136
11	3	3.0	$40,575	$121,725	$7,304	$1,035	$150	$2,435	$0	$110,802	0.628412	$69,629
12	3	0.0	$40,575	$121,725	$7,304	$517	$75	$2,435	$0	$111,395	0.602425	$67,107
	36			$1,358,376	$81,503	$36,530	$5,850	$27,168	$0	$1,207,326		$917,978

Indicated Bulk Sale Value $917,978
Rounded $920,000
Time Value Profit $289,348

Exhibit 12.3
Ridgewood Bulk Sales Comparison

	Analysis Results	
	Scenario 1 Shorter Absorption	Scenario 2 Longer Absorption
Description		
Bulk sale value	$918,028	$917,978
Holding & sales costs		
Sales	76,734	81,503
Taxes	13.508	36,530
Association dues	2,250	5,850
Miscellaneous	25,578	27,168
Profit		
Line-item profit	0	0
Discount rate	242,802	289,348
Gross proceeds	$1,278,900	$1,358,376
Line-item profit	0.0%	0.0%
(as a percentage of gross sales)	40.00%	17.25%
Total dollar profit	$242,802	$289,348
Profit per year	$242,802	$96,449
Absorption time frame years	1	3

Note. Numbers may vary slightly due to rounding.

and generate the greatest profit. The distinction that must be made in this situation and all time discounting problems is that the dollar profit, yield, and time frame involved should be evaluated together.

This question brings to the forefront one of the most difficult concepts to understand in subdivision valuation and in general appraisal practice: the interaction of the holding period and time value concepts in relation to dollar profit and yield. Choosing Scenario 2 as the most profitable ignores the yield rates and the length of the absorption period. Profit can be expressed as a dollar amount or as a yield rate (i.e., *IRR*). In Ridgewood Scenario 1, the total dollar profit was $242,802, with a relatively short absorption period of four quarters. However, Scenario 2 reflects a slower market, and a longer absorption period of 12 quarters generated a total dollar profit of $289,348. This book clearly explains that the goal in subdivision development is to sell the lots as quickly as possible to achieve the greatest profit. The results from Scenario 2 based on dollar profit appear to contradict this statement. How can Scenario 1 be more attractive to a potential buyer, while Scenario 2 generates a higher dollar profit?

The answer is explained by the time periods involved. In Scenario 2, the total time period involved in the investment is 12 quarters. The $920,000 investment by the purchaser in Scenario 2 produced a total profit of $289,348 over 12 quarters and generated a yield rate of only 17.25% on an annual basis with the same purchase price as Scenario 1. Over the same time period, the investor under Scenario 1 could have purchased three separate groups of lots each year on a bulk sale basis. If each group was purchased for the same initial investment of about $920,000 and sold in four quarters, the three projects would have earned a total profit of $728,406 ($242,802 × 3) over the same three-year period. The internal rate of return from the investment would be 40.0% each year. This is far superior to the investment Scenario 2, reflecting a total profit of $289,348 over the same three-year time frame. The correct test of profit is to compare the investment results over the same time frame and recognize the influences of the time-value calculations. Clearly, total dollar profit alone is not the only measure. Total dollar profit cannot be considered alone by ignoring the time value of money.

Don't be misled into the mindset that total dollar profit can be evaluated without considering the time periods involved and the yield rates (or *IRR*) associated with each alternative. Dollar profit, time, and yield must always be evaluated together and never separately.

Time Zero Profit Dilemma

The time zero profit dilemma topic explores the valuation issues involved when estimating market bulk sale values for relatively short absorption periods and selecting an appropriate yield rate. Yield rate selection becomes problematic as the absorption time frame decreases. The problem arises when discounting is performed for holding periods of less than about one or two years. A comprehensive example is provided for the Serenola Hills subdivision project. In this example, the absorption forecasts have been engineered by considering a short-term demand spike to enhance the differences for illustration purposes. Both the time zero profit element and the effect of the short holding period are considered as part of a market demand for Serenola Hills and are presented in Exhibits 12.4 through 12.12. This example is different from the presales discussion in Chapter 7 that considered developer yield. The buyer's perspective is considered by evaluating the profit margins reflected in the bulk sale appraised value.

The Serenola Hills subdivision project contains 72 lots on 18 acres, and all infrastructure and subdivision site improvements were 100% installed and completed as of January 1, 2018. Exhibit 12.4 provides a cost approach analysis for the property and considers both direct and indirect construction costs, together with the profit achieved over the permitting and construction phase. Accordingly, this is a "when complete" value estimate by the cost

Exhibit 12.4
Serenola Hills Cost Data

Current Date—Construction 100% completed	1/1/18		
Project Information	72 lots on 18.0 acres (4 units/ac.)		
Cost New		**Total Cost**	**Cost per Lot**
Permitting Phase Expenses			
Planning and conceptual drawings		$23,896	$332
Holding costs & taxes		10,000	139
Permitting fees		22,000	306
Environmental audit		20,000	278
Survey & topographical		26,104	363
	Subtotal	$102,000	$1,417
Construction Phase Expenses			
Direct construction costs		$2,340,000	$32,500
Survey, engineering, & final plat		25,000	347
Front entrance with landscaping		15,000	208
Holding costs & taxes		38,000	528
	Subtotal	$2,418,000	$33,583
Permitting phase & construction phase profit		72,000	1,000
Replacement cost new		$2,592,000	$36,000
Less: Depreciation—none		0	0
Depreciated improvement value		$2,592,000	$36,000
Add: Land value (raw land value excluding profit)			
	18.0 acres @ $40,000	720,000	$10,000
Indicated Value—When Complete Date		$3,312,000	$46,000
Absorption Forecast:			
Estimated retail value per lot		$5,400,000	$75,000
Less: Cost per lot		-3,312,000	-46,000
Less: Developer's required absorption phase profit (35% of total costs plus land value)	35.0%	-1,159,200	-16,100
Note: This amount is 21.5% "retail" value/lot			
Residual Available to Cover Holding & Sales Costs		$928,800	$12,900
Absorption Forecast			
Normal market absorption	6	Lots per quarter @	$75,000
Micro-market demand spike			
Initial lot reservations	36	Lot reservations @	$75,000
Remaining lots	9	Lots per quarter @	$75,000

Note. Numbers may vary slightly due to rounding.

approach at the point in time when construction is 100% complete, reflecting a value of $3,312,000.

The estimated retail value per lot is $75,000. The project developer indicates that the minimum required profit over the absorption phase is about 35% of direct and indirect costs, or $1,159,200, as shown at the bottom of Exhibit 12.4. Subtracting the cost per lot as of the "when complete" date as well as the developer's minimum required profit of $16,100 per lot reflects a residual available to cover any holding and sales costs over the future absorption period of about $12,900 per lot, or $928,800. This type of cost-oriented scenario is a typical scenario that is employed by many builders in pricing lots and estimating future profit from lot sales recognizing holding and sales costs over the future absorption period. The fundamental demand forecast concludes a market demand of six units per quarter prior to the demand spike.

Just after the construction was started about one year ago, a new large upscale innovation office development was announced for the subject neighborhood. The first phase is currently under construction; this will bring new home demand to the area. In fact, the developer has 36 lot reservations as of time zero as of the "when complete" date on January 1, 2018. The reservations are lot purchase agreements with individual homeowners that will build homes for owner occupancy on individual lots. A $2,000 non-refundable deposit clause is included in each contract. However, the contracts can be cancelled. Because of the new short-term demand generated by the office development, future absorption is estimated above the initial fundamental forecast at nine lots per quarter. This speculative figure is higher than the fundamental demand of six lots per quarter. All reservations are at $75,000 per lot. To keep this example simple, no inflation is considered over the holding period in terms of the retail lot values; future lot sales are at the same price as the market retail value, or $75,000 per lot. A cost approach was performed as of the *when complete* date and is shown in Exhibit 12.4. The developer's required profit is $1,159,200, or about 35% of total costs plus land value. This amount is about 21.5% of the retail lot value.

Whenever a proposed project or, for that matter, any group of lots is appraised on an *as is* basis, the initial analysis is always performed on a market-oriented basis, in which market absorption considering six-step fundamental demand analysis is considered. Even with lot reservations or presale agreements, a fundamental forecast is required to address highest and best use in the appraisal. This is the absorption rate to end users based on market research, and it establishes the required sell-out period or time frame for the cash flow analysis. This is the appraiser's market-oriented absorption forecast ignoring the market spike caused by the new office development and any presales of lots. A second calculation or multiple calculations are then performed to consider the lot reservations and the resulting up-tick in demand and its effect on the resulting bulk sale value conclusions.

The first scenario considered for Serenola Hills is a developer sensitivity analysis shown in Exhibit 12.5. This bulk sale conclusion was made to determine if the developer will achieve the minimum level of required profit over a typical market-oriented holding period to end users (fundamental forecast) using a market yield rate of 20% with a zero line-item profit and a market absorption of six lots per quarter. The yield rate is based on the market absorption period of three years, with quarterly discounting based on market data and/or market rate surveys consistent with the three-year absorption period. This calculation is presented in Exhibit 12.5. This is the market value supported by the income capitalization approach, with no lot reservations and typical market demand reflecting a bulk value of $3,460,000, which is just above the cost approach indication of $3,312,000. The value conclusion under the market absorption scenario with about equal weight to each approach is rounded to $3,400.000. This is a reference value without considering the lot reservations and the market spike.

The market absorption is estimated based on the fundamental forecast considering research at normal market levels unaffected by the new office development. Retail lot value is $75,000 per lot. The holding and sales costs over the absorption period include sales costs estimated at 6% of gross sales and a real estate tax based on an 85% assessment ratio, with taxes of 2% of lot value (i.e., tax rate of 20.00 mills) per year on the remaining lot inventory that gradually decrease over time until the last lots are sold. Also, association dues are $25 per lot per quarter on remaining inventory, which also decreases as lots are sold. Miscellaneous costs are 4% of gross sales, as shown in Exhibit 12.5. These expenses are the same in all forecasts.

Scenario 1 provides a present value conclusion with a sensitivity analysis based on the bulk sale value supported by market criteria, ignoring the demand spike. Discounting the net proceeds at the market yield rate of 20% with zero line-item profit reflects a bulk sale value rounded to $3,460,000. Under this scenario, the average profit per lot is $17,207. This amount exceeds the required developer profit of $16,100 per lot and allows the developer to achieve a yield rate of 23.1%. Accordingly, the developer will have achieved a minimum level of profit of $1,159,169, together with a residual profit of about $148,000. This is because the bulk sale value of $3,460,227 is higher than the cost of $3,312,000, so the total profit achieved by the developer is the minimum required profit of $1,159,169 together with the dollar difference between the cost and the indicated bulk sale value, or about $148,000.

Exhibit 12.5 was constructed to include two additional columns at the right side of the table reflecting the dollar profit per period and the profit per lot sold. Characteristic of yield calculations, the greatest dollar profit is in the later time periods, and minimal profit is extracted in the initial time periods. For this reason, it is important to extract market yield rates from proper-

Exhibit 19.5
Serenola Hills Scenario 1: Market Value Scenario–No Lot Reservations

Absorption Holding & Sales Costs

Quarter	Lots Sold	Remaining Lots	Retail Lot Value*	Gross Sales	Sales 6.0%	Tax	Assoc. Dues	Misc. 4.0%	Line-Item Profit 0.0%	Net Proceeds	PV Factor 20.00%	Present Value	Dollar Profit per Period	Profit per Lot Sold
		72												
0	0	72	$75,000	$0	$0	$0	$0	$0	$0	$0	1.000000	$0		$0
1	6	66	$75,000	$450,000	$27,000	$22,950	$1,800	$18,000	$0	$380,250	0.952381	$362,143	$18,107	$3,018
2	6	60	$75,000	$450,000	$27,000	$21,038	$1,650	$18,000	$0	$382,313	0.907029	$346,769	$35,544	$5,924
3	6	54	$75,000	$450,000	$27,000	$19,125	$1,500	$18,000	$0	$384,375	0.863838	$332,038	$52,337	$8,723
4	6	48	$75,000	$450,000	$27,000	$17,213	$1,350	$18,000	$0	$386,438	0.822702	$317,923	$68,515	$11,419
5	6	42	$75,000	$450,000	$27,000	$15,300	$1,200	$18,000	$0	$388,500	0.783526	$304,400	$84,100	$14,017
6	6	36	$75,000	$450,000	$27,000	$13,388	$1,050	$18,000	$0	$390,563	0.746215	$291,444	$99,119	$16,520
7	6	30	$75,000	$450,000	$27,000	$11,475	$900	$18,000	$0	$392,625	0.710681	$279,031	$113,594	$18,932
8	6	24	$75,000	$450,000	$27,000	$9,563	$750	$18,000	$0	$394,688	0.676839	$267,140	$127,548	$21,258
9	6	18	$75,000	$450,000	$27,000	$7,650	$600	$18,000	$0	$396,750	0.644609	$255,749	$141,001	$23,500
10	6	12	$75,000	$450,000	$27,000	$5,738	$450	$18,000	$0	$398,813	0.613913	$244,836	$153,977	$25,663
11	6	6	$75,000	$450,000	$27,000	$3,825	$300	$18,000	$0	$400,875	0.584679	$234,383	$166,492	$27,749
12	6	0	$75,000	$450,000	$27,000	$1,913	$150	$18,000	$0	$402,938	0.556837	$224,371	$178,567	$29,761
	72			$5,400,000	$324,000	$149,175	$11,700	$216,000	$0	$4,699,125		$3,460,227	$1,238,898	$17,207
Annual increase 0%											Rounded	$3,460,000		

*

Exhibit 12.5
Serenola Hills Scenario 1: Market Value Scenario—No Lot Reservations (continued)

DCF Summary		$	Per Lot	IRR Summary		Developer Cost Basis	Market Bulk Sale Estimate
Sum of the retail values—Time 0		$5,400,000	$75,000			-$3,312,000	-$3,460,227
Add: Lot value inflation		$0	$0	Income	Quarter 1	$380,250	$380,250
Gross proceeds		$5,400,000	$75,000		Quarter 2	$382,313	$382,313
Less: Absorption holding & sales costs					Quarter 3	$384,375	$384,375
Sales		$324,000	$4,500		Quarter 4	$386,438	$386,438
Tax		$149,175	$2,072		Quarter 5	$388,500	$388,500
Association dues		$11,700	$163		Quarter 6	$390,563	$390,563
Miscellaneous		$216,000	$3,000		Quarter 7	$392,625	$392,625
Subtotal holding & sales costs		$700,875	$9,734		Quarter 8	$394,688	$394,688
Profit: Line-item profit	$0		$0		Quarter 9	$396,750	$396,750
Time value profit	$1,238,898		$17,207		Quarter 10	$398,813	$398,813
Subtotal profit	$1,238,898	$1,238,898	$17,207		Quarter 11	$400,875	$400,875
Total adjustment		$1,939,773	$26,941		Quarter 12	$402,938	$402,938
Bulk sale value		$3,460,227	$48,059		Indicated IRR	23.11%	20.00%
Rounded		$3,460,000	$48,056				
Project cost as of *when complete* date		$3,312,000					
Residual profit (if any)		$148,000					
Profit as % of gross sales (sum of retail values)		22.9%					

Conclusions:

1. The developer's minimum required profit is achieved and exceeded under the market absorption scenario
2. The required level of profit is $16,100 per lot and the profit reflected in the market value bulk sale calculation is $17,207 per lot.
3. The developer's yield is 23.11%, which is higher than the required market yield of 20%.

Matched pairs yield and line-item profit are as follows:

Line-Item	Yield
0.00%	20.00%
10.00%	11.67%
22.94%	0.00%

ties that have the same or similar absorption time frames. If sales are not available, then adjustments should be made to the yield rate and/or the selection of matched pairs of line-item profit and yield to ensure that sufficient profit is considered.

The conclusions drawn under market Scenario 1 are as follows:

- The developer's minimum required profit is achieved and exceeded under the market fundamental absorption for this scenario, prior to consideration of any lot reservations.
- The developer's required level of profit is $16,100 per lot, and the profit reflected in the market value bulk sale calculation is $17,207 per lot.
- The developer's yield is 23.11%, which is higher than the market yield of 20%.

The matched pairs yield and line-item profit are extracted from market Scenario 1 as follows:

Line-Item	Yield
0.00%	20.00%
10.00%	11.67%
22.94%	0.00%

The Serenola Hills example is expanded to consider lot reservations and a higher demand forecast in Exhibit 12.6, Scenario 2. Under this scenario, the appraiser is performing a DCF at the same market yield rate of 20% with zero line-item profit and places the initial sale of 36 lots as of time period zero before the Quarter 1 present value calculation. The appraiser reasons that because the lots will sell immediately after construction on the *when complete* date, no profit will be considered. The appraiser does consider the lot sales expenses of $162,000 (see Exhibit 12.6, Scenario 2), together with miscellaneous costs of $108,000. No real estate tax or association dues are allocated because the calculation is in time period zero. There is no discounting for the initial lot sales using this method. Accordingly, zero profit is taken out of the initial lot purchase of 36 lots at $2,700,000. Absorption is nine lots per quarter over the remaining holding period, anticipating a continued demand push by the new office development. In Quarters 2 through 5, the appropriate holding and sales costs as well as profit reflected in the discount rate of 20% is taken out, reflecting a total profit of $373,055. This is the only profit considered in the present value calculation and is significantly lower than the profit level under the market value scenario. This analysis indicates a bulk sale value rounded to $4,431,000, which is the appraised value assuming time zero lot sales with no profit allocation taken out of the initial sale of 36 lots.

Exhibit 12.6
Serenola Hills Scenario 2: Considering Lot Sales at Time Zero without Discounting

Quarter	Lots Sold	Remaining Lots	Retail Lot Value*	Gross Sales	Absorption Sales 6.0%	Holding & Sales Costs Tax	Assoc. Dues	Misc. 4.0%	Line-Item Profit 0.0%	Net Proceeds	PV Factor 20.00%	Present Value	Dollar Profit per Period
		72											
0	36	36	$75,000	$2,700,000	$162,000	$0	$0	$108,000	$0	$2,430,000	1.000000	$2,430,000	$0
1	0	36	$75,000	$0	$0	$22,950	$1,800	$0	$0	-$24,750	0.952381	-$23,571	-$1,179
2	9	27	$75,000	$675,000	$40,500	$11,475	$900	$27,000	$0	$595,125	0.907029	$539,796	$55,329
3	9	18	$75,000	$675,000	$40,500	$8,606	$675	$27,000	$0	$598,219	0.863838	$516,764	$81,455
4	9	9	$75,000	$675,000	$40,500	$5,738	$450	$27,000	$0	$601,313	0.822702	$494,701	$106,612
5	9	0	$75,000	$675,000	$40,500	$2,869	$225	$27,000	$0	$604,406	0.783526	$473,568	$130,838
	72			$5,400,000	$324,000	$51,638	$4,050	$216,000	$0	$4,804,313		$4,431,258	$373,055
											Rounded	$4,431,000	

* Annual increase 0%

DCF Summary

	$	Per Lot			
Sum of the retail values—Time Ø	$5,400,000	$75,000	**Developer IRR**		
Add: Lot value inflation	0	0	Developer IRR*		
Gross proceeds	$5,400,000	$75,000	Based on cost		
Less: Absorption holding & sales costs			($3,312,000 – $2,430,000)		-$882,000
Sales	$324,000	$4,500	Income	Quarter 1	-$24,750
Tax	51,638	717		Quarter 2	$595,125
Association dues	4,050	56		Quarter 3	$598,219
Miscellaneous	216,000	3,000		Quarter 4	$601,313
Subtotal holding & sales costs	$595,688	$8,273		Quarter 5	$604,406
Profit: Line-item profit	$0	$0	Indicated IRR		137.14%
Time value profit	$373,055	$5,181	* Assumes developer sells the lots over the 5-quarter absorption period		
Subtotal profit $373,055	$373,055	$5,181			
Total adjustment	$968,742	$13,455	**Proposed Purchase IRR**		
Bulk sale value	$4,431,258	$61,545	Appraised value IRR		
Rounded	$4,431,000	$61,542	Purchase at bulk value		-$2,001,258
Project cost as of when complete date	$3,312,000		($4,431,258 – $2,430,000)		
Residual profit (if any)	$1,119,258		Income	Quarter 1	-$24,750
				Quarter 2	$595,125
				Quarter 3	$598,219
				Quarter 4	$601,313
				Quarter 5	$604,406
			Indicated IRR		20.00%

Conclusions:
1. Total dollar profit is significantly reduced based upon the Time 0 transaction without discounting.
2. The project profit reflected in the appraised value of $4,431,000 is only $373,055.
3. If the purchase reservations fall through and market demand decreases, the bulk sale value would drop from $4,431,000 in Scenario 2 to $3,460,000 reflected in Scenario 1.
4. The short marketing time frame of five quarters does not allow the yield capitalization math to generate sufficient profit, and value is overstated.

For informational purposes, the original developer's *IRR* is based on the developer's cost of $3,312,000, less the time zero net purchase net proceeds of $2,430,000. The developer's *IRR* summary can be found at the bottom of Exhibit 12.6. The developer's *IRR* reflects a yield rate of about 137% developer yield based upon the time zero calculation, when no profit is taken on the initial purchase of 36 lots as part of the lot sale agreements. This significantly enhances the developer's actual return and significantly reduces the profit considered in the DCF analysis with a relatively minimal total profit of 373,055, as reflected in the DCF calculations.

While this is beneficial to the developer, it is very problematic to a potential buyer who purchases the property at the appraised value. If this property (all 72 lots) was purchased at $4,431,258, the buyer would receive a total profit of $373,055. The difficulty with this calculation is that eliminating the profit in the present value calculation by using a time zero calculation with no profit considered substantially increases the bulk sale value when no profit was removed through the discounting process. In fact, the profit adds to the bulk sale value conclusion because it was not considered in the present value calculation. The total dollar profit reflected in the calculation is only $373,055. While this is beneficial to the developer, it is very problematic to a potential buyer who purchases the property at the appraised value.

The Scenario 2 conclusions are as follows:

- The total dollar profit is significantly reduced based on the time zero transaction without discounting.
- The total profit reflected in the appraised value of $4,432,000 is only $373,055 to a potential buyer.
- If the purchase contracts fall through, the bulk sale market value would drop from $4,431,000 in Scenario 2 to $3,460,000, as reflected in Scenario 1.
- The short marketing time frame of five quarters does not allow the yield capitalization math to generate sufficient profit, and the value is overstated.

The bulk sale value under this scenario is entirely dependent upon whether or not the pending lot reservations are realized and come to fruition. The time zero placement of sales with no profit allocation significantly overstates market value because insufficient profit was deducted in the time period zero calculations. Essentially, the profit that should have be taken in the initial lot takedown is allowed to flow through into the calculation of market value, overstating the present value estimate.

One solution that may be applied to rectify this situation is to include the initial sale of the 36 lots as part of the discounting for the first quarter and not in time zero. This scenario is presented in Exhibit 12.7 (Serenola Hills Scenario 3), in which the presales are considered in the first quarter and not in time period zero, allowing for the yield rate calculation to consider profit earned as part of the presale transaction. This scenario is very similar to Scenario 2, with the exception that the initial transaction of 36 lots is performed in Quarter 1, which allows the net proceeds to be discounted at 20% for Period 1.

This calculation provides for a relatively minimal increase in the profit that is considered in the discounting. Total dollar profit is increased to $488,770 and reduces the bulk sale value conclusion to $4,316,000. Under this scenario, the proposed purchaser at the appraised value would achieve the market-oriented yield rate of 20%. However, the question in this analysis is the same as in the previous analysis. Does this generate significant profit to reflect the risk inherent in the bulk sale value of $4,316,000? The answer is probably not.

Profit is $488,770 under this scenario, which is substantially less than the initial subdivision developer's required minimum profit. So why would an investor purchase the property at the appraised value of $4,316,000 and only earn $488,770 in return? The investor could become a developer, purchase a vacant site, build a competing subdivision, and achieve a substantially higher profit.

The following conclusions can be made under Scenario 3 regarding profit and appraised value:

- Total profit earned on the purchase at the appraised value is still minimal, increasing from $373,055 in Scenario 2 to $488,770 in Scenario 3.
- Profit is still significantly below the required amount needed by developers or investors.

To remedy this situation, the appraiser begins to revise the analysis. Instead of using straight discounting with zero line-item profit, the appraiser converts to the split-rate method. This calculation is shown in Exhibit 12.8. Under Scenario 4, the split-rate method uses a line-item profit of 10% of gross sales, together with the matched pair discount rate of 11.67. The matched pair of yield and discount rates was solved under Scenario 1 based on the three-year holding period for the initial market value conclusion.

Under Scenario 4, the total dollar profit is the sum of profit generated by the line-item profit at 10% of gross sales, together with the present value calculation of 11.67%. This indicates a total dollar profit of $803,799 as shown in the DCF summary for Scenario 4, which is moving closer to the developer's minimal required profit of $1,159,200. Accordingly, by switching to the split-rate method, a higher level of dollar profit is generated by the DCF analysis more consistent with expected profit levels that would be achieved in the

Exhibit 12.7
Serenola Hills Scenario 3: Considering Lot Sales in Period 1

Quarter	Lots Sold	Remaining Lots	Retail Lot Value*	Gross Sales	Absorption Holding & Sales Costs					Net Proceeds	PV Factor 20.00%	Present Value	Dollar Profit per Period
					Sales 6.0%	Tax	Assoc. Dues	Misc. 4.0%	Line-Item Profit 0.0%				
		72											
0	0	72	$75,000	$0	$0	$0	$0	$0	$0	$0	1.000000	$0	$0
1	36	36	$75,000	$2,700,000	$162,000	$22,950	$1,800	$108,000	$0	$2,405,250	0.952381	$2,290,714	$114,536
2	9	27	$75,000	$675,000	$40,500	$11,475	$900	$27,000	$0	$595,125	0.907029	$539,796	$55,329
3	9	18	$75,000	$675,000	$40,500	$8,606	$675	$27,000	$0	$598,219	0.863838	$516,764	$81,455
4	9	9	$75,000	$675,000	$40,500	$5,738	$450	$27,000	$0	$601,313	0.822702	$494,701	$106,612
5	9	0	$75,000	$675,000	$40,500	$2,869	$225	$27,000	$0	$604,406	0.783526	$473,568	$130,838
	72			$5,400,000	$324,000	$51,638	$4,050	$216,000	$0	$4,804,313		$4,315,543	$488,770
											Rounded	$4,316,000	
Annual increase 0%											Total Dollar Profit		$488,770

*

Conclusions:
1. Total profit earned on the purchase at appraised value is still minimal, increasing from $373,055 in Scenario 2 to $488,770 in Scenario 3.
2. Profit is still significantly below the required amount needed by developers.

Exhibit 12.8
Serenola Hills Scenario 4: Considering Lot Sales in Period 1 with Line-Item Profit

Quarter	Lots Sold	Remaining Lots	Retail Lot Value*	Gross Sales	Absorption Holding & Sales Costs				Line-Item Profit 10.0%	Net Proceeds	PV Factor 11.67%	Present Value
					Sales 6.0%	Tax	Assoc. Dues	Misc. 4.0%				
0	0	72	$75,000	$0	$0	$0	$0	$0	$0	$0	1.000000	$0
1	36	72	$75,000	$2,700,000	$162,000	$22,950	$1,800	$108,000	$270,000	$2,135,250	0.971652	$2,074,720
2	9	36	$75,000	$675,000	$40,500	$11,475	$900	$27,000	$67,500	$527,625	0.944108	$498,135
3	9	27	$75,000	$675,000	$40,500	$8,606	$675	$27,000	$67,500	$530,719	0.917344	$486,852
4	9	18	$75,000	$675,000	$40,500	$5,738	$450	$27,000	$67,500	$533,813	0.891339	$475,808
5	9	9	$75,000	$675,000	$40,500	$2,869	$225	$27,000	$67,500	$536,906	0.866072	$464,999
	72	0		$5,400,000	$324,000	$51,638	$4,050	$216,000	$540,00	$4,264,313		$4,000,514
											Rounded	$4,001,000
											Total Dollar Profit	$803,799

Annual increase 0%

*

Conclusions:

1. Under this scenario, profit is increased to $803,799 from the minimal level of $488,770 in Scenario 3 and the $373,055 level in Scenario 2.
2. The profit under this scenario is higher but significantly below the minimum profit by the developer of $1,159,200. This is more in line with profit levels that would be expected considering the magnitude of the bulk sale purchase price and typical profit levels expected in subdivision development.

market. The matched pair of line-item profit and yield is from the original Scenario 1, considering the market-oriented, three-year absorption time frame. The following conclusions can be made:

- Under this scenario, profit is increased to $803,799 from the minimal levels of $488,770 in Scenario 3 and the $373,055 level in Scenario 2.
- The profit under this scenario is moving closer to the required minimum profit by the developer of $1,159,200. This is more in line with profit levels that would be expected considering the magnitude of the bulk sale purchase price and typical profit levels expected in subdivision development.

Scenario 5 is the next projection and provides a similar calculation, except that no discounting is provided and all profit is represented in a line-item profit of 22.94% of gross sales. The calculations are shown in Exhibit 12.9. This is an unconventional analysis that was a matched pair that was solved as part of the initial market value in Scenario 1, where a 22.94% line-item profit with a zero discount rate was reflected in the DCF over the initial three-year absorption period.

This calculation delivers a bulk sale value of $3,565,553 that is above the cost approach estimate of $3,312,000 and reflects a dollar profit of $1,238,760. This method delivers a higher level of profit compared to Scenarios 2 through 4, as shown in the analysis summary in Exhibit 12.11. However, this is about the same amount of dollar profit as was generated under market Scenario 1. This is expected because the line-item profit percentage came from Scenario 1, and the analysis ignores the time value aspects measured by yield rates.

This method (i.e., a matched pair line-item profit with 0% yield) is rarely used on any time period greater than about one year. It is provided here for illustration purposes only and could be a method that is needed for extremely short marketing time frames to generate sufficient profit. In this example, applying the full line-item profit with a zero yield rate significantly overestimates the profit considering the presales and ignores time value considerations.

Conclusions for this scenario are as follows:

- This method ignores the time value influence of the yield rate and delivers the same dollar amount of profit as Scenario 1.
- The "line-item profit only" method would inherently yield the same results as Scenario 1, except for the negative cash flows.
- This method probably extracts more profit than would be justified given the presales benefit and reduced holding period.

Appraisers have long recognized that there is a profit dilemma when discounting cash flows for very short holding periods.

Exhibit 12.9
Serenola Hills Scenario 5: Considering Lot Sales Period 1–Line-Item Profit Only

					Absorption Holding & Sales Costs							
Quarter	Lots Sold	Remaining Lots	Retail Lot Value*	Gross Sales	Sales 6.0%	Tax	Assoc. Dues	Misc. 4.0%	Line-Item Profit 22.94%	Net Proceeds	PV Factor 0.00%	Present Value	Dollar Profit per Period
		72											
0	0	72	$75,000	$0	$0	$0	$0	$0	$0	$0	1.000000	$0	$0
1	36	36	$75,000	$2,700,000	$162,000	$22,950	$1,800	$108,000	$619,380	$1,785,870	1.000000	$1,785,870	$619,380
2	9	27	$75,000	$675,000	$40,500	$11,475	$900	$27,000	$154,845	$440,280	1.000000	$440,280	$154,845
3	9	18	$75,000	$675,000	$40,500	$8,606	$675	$27,000	$154,845	$443,374	1.000000	$443,374	$154,845
4	9	9	$75,000	$675,000	$40,500	$5,738	$450	$27,000	$154,845	$446,468	1.000000	$446,468	$154,845
5	9	0	$75,000	$675,000	$40,500	$2,869	$225	$27,000	$154,845	$449,561	1.000000	$449,561	$154,845
	72			$5,400,000	$324,000	$51,638	$4,050	$216,000	$1,238,760	$3,565,553		$3,565,553	$1,238,760
											Rounded	$3,566,000	
											Total Dollar Profit		$1,238,760

* Annual increase 0%

Conclusions:

1. This method ignores the time value influence of the yield rate, but delivers exactly the same dollar profit as Scenario 1 except for rounding.
2. This method probably extracts more profit than would be justified given the presales benefit and reduced holding period.

Exhibit 19.10
Serenola Hills Scenario 6: Required Yield

Quarter	Lots Sold	Remaining Lots	Retail Lot Value*	Gross Sales	Absorption Holding & Sales Costs					Net Proceeds	PV Factor 40.52%	Present Value	Dollar Profit per Period
					Sales 6.0%	Tax	Assoc. Dues	Misc. 4.0%	Line-Item Profit 0.0%				
0	0	72	$75,000	$0	$0	$0	$0	$0	$0	$0	1.000000	$0	$0
1	36	36	$75,000	$2,700,000	$162,000	$22,950	$1,800	$108,000	$0	$2,405,250	0.908008	$2,183,987	$221,263
2	9	27	$75,000	$675,000	$40,500	$11,475	$900	$27,000	$0	$595,125	0.824479	$490,668	$104,457
3	9	18	$75,000	$675,000	$40,500	$8,606	$675	$27,000	$0	$598,219	0.748634	$447,847	$150,372
4	9	9	$75,000	$675,000	$40,500	$5,738	$450	$27,000	$0	$601,313	0.679766	$408,751	$192,562
5	9	0	$75,000	$675,000	$40,500	$2,869	$225	$27,000	$0	$604,406	0.617233	$373,059	$231,347
	72			$5,400,000	$324,000	$51,638	$4,050	$216,000	$0	$4,804,313		$3,904,312	$900,001
											Rounded	$3,900,000	
											Total Dollar Profit		$900,001

* Annual increase 0%

Conclusions:
1. When using the full yield rate calculation with zero line-item profit, the discount rate needs to be increased for relatively short maketing periods.
2. Whenever the forecast holding period is significantly less than the market supported absorption period to end users, the appraiser should perform a sensitivity analysis similar to the sequence of calculations in this example to support the analysis results.

Exhibit 12.11
Time Zero Profit Dilemma Analysis Summary

Scenario	Exhibit	Analysis Premise	Bulk Sale Value	Total Profit	Profit as Percentage of Bulk Value	Indicated Flat Discount	Matched Pairs Y	Matched Pairs Line-item Profit %	Absorption Period Qtrs.
1	12.5	Market value scenario—normal absorption	$3,460,227	$1,238,898	35.8%	-35.9%	20.00%	0.00%	12
2	12.6	Lot sales Time Ø, no discounting	$4,431,258	$373,055	8.4%	-17.9%	20.00%	0.00%	5
3	12.7	Lot sales Period 1, profit reflected in Y	$4,315,543	$488,770	11.3%	-20.1%	20.00%	0.00%	5
4	12.8	Lot sales Period 1, both line-item profit and Y	$4,000,514	$803,799	20.1%	-25.9%	11.67%	10.00%	5
5	12.9	Lot sales Period 1, line-item profit only	$3,565,553	$1,238,760	34.7%	-34.0%	0.00%	22.94%	5
6	12.10	IRR calculation with required profit of $900,000	$3,904,312	$900,001	23.1%	-27.7%	40.52%	0.00%	5

Note: Developer minimum profit with normal market absorption $1,159,200

Y = yield rate or discount rate

The problem is that the effect of the yield method alone generates minimal profit for short marketing periods, with most of the profit in later years as a normal function of the time value of money. Whenever a short time frame is involved, the yield rate alone typically does not generate significant profit. The yield rate must be increased significantly to generate an appropriate level of profit to attract a buyer or investor to a purchase given the risk characteristics inherent in subdivision development.

This dilemma is illustrated in Exhibit 12.11. This table provides a summary of Scenarios 1 through 6 with the indicated bulk sale value, total profit reflected in the analysis, profit as a percentage of the bulk value, and the contrast between the yield rate and the line-item profit percentage provided for each Scenario. Scenario 1 in Exhibit 12.11 is the initial or typical market scenario, in which the developer builds the subdivision and markets lots at an absorption rate to typical end users over three years. The bulk sale value is based on a market-oriented yield rate of 20% with zero line-item profit over a 12-quarter (3-year) holding period. Accordingly, the rates and matched pair calculations are appropriate for a similar forecast of three years.

This example was constructed using a creative demand spike scenario for illustration purposes. It was introduced to demonstrate the effect of the short marketing time frame. This is not an example to evaluate sales contacts or demand spikes. Rather, it is an example designed to evaluate short marketing time frames in which the market data in support of the conclusions is extracted from comparable data with longer market-oriented time frames. The observation can be made that it is the remaining 36 lots and not the full inventory of 72 lots that is being appraised, since the first 36 lots are sold immediately after construction at time zero. This is a rationale for including the 36 lots in the DCF at time zero without discounting. However, for all purposes the entire sales proceeds (except for subtracting minimal holding and sales costs) go straight to the present value bottom line. If the goal is to appraise the remaining 36 lots, then the initial 36 lot sales would not be included in the analysis and the profit levels may be more appropriate for the remaining inventory of 36 lots. An appraisal under these conditions may require consultation with the client to clarify the appraisal problem. Is the appraisal of the entire inventory of 72 lots as of the "when complete" date or some other scenario?

It is not uncommon to have some level of presales for the appraisal of a proposed subdivision. Financing is arranged as part of the initial project construction, and all the lots must be considered in the market value conclusion for the bulk sale. This introduces the possibility of an analysis with a reduced holding period. Whenever discounting is made over relatively short holding periods (typically less than two years), there is the potential to significantly overstate market value in terms of the bulk sale value conclusion because insufficient profit is considered in the analysis. This is especially evident when yield capitalization only is used without application of the split-rate method.

An appropriate method would be to consider profit as part of any presales, even when the lot sales occur immediately upon construction of the subdivision as of the *when complete* date. Scenario 2 made this mistake and placed the presales in time period zero without any consideration of profit. Essentially all the presale profit flowed into the present value calculation, overstating the bulk value. Also, this scenario reflected the lowest amount of dollar profit. In conclusion, profit should always be considered, even when there are presales as of the *when complete* date.

The results of Scenario 3 yielded minimal improvement for the profit dilemma. Scenario 3 moved the sales proceeds to Quarter 1, which allowed the yield rate calculation to extract a minimal level of profit. Profit was increased from $373,055 in Scenario 2 to $488,770 in Scenario 3. In addition, Scenario 3 was similar to Scenario 2 in employing the yield rate only to support the profit calculation.

The split-rate method was applied in Scenario 4. A matched pair of a 10% line-item profit and an 11.67% yield rate was applied and generates a profit more in line with typical profit expectations of about $803,799 with a bulk sale value of $4,000,514, which is more appropriate for the subject property. However, this profit level is still significantly below the original developer's minimum required profit of $1,159,200. It makes sense that the profit would be reduced on a bulk sale in which the holding period is reduced and some risk is removed because of the lot sales agreements. However, the market value conclusion is totally dependent upon the actual closing of any presales. If presales do not occur, the value essentially falls back to the initial valuation under Scenario 1 with the three-year holding period of $3,460,227, which is a significantly lower market value than the value generated over the shorter time frame.

Scenario 5 provides an analysis in which a 22.94% line-item profit was used with a 0.0% yield rate. This generated a significantly higher level of profit but reduced the bulk sale value significantly and ignores the time value of money. The profit was the same as in Scenario 1 and is clearly too high since the absorption time frame was reduced.

Scenario 6 is the last scenario considered. This is a sensitivity analysis to determine what yield rate would be required to generate an approximate level of profit. The profit is estimated at about $900,000. This amount is above the levels obtained in Scenarios

2 through 4 with a maximum of about $803,799, and below the level of about $1,238,000 in Scenarios 1 and 5. This appears to be a realistic estimate given the reduced marketing time frame. The value is higher than Scenario 1 with the longer holding period and below the unrealistic bulk values reflected in Scenarios 2 and 3. With the given profit level of $900,000 in Scenario 6, the bulk sale value conclusion is about $3,900,000. The indicated *IRR* with zero line-item profit is 40.52%. Stated differently, the appropriate yield rate for the five-quarter holding period with the pattern of lot sales reflected in the analysis must be increased from 20.0% with zero line-item profit in Scenarios 1-3 to 40.52% to reflect an appropriate bulk sale value in Scenario 6.

These scenarios are provided to reinforce what many appraisers have observed in the market. Whenever the absorption period decreases to very brief time frames in a range of one to two years or less, yield rates must be increased significantly to deliver the minimum required profit as compared to rates observed for longer holding periods. It would help if the analysis was converted to the split-rate method, but the profit may still be understated.

Inappropriate reasoning would be as follows: If the appropriate yield rate for a three-year forecast is 20%, and the forecast is revised with a holding period of only one year and then the risk is reduced, the yield rate should be adjusted downward to a number less than 20%. This is the opposite of what the appraiser should be considering.

This profit dilemma is different from most time discounting valuation problems seen in typical commercial real estate markets. For example, compare subdivision development cash flow characteristics with a typical office or apartment commercial property. For an office or apartment property, the yield calculation on a commercial DCF is typically performed over a 5- to 10-year time frame or holding period, in which the present value of the net income is discounted together with the reversion or resale value of the property reversion at the end of the holding period.

Yield rates tend to be more predictable and have less variability under these scenarios because the reversion value at the end of the analysis helps "modulate" the range of applicable yield rates. This is because the reversion often makes up 40%-60% of the total present value as part of an investment calculation for an apartment or office property. This is significantly different than discounting for subdivision valuation because the reversion value is always zero. There is no relatively large single reversion value at the end of the absorption period that makes up a component part of the present value calculation to help "modulate" the range of yield rates that are supported on a purchase. This also partially explains why yield rates vary significantly in published rate surveys for subdi-

vision development. It would be helpful if survey providers report the absorption time periods associated with the various yield rates.

For this reason, yield rates (with zero line-item profit) can vary significantly in subdivision development, depending on the time periods involved. Appraisers should recognize that the yield rates alone—without applying the split-rate method—must be increased significantly for short holding periods of less than about two years. However, use of the matched pair split-rate method can to some extent help "modulate" the range of yield rates applicable and reduce the relatively wide range of rates when using the yield rate only with zero line-item profit. The appraiser should always perform a sensitivity analysis for the present value generated when presales or other circumstances generate short absorption periods. This will allow for an appropriate selection of the applicable yield rate or rates used in the split-rate method to provide well-supported market value conclusions.

Exhibit 12.12 provides a graphic presentation of the effect of the absorption period on the selection of matched pairs of line-item profit (as a percentage of gross sales each period) and the yield rate for three scenarios. All of the calculations are based on a given market value (bulk sale value) of $3,900,000, targeting a total dollar profit of about $900,000. A lot value inflation of 2% per year was added to the calculation, and the initial forecast is made for 12 quarters with 0% line-item profit and a yield rate of 13.08%. A yield rate sensitivity analysis is performed under three scenarios. Under all three forecasts, the marketing time frame was evaluated at a holding period of 2, 4, 6, 8, 10, and 12 quarters. Lot absorption was evenly distributed over each marketing time frame. The data points were calculated by extracting the required matched pairs of line-item profit and yield needed to reflect a bulk value conclusion of $3,900,000.

The first forecast is for zero line-item profit and is shown in blue on the chart. With zero line-item profit, the yield rates range from a low of 13.08% with an absorption period of 12 quarters to a high of 61.58% for 2 quarters. As the absorption period decreases, the yield rate must increase to reflect the same value of 3,900,000 with about $900,000 in total dollar profit. This reflects a very wide spread of 48.5%. Line-item profit is introduced in Scenarios 2 and 3. Both scenarios reduce the required range of yield rates to deliver the same value over the various absorption periods.

As shown at the bottom of Exhibit 12.12, when a 5% line-item profit is introduced into the forecast, the overall range in required yield rates is reduced from 9.2% to 43.84%, with a total spread of 34.64%. Increasing the line-item profit to 8% reflects a yield rate range from 6.82% to 33.09%. The spread is reduced to 26.27%. The trend is particularly pronounced on holding periods

Exhibit 12.12
Yield vs. Line-Item Profit with Matched Pairs

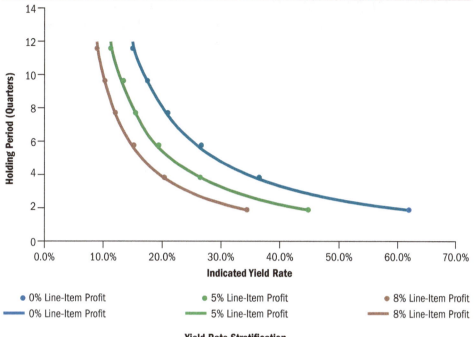

Premise	Yield Rate Range %		
	Low	High	Spread
Scenario 1—0% line-item	13.08%	61.58%	48.50%
Scenario 2—5% line-item	9.20%	43.84%	34.64%
Scenario 3—8% line-item	6.82%	33.09%	26.27%

Yield Rate Stratification

of less than two years. Appraisers should be very careful with their selection of yield rates and the method used for time periods of less than two years.

Like the effect of a "reversion" in a more typical commercial income DCF analysis, the use of line-item profit to some extent helps to "modulate" the range of rates that may be considered in the subdivision analysis. For this reason, appraisers may be well advised to employ the split-rate method on absorption forecasts for short time frames of less than about two years. This may significantly reduce the problem of selecting an appropriate yield for the analysis. At a minimum, it will help reduce the range of rates that may be applicable.

However, it should be recognized that the chart in Exhibit 12.12 cannot be used for the selection of a yield rate in a specific analysis because it ignores the risk associated with the various time periods and solves for the same value and level of profit in each matched pair trend line. Accordingly, it does not consider that a shorter absorption may have less risk than a longer time frame and that profit would be less than the fixed amount of $900,000 used for each trend line calculation. It does, however, emphasize the wide range of rates that may be applicable as the absorption period decreases.

In summary, yield rate selection is problematic in subdivision analysis, especially for relatively short absorption periods. The length of the absorption period and associated yield rates and resulting profit must always be evaluated. A sensitivity analysis should be performed to ensure that the appropriate level of profit is considered. There is no such thing as a single, "one size fits all" market yield rate applicable to all income forecasts and absorption periods. This concept escapes many developers, appraisers, lenders, and other participants in the market. To some extent, the difficulty associated with selecting an appropriate yield rate may explain the rationale of the developer who determines a profit forecast on the "back of a napkin" at the local restaurant. Appraisers, on the other hand, must have a reasoned analysis supported by market data and appropriate analytical techniques.

Developer Risk Reduction Strategies

Developer risk reduction strategies consider various methods that may be used by developers to minimize or otherwise reduce the risk associated with subdivision development. These strategies have evolved over time, with most of the strategies considering the relatively long time horizons required to achieve permitting and reducing costs associated with the initial land development and holding costs over the absorption period.

Obtaining Entitlements Prior to Land Purchase

In many markets, there are significant holding periods from the point in time when a vacant tract of land is being considered for subdivision development and going through the governmental process to achieve site plan approval for a proposed project with full entitlements in place for immediate development. Time frames can range anywhere from six months to several years, depending on the character of the property, the governmental environment with the local community, and the type of project being considered.

It is common for proposed developments, whether they are vacant land or any other commercial projects, to have land purchase contracts contingent upon receiving entitlements. Entitlements are required in order to construct the project as initially conceived by the project developer. Accordingly, land contracts can have a relatively long time horizon within the contract that allows for a due diligence period with periodic extensions that may be exercised either with or without additional deposits. This would allow the developer sufficient time to take the vacant land through a site plan review process with the local governmental authorities to the point at which sufficient entitlements are in place to purchase the land and develop the project.

Under this strategy, the developer is delaying the land purchase prior to any development and is avoiding the risk of having the project significantly scaled down or the marketing concept rejected. This allows the developer to drop the contract, which may involve the loss of initial deposits and permitting costs. However, on an overall basis, this significantly reduces the risk of buying land up-front at relatively prohibitive costs and not being able to achieve significant building density or a development concept that would be financially feasible given the initial land purchase price. This strategy has evolved over time and is a widespread practice in most commercial developments for subdivision development and other commercial projects.

Project Design with Multiple Price Points

Another strategy commonly used in subdivision development is to provide for a site plan and marketing concept that supports multiple price points within the same development. This allows for simultaneous absorption in several price point categories, which ultimately increases the overall absorption for the entire project, enabling the developer to get in and out of the project within a shorter marketing time frame than otherwise might be achieved when only one product category is considered. An example of a simultaneous absorption for a proposed subdivision project is provided in Exhibit 12.13. This project supports a total of 132 lots, with 72 lots in the lower price points with an average home price of about $200,000, 36 lots in the middle price points with an average home price of about $350,000, and 24 lots for upper price point homes with a typical price point of about $600,000.

A typical subdivision developer forecast is provided based on market-supported absorption rates for each price point and the pattern of retail values that are expected over the absorption period. As shown in Exhibit 12.13, the absorption forecast for the lower price points is about six homes per quarter, with a total holding period of about twelve quarters, or three years. The middle price points have an estimated absorption of about three lots per quarter with the same time horizon of three years, together with an estimate of two lots per quarter for the upper price point homes.

Exhibit 12.15
Simultaneous Sales with Multiple Price Points

	Lots Sold				Retail Lot Value*				Absorption Holding & Sales Costs							
Qtr.	Lower End	Middle Range	High End	Remaining Lots	Lower End	Middle Range	High End	Gross Sales	Sales 6.0%	Tax	Assoc. Dues	Misc. 4.0%	Line-Item Profit 0.00%	Net Proceeds	PV Factor 20.00%	Present Value
				132												
1	6	3	2	121	$40,000	$70,000	$120,000	$690,000	$41,400	$35,190	$3,300	$27,600	$0	$582,510	0.952381	$554,771
2	6	3	2	110	$40,000	$70,000	$120,000	$690,000	$41,400	$32,258	$3,025	$27,600	$0	$585,718	0.907029	$531,263
3	6	3	2	99	$40,000	$70,000	$120,000	$690,000	$41,400	$29,325	$2,750	$27,600	$0	$588,925	0.863838	$508,736
4	6	3	2	88	$40,000	$70,000	$120,000	$690,000	$41,400	$26,393	$2,475	$27,600	$0	$592,133	0.822702	$487,149
5	6	3	2	77	$40,800	$71,400	$122,400	$703,800	$42,228	$23,460	$2,200	$28,152	$0	$607,760	0.783526	$476,196
6	6	3	2	66	$40,800	$71,400	$122,400	$703,800	$42,228	$20,938	$1,925	$28,152	$0	$610,557	0.746215	$455,607
7	6	3	2	55	$40,800	$71,400	$122,400	$703,800	$42,228	$17,947	$1,650	$28,152	$0	$613,823	0.710681	$436,233
8	6	3	2	44	$40,800	$71,400	$122,400	$703,800	$42,228	$14,956	$1,375	$28,152	$0	$617,089	0.676839	$417,670
9	6	3	2	33	$41,616	$72,828	$124,848	$717,876	$43,073	$11,965	$1,100	$28,715	$0	$633,024	0.644609	$408,053
10	6	3	2	22	$41,616	$72,828	$124,848	$717,876	$43,073	$9,153	$825	$28,715	$0	$636,110	0.613913	$390,517
11	6	3	2	11	$41,616	$72,828	$124,848	$717,876	$43,073	$6,102	$550	$28,715	$0	$639,436	0.584679	$373,865
12	6	3	2	0	$41,616	$72,828	$124,848	$717,876	$43,073	$3,051	$275	$28,715	$0	$642,762	0.556837	$357,914
	72	36	24		$489,664	$856,912	$1,468,992	$8,446,704	$506,802	$230,736	$21,450	$337,868	$0	$7,349,847		$5,397,974
													Indicated Bulk Sale Value			$5,398,000

* Annual increase 2%

Note: Numbers may vary slightly due to rounding.

It is common to have lower absorption rates for higher price points, but obviously the absorption ultimately depends on the current velocity of sales consistent with the price points in the proposed project. It should also be recognized that the absorption may be different for the various price points. This example has the absorption for all three price points ending in three years. It is possible for the three price points to have different eventual holding periods, depending on market absorption at the date of valuation. In this example, retail lot values are anticipated to increase over time consistent with inflation, and typical expenses are considered for sales costs, real estate taxes over the holding period, association dues, and any miscellaneous costs. The example provides for a yield rate of 20% with zero line-item profit, reflecting a present value with the simultaneous absorption of about $5,398,000.

Multiple price points within the same project must be supported by the development concept. The subdivision design is typically oriented so that different "pods" within the project have lot sizes that vary depending on the price points, providing for support for larger lots for the upper-end homes and smaller lots for the lower-end patio homes or other building concepts. Streetscaping within each pod is designed consistent with the price point of the homes considered within a unified development concept. The ability to have multiple absorptions within numerous price points is a beneficial marketing factor for most projects and is a common strategy used to develop large tracts of land where absorption can be achieved throughout the entire stratification of home price points supported in the market.

Installing Common Improvements in Phases

Years ago, it was common for developers to install 100% of all common infrastructure immediately up front, prior to the sale of lots within a project. Over time, the installation of common infrastructure has been modified in most areas where developers recognize that reducing up-front development costs and spreading costs throughout the various phases of development for a large multiphase project is beneficial by reducing holding costs over time and spreading common infrastructure costs over several phases of development. Typically, the infrastructure installed in the project—which may include a clubhouse with a swimming pool, tennis courts, and walking or biking trails—is phased and implemented within each new phase.

In many communities, larger planned developments have a required phasing schedule in which specific infrastructure is timed for construction consistent with the timing and completion of the various pods within the planned development. The project approval will have a schedule of phases that must be completed

within certain time frames as well as a specific infrastructure installed for the overall project. For example, the initial phase may include the walking and biking trails and part of the common amenities, possibly for the tennis courts only, while the second phase might include installation of the clubhouse facility with a swimming pool and a third phase might include the completion of basketball courts and open park areas with playground equipment as part of a required infrastructure plan for common amenities for the overall development. Installing infrastructure over time reduces the up-front costs and the associated carrying costs. This is a common risk-reduction strategy in contemporary development for a wide range of projects, including subdivision development.

Presales of Lots to Participating Homebuilders

The strategy of selling lots to participating homebuilders is presented in Chapter 7, where examples of presales are explored for subdivision valuation. Presales reduce the holding costs for the project but often require a reduction in the retail lot value in order to achieve presales to homebuilders within the project. It is not uncommon for subdivision projects to be built by a group of investors that have a separate "team" of homebuilders. The developer installs the subdivision infrastructure, making the lots available for building homes within the project. The homebuilders are usually selected as part of an approved panel of builders and may or may not be the only homebuilders that are approved to build homes within the project. Each builder typically has a required takedown purchase contract for lots, buys small groups of lots usually at a discount, and builds spec homes within the project.

The presale of lots ensures immediate cash flow from lot sales from the developer's perspective and ensures that significant spec home construction would be completed within the project to draw interest to the development, especially when multiple homebuilders might be involved. In many projects, there is a synergy when multiple builders with multiple marketing efforts generate a higher level of demand than would be achieved by one builder only in the same project. This common strategy for most new subdivision developments in expanding communities provides for a level of "selection" for buyers within the project and is often employed for projects that have multiple price points when selected groups of homebuilders are building homes in all price point stratifications within a proposed project. While the retail value is initially reduced as part of the takedown contracts, the ability for an investor/developer to get in and out of a development in a relatively brief time horizon is beneficial and can generate higher returns, as described in Chapter 7.

Lot Sales to Potential Homeowners

The strategy of selling lots to potential homeowners is often employed when one or relatively few homebuilders are building homes within the project. This method is probably used more for upper-end priced homes, which are most often custom homes built for individual homebuyers within a project, but it can apply to a wide range of housing types and is common in many areas.

Under this strategy, the homebuilder typically has one spec home in a development that may also serve as a sales office. Typically, homebuyers select a home from a menu of various model plans. Interior color schemes, cabinets, and other features are chosen by the homebuyer prior to construction of the house. The homebuilder will sell the vacant lot to the purchaser with a contract for construction of the new home. The buyer then obtains financing for the new home, and an appraisal is made for the proposed home based on construction plans. At that point in time, the buyer owns the lot and is paying interest on the loan during the construction period as construction draws are made throughout the construction period. The custom home is eventually completed and occupied to the buyer. Under this scenario, the homebuilder is not responsible for any of the interest carrying costs during construction and has transferred all financing costs over the construction period to the homebuyer.

This method significantly reduces the carrying costs to the homebuilder and relieves the homebuilder from building spec homes that may or may not ideally be what the prospective purchaser is looking for in terms of the internal features and amenity selections. Because of the time frames involved and the loan approval process prior to construction, this strategy is seen more frequently in the upper-end price point homes rather than lower-end, entry-level homes.

Proposed Construction Performance Bonds

As a general statement, any techniques that can be used to accelerate the ability to buy, develop, and sell are risk-reduction strategies for homebuilders and for subdivision development. The goal often is to have a new project and home sales commence as soon as possible. One strategy that is often used is to obtain a performance bond to ensure construction of the subdivision project if for any reason the developer defaults on the project. In fact, many lenders require performance bonds as part of any loan activity for a proposed project. This ensures that project development will continue and finish even if the initial developer is unable to perform.

A secondary benefit–and in many cases a primary benefit–of the performance bond is that the local community will allow the construction of single-unit homes in the project prior to the actual completion of the subdivision infrastructure. Because there is a performance bond, the governmental authorities have assurance that the city streets and all infrastructure will be 100% built and have a higher "comfort level" in providing the ability to achieve building permits prior to the actual completion of the subdivision infrastructure. This allows for simultaneous construction of the subdivision infrastructure with streets and common utilities as well as single-unit home construction occurring simultaneously with the construction of the subdivision development. This is a win/win scenario for both the project developer and the prospective homebuyer because it reduces the required time frame before new homes can be delivered for immediate occupancy. This is also a common strategy used in new subdivision development and is often required by lenders.

Super Pad Sites

The real estate industry is constantly changing and introducing new building concepts, marketing strategies, and land development patterns. Subdivision development is no exception, and an emerging trend in this industry is known as "super pads." This is a development concept that is an extension of the common planned developments or mixed-use planned communities. Many of these developments are in the Southwest region of the United States and have taken the familiar concept of a planned development to a whole new level.

Under this development concept, large tracts of land–typically on the fringe of urban development in established communities–are developed into very large subdivisions. For example, a 600-acre parcel of land may be purchased and developed into a subdivision supporting ten 50-acre super pads on 500 acres. The remaining land area is improved with site infrastructure to support the 10 super pad sites. The developer will install a main interior collector road on the acreage with access to the city street system, with supporting on-site utilities to service the 10 pad sites. The road will stub out utilities to each pad site and will have supporting water retention basins for the roadway that may also be used to support off-site water retention for the pad sites and any required streetscaping, streetlights, and other required common infrastructure. The street may or may not be a dedicated public right-of-way. In any case, there will be a master owner's association for any common upkeep of the road and related infrastructure. The product sold (the super pad site) is vacant land containing 50 acres without any installed roads or other site infrastructure. The pad will have the ability to connect to the collector road and will have access to central utilities provided adjacent to the roadway. All other infrastructure will be provided by the buyer of the pod acreage, who will then develop a more conventional subdivision on the 50-acre parcel.

Like many planned developments, the project will be taken through a site plan review process where uses and densities are established for each pad site prior to development of the collector road. Typically, the development will have full entitlements for the overall 600-acre parcel, which will entail the required infrastructure to be installed to make the pad sites available for purchase. The level of detail in terms of the type of uses supported on each pad site may be general uses and densities under a general zoning category (such as residential development with a maximum density of four units per acre) or more specific site plans for each pad site. Also, the various pads may have a wide range of uses. For example, pads at the front of the development near the city street may support a mix of retail, office, multiunit, or other commercial uses in a mixed-use environment. Rear pads in the project may have a lower residential density that could support a wide range of residential housing types and price points. Individual site plan approval may be required of each individual pad within the context of the general uses established as part of the initial development. As with any subdivision development, entitlements are considered in the valuation of vacant land.

Other than the scale of the individual pads, an appraisal of the super pad subdivision is not significantly different than the appraisal of a more conventional subdivision project. An appraisal of the super pad proposed subdivision considers the same three phases of development, starting with entitlement and progressing through construction and the sale or absorption of the 10 pad sites. In this case, the "user" is a different developer who will purchase the vacant pad site for future subdivision development to eventual "end users." The most difficult aspect of the valuation is the absorption forecast. The forecast should support the full six-step fundamental demand analysis considering market demand for various building types and products supported on the pad sites. The sites may support a wide spectrum of uses, including retail, office, commercial, hotel, industrial, multiunit, and low-density residential. Demand support for each category must be supported, and it may be different for each pad site.

The project may have one uniform building concept in one building sector–such as low-density residential for all 10 pad sites—which would help reduce the complexity of the demand forecast. However, the demand to "eventual end users" is the final criteria. For example, assume residential use for all 10 pad sites at an average density of six units per acre. The fundamental forecast is for 20 units per month or 240 units per year in the subject project (i.e., all 10 pad sites). The project has 500 acres available for development, supporting about 3,000 housing units with full build-out of all 10 pad sites. With an average distribution of density, each pad site would support about 300 units with an absorption time horizon of about 1.25 years. The time frame to absorb the entire project with all 10 pad sites is about 12.5 years. In this simplistic example, an absorption forecast of 12.5 years would be supported.

The appraisal problem can be expanded by considering the appraisal of individual subdivisions proposed on multiple pad sites. Consider an appraisal problem in which the appraiser is engaged to appraise three of the pad sites, each with a proposed residential subdivision in competing price points supporting a density of six units per acre. Each new residential project will be competing with the other two proposed subdivisions. Dividing the total absorption of 240 units per year between the three competing pads indicates a component absorption of 80 units per year per pad, resulting is a 3.75-year absorption period for each pad. If more pads are developed, the dilution in the individual demand profile for each pad is further reduced and may put the projects at risk for failure. The analysis must consider that demand is allocated when multiple pads are being developed and that the overall fundamental forecast of 20 units per month only applies to the overall super pad subdivision and is not representative of the demand for each individual pad when multiple pads are competing for absorption.

In conclusion, any appraisal of a mixed-use subdivision—whether it is one unified plan on 20 acres or a super pad subdivision on 600 acres—must consider that simultaneous absorption in component parts of the development may be competing with other pads and the effect on the valuation of an individual segment.

APPENDIX
Frequently Asked Questions on Residential Tract Development Lending

Board of Governors of the Federal Reserve System
Federal Deposit Insurance Corporation
National Credit Union Administration
Office of the Comptroller of the Currency
Office of Thrift Supervision

September 8, 2005

Purpose

The Board of Governors of the Federal Reserve System (FRB), the Federal Deposit Insurance Corporation (FDIC), the National Credit Union Administration (NCUA), the Office of the Comptroller of the Currency (OCC), and the Office of Thrift Supervision (OTS) (the agencies) are jointly issuing the attached frequently asked questions (FAQs) to assist institutions in complying with the agencies' appraisal and real estate lending requirements for residential tract developments. A residential tract development is a project of five or more units that are constructed as a single development.

Overview

Institutions employ a variety of credit structures for financing a residential tract development. When the agencies adopted their appraisal and real estate lending regulations in the early 1990s, it was common practice for institutions to provide a developer with a credit facility to fund an entire tract development project or subdivision. More recently, institutions tend to finance land acquisition and development separately from home construction and limit the number of speculative homes under construction at any one time. These trends help institutions to better identify, manage, and control risk to a particular borrower.

Recognizing changes in lending practices, the attached FAQs provide clarification on the agencies' appraisal and real estate lending requirements for financing residential construction in a tract development. The FAQs address how institutions determine collateral value and calculate the loan-to-value ratio for these credits. Institutions should review these FAQs in conjunction with the agencies' real estate appraisal and lending regulations and guidelines, including the Interagency Guidelines for Real Estate Lending Policies (lending guidelines)[1] and the Interagency Appraisal and Evaluation Guidelines (appraisal and evaluation guidelines).[2]

Frequently Asked Questions on Residential Tract Development Lending

1. **What is a residential tract development?**
   Answer: The agencies' appraisal regulations define a "tract development" as a project with five or more units that is constructed or is to be constructed as a single development. For purposes of this document, a "unit" refers to: a residential building lot; a detached single-family home; an attached single-family home; or a residence in a condominium building.

2. **What are the appraisal requirements when an institution finances residential tract developments?**
   Answer: An appraisal for a residential tract development must meet the minimum appraisal standards in the agencies' appraisal regulations and guidelines. Appraisals for these properties must reflect deductions and discounts for holding costs, marketing costs, and entrepreneurial profit. In some circumstances, as discussed in FAQ 11, an institution may rely on an appraisal of the individual unit(s) to meet the agencies' appraisal requirements and to determine market value for calculating the loan-to-value (LTV) ratio.

   An institution may exclude presold units to determine whether an appraisal of a tract development is required. A unit may be considered pre-sold if a buyer has entered into a binding contract to purchase the unit and has made a substantial and nonrefundable earnest money deposit. Further, the institution should obtain sufficient documentation that the buyer has entered into a legally binding sales contract and has obtained a written pre-qualification or commitment for permanent financing.

3. **What are the appraisal requirements when an institution finances raw land, lot development or lot acquisition as part of a residential tract development?**
    Answer: The institution must obtain an appraisal, which includes appropriate deductions and discounts, of the entire tract of raw land or lots. The appraisal should reflect the value of the property in its current condition and existing zoning as well as the market value of land upon completion of land improvements, if applicable. The land improvements may include the construction of utilities, streets, and other infrastructure necessary for future development. An appraisal of raw land to be valued as developed lots should reflect a reasonable time frame during which development will occur. The feasibility study or the market analysis in the appraisal should support the absorption period for the developed lots; otherwise, a portion of the tract development should be valued as raw land.

4. **What are the supervisory LTV limits for residential tract developments?**
    Answer: An institution may lend up to 65 percent of the value for raw land, 75 percent for land development or finished lots, 80 percent for multifamily residential construction, and 85 percent for 1- to 4-family residential construction.[3] If a loan funds both land development and home construction, the applicable supervisory LTV limit is 85 percent, which corresponds to the limit for the final phase of the project. However, loan disbursements should not exceed actual development or construction costs, and the institution should ensure that the borrower maintains appropriate levels of hard equity throughout the term of the loan.

5. **When should institutions calculate the LTV ratio for residential tract development loans?**
    Answer: An institution should calculate the LTV ratio at the time of loan origination and recalculate the ratio whenever collateral is released or substituted. If the LTV ratio is in excess of the supervisory LTV limits, the institution should comply with the lending guidelines for high LTV loans.

6. **What is the loan amount to be used to calculate the LTV ratio for residential tract development loans?**
    Answer: As defined in the lending guidelines, the loan amount refers to the total amount of a loan, line of credit, or other legally binding commitment. For a line of credit, the

legally binding commitment is based on the terms of the credit agreement.

7. **How should institutions determine the loan amount to calculate the LTV ratio for a loan to finance a phase of a multi-phase tract development?**
Answer: If an institution commits to finance only a phase of development or construction rather than an entire multi-phase tract development project, the loan amount is the legally binding commitment for the phase.

8. **What collateral value is used to calculate an LTV ratio for a residential tract development loan?**
Answer: The value of the real estate collateral for the calculation of the LTV ratio is the "market value" as defined in the agencies' appraisal regulations. The appraisal should reflect a market value upon completion of construction of the home(s) and the market value of any other collateral, such as lots or undeveloped land. Further, the appraisal must consider an analysis of appropriate deductions and discounts for unsold units, including holding costs, marketing costs, and entrepreneurial profit. For loans to purchase land or existing lots, "value" means the lesser of the actual acquisition cost or the appraised market value.

9. **How can an appraisal of a model(s) home be used to establish a market value for calculating the LTV ratio?**
Answer: An appraisal of a model(s) provides a market value of a particular home in a given development, considering the cost of construction and the market value of the model's unique features and floor plan on a typical lot. Normally, an institution will obtain an appraisal for each model or floor plan that a borrower is planning to build and offer for sale. The model appraisal is based on the price of a "base" lot in a particular development without consideration to the costs of, or value attributed to, specific options, upgrades, or lot premiums.

If the institution is financing the construction of a residential tract development, an appraisal of the model(s) would provide relevant information for the appraiser to consider in providing a market value of the development. That is, the value attributable to the models is used as a basis for estimating a market value for the tract development by reflecting the mix of units and adjusting for options, upgrades, and lot premiums. The market value should also reflect an analysis of appropriate deductions and discounts for holding costs, marketing costs, and entrepreneurial profit.

For the construction of units that are not part of a tract development, the appraisal of a model may be used to estimate the market value of the individual home, if the model and base lot are substantially the same as the subject home and the appraisal meets the agencies' appraisal requirements and is still valid. In assessing the validity of the appraisal, the institution should consider the passage of time and current market conditions. When underwriting a loan to finance construction of a single home, the institution should consider the value of the actual lot and any options and upgrades relative to the values in the appraisal of the model.

10. **What are some common underwriting characteristics of revolving lines of credit in which a borrowing base sets the availability of funds?**
Answer: A borrowing base is a lending condition incorporated into many revolving credit agreements that limits the institution's legally binding commitment to advance funds to the borrower. The borrowing base specifies the maximum amount the institution will lend to the borrower as a function of the collateral's type, value, eligibility criteria, and advance rates. The credit agreement also specifies a maximum commitment amount regardless of the amount of the borrowing base availability.

Typically, the borrowing base formula specifies different advance rates for each collateral type, such as land, developed lots, homes under construction, and completed and unsold homes. The amount of collateral in each category and the corresponding advance rates limit the borrower's ability to draw additional funds. The advance rates are generally higher for collateral with lower development, construction, and marketing risk. For example, the advance rate for developed lots is likely to be lower than that for a completed home. In addition, advance rates may vary among borrower credit agreements. Generally, institutions grant more liberal advance rates to borrowers that have greater financial strength. Collateral must meet specified eligibility criteria to be included in the borrowing base. These commonly include limitations on the number of speculative units and the duration of time a completed unit may remain in the borrowing base.

This type of facility enables an institution to control loan advances and proceeds from home sales. The funds available under the revolver are based on frequent (usually monthly) borrower-prepared reports, commonly referred to as a borrowing base certificate. The borrowing base certificate details and certifies the quantity and value of collateral in each category that meets the borrowing-base eligibility criteria and a total amount of the borrowing base (the outstanding balance of the facility plus any available funds). The institution periodically performs on-site verification of the information provided by the borrower.

When constructing the borrowing base formula, the institution should require the borrower to maintain appropriate levels of hard equity throughout the project's construction and marketing periods.

11. **Are there instances when an appraisal that reflects deductions and discounts is not necessary for financing construction of single-family homes in a residential tract development?**

    Answer: An appraisal of a tract development must analyze and report appropriate deductions and discounts. However, there are circumstances when the structure of the proposed loan mitigates the need to obtain an appraisal of a tract development.

    If an institution finances construction starts on an individual unit basis, an institution may be able to use appraisals of the individual units to satisfy the agencies' appraisal requirements and as a basis for computing the LTV ratio. In this case, the institution should be able to demonstrate, through a feasibility study or market analysis conducted independently of the borrower and loan production staff, that all units collateralizing the loan are likely to be constructed and sold within 12 months. For LTV purposes, the value is the lower of the market value of the collateral or the borrower's actual development and construction costs. The borrower should maintain appropriate levels of hard equity (for example, cash or unencumbered investment in the underlying property) throughout the construction and marketing periods.

    If an institution finances a unit's construction under a revolving line of credit in which a borrowing base sets the availability of funds, an institution may be able to use appraisals on the individual units to satisfy the agencies' appraisal requirements and as a basis for computing the LTV ratio. This is the case if the institution limits the number of construction starts and completed, unsold homes included in the borrowing base and if the institution satisfies the conditions described in the preceding paragraph. If the borrowing base includes developed lots or raw land to be developed into lots, the institution must obtain an appraisal of the collateral that reflects deductions and discounts.

Institutions should also ensure that residential construction loans meet prudent real estate underwriting standards reflected in the lending guidelines. Among other standards, institutions should (a) establish appropriate limits on construction starts for speculative homes; (b) address any concentration risk to a particular builder or a specific development; (c) monitor market conditions and analyze demand and supply for residential housing; (d) maintain prudent controls for the advancement of funds for construction costs; (e) perform periodic collateral inspections to verify construction progress; and (f) confirm compliance with supervisory LTV limits.

12. **What are the appraisal requirements when an institution finances construction of a condominium building(s)?**
Answer: For a condominium building with five or more units, an institution must obtain an appraisal of the building that reflects appropriate deductions and discounts for holding costs, marketing costs, and entrepreneurial profit. An institution may not use the aggregate retail sales prices of the individual units as the market value to calculate the LTV ratio. For purposes of this document, condominium buildings are distinguished from other types of residential properties if construction of the entire building has to be completed before any one unit is occupied.

If an institution finances the construction of a single condominium building with less than five units or a condominium project with multiple buildings (e.g., clustered condominiums and town homes) with less than five units in a building, the institution may be able to rely on appraisals of the individual units to satisfy the agencies' appraisal requirements and to determine the market value for calculating the LTV ratio. In this regard, the institution should be able to control starts on an individual building basis and demonstrate by a feasibility or market analysis, conducted independently of the borrower and loan production staff, that all units in each building can be constructed and sold within 12 months.

13. **For revolving lines of credit in which a borrowing base sets the availability of funds, what loan amount and collateral value should be used to determine the LTV ratio?**

    Answer: The *loan* amount is the institution's legally binding commitment (that is, the outstanding balance of the facility plus any availability under the borrowing base). *Value* is the lower of the borrower's actual development or construction costs or the market value of completed units securing the loan multiplied by their percentage of completion.

---

1. OCC: 12 CFR 34, C and D; FRB: 12 CFR 208, E and appendix C, and 12 CFR 225, G; FDIC: 12 CFR 323 and 12 CFR 365; and OTS: 12 CFR 564, and 12 CFR 560.100, and 12 CFR 560.101. NCUA was not a party to the lending guidelines; however, these guidelines, to the extent they are consistent with NCUA Rules and Regulations, establish best practices that credit unions should follow.
2. The appraisal and evaluation guidelines may be found in: *Comptroller's Handbook for Commercial Real Estate and Construction Lending* for OCC; SR letter 94-55 for FRB; FIL-74-94 for FDIC; and Thrift Bulletin 55a for OTS. NCUA was not a party to the appraisal and evaluation guidelines; however, these guidelines, to the extent they are consistent with NCUA Rules and Regulations, establish best practices that credit unions should follow.
3. NCUA Rules and Regulations Part 723 (Member Business Loans) has specific LTV requirements that vary from these guidelines. Credit Union State Supervisory Authorities may also have regulatory LTV requirements that vary from these guidelines. Credit Unions supervised by these agencies should review the LTV limits and ensure compliance.

Glossary

absorption.
In market analysis, short-term capture. In subdivision analysis, the process whereby lots or units in a subdivision are sold off.[1]

absorption period.
The actual or expected period required from the time a property, group of properties, or commodity is initially offered for lease, purchase, or use by its eventual users until all portions have been sold or stabilized occupancy has been achieved. Also referred to as "holding period," "project marketing period," or "sell-out period."

absorption rate.
In subdivision analysis, the rate of sales of lots or units in a subdivision.

allocation.
A method of estimating land value in which sales of improved properties are analyzed to establish a typical ratio of land value to total property value and this ratio is applied to the property being appraised or the comparable sale being analyzed.

bulk value.
The value of multiple units, subdivided plots, or properties in a portfolio as though sold together in a single transaction.

Historically, this term has been used incorrectly to express a specific type of value. Actually, "bulk sale value" is the market

---

1. Definitions that appear in italics have been taken from *The Dictionary of Real Estate Appraisal*, 6th ed. (Chicago: Appraisal Institute, 2015). All other definitions have been provided by the author.

value for a group of lots under a specific valuation scenario rather than a separate definition of value. For the sake of convenience, the term "bulk value" is used in this text to describe the bulk value scenario. See also **bulk value scenario.** Historically, "bulk value" has sometimes been referred to as the "present value of the sell-out," "bulk sale value," "lump-sum bulk value," or "wholesale value." In subdivision analysis, "bulk value" is the market value of a group of lots to one purchaser.

bulk value scenario.

The valuation scenario employed in subdivision valuation and other appraisal problems in which a group of properties are evaluated under a bulk sale scenario. This valuation scenario has as its premise the valuation of a group of lots or units to one purchaser; it is a "market value" estimate that recognizes a specific valuation scenario that is based on the presumption of a transaction in which a group of lots are to be sold to one purchaser as one sales transaction. The value estimate must reflect this bulk sale scenario and recognize that the only way the purchaser can earn a profit on the investment is to eventually sell the lots or units over time to eventual end users. The bulk sale scenario considers the absorption period needed to market the lot inventory over time with appropriate deductions and discounts for holding and sales costs as well as profit. This analysis assumes that time is of the essence and lot or unit inventory will be made available for sale to match available market demand at the market-supported retail lot or unit values.

capture rate.

The percentage of total market demand a specific property or group of properties is expected to capture, which is derived by comparing the competitive attributes of the specific property to the attributes of all the competitive properties in the area; also called market share.

developer's fee.

Typically, a payment by a property owner to a third party for overseeing the development of a project from inception to completion, included among the direct and indirect costs of development. Sometimes, the term is used to describe the time, energy, and experience a developer invests in a project as well as a reward for the risk undertaken.

developer's profit.

The profit earned by the developer of a real estate project. See also **entrepreneurial incentive; entrepreneurial profit.**

development.
> The transformation of formerly raw land into improved property through the application of labor, capital, and entrepreneurship.

discounted cash flow (DCF) analysis.
> The procedure in which a discount rate is applied to a set of projected income streams and a reversion. The analyst specifies the quantity, variability, timing, and duration of the income streams and the quantity and timing of the reversion, and discounts each to its present value at a specified yield rate.

entitlement.
> In the context of ownership, use, or development of real estate, governmental approval for annexation, zoning, utility extensions, number of lots, total floor area, construction permits, and occupancy or use permits.

entrepreneur.
> One who innovates or assumes the risks of a business or enterprise in exchange for possible gains; a promoter who initiates development.

entrepreneurial incentive.
> The amount an entrepreneur expects to receive for his or her contribution to a project. Entrepreneurial incentive may be distinguished from entrepreneurial profit (often called developer's profit) in that it is the expectation of future profit as opposed to the profit actually earned on a development or improvement. The amount of entrepreneurial incentive required for a project represents the economic reward sufficient to motivate an entrepreneur to accept the risk of the project and to invest the time and money necessary in seeing the project through to completion. See also **entrepreneurial profit**.

entrepreneurial profit.
> 1. *A market-derived figure that represents the amount an entrepreneur receives for his or her contribution to a project and risk; the difference between the total cost of a property (cost of development) and its market value (property value after completion), which represents the entrepreneur's compensation for the risk and expertise associated with development. An entrepreneur is motivated by the prospect of future value enhancement (i.e., the entrepreneurial incentive). An entrepreneur who successfully creates value through new development, expansion, renovation, or an innovative change of use is rewarded by entrepreneurial profit. Entrepreneurs may also fail and suffer losses.*
> 2. *In economics, the actual return on successful management practices, often identified with coordination, the fourth*

factor of production following land, labor, and capital; also called **entrepreneurial return** *or* **entrepreneurial reward.** *See also* **entrepreneurial incentive.**

excess land.
Land that is not needed to serve or support the existing use. The highest and best use of the excess land may or may not be the same as the highest and best use of the improved parcel. Excess land has the potential to be sold separately and is valued separately. See also **surplus land.**

frictional vacancy.
The amount of vacant space needed in a market for its orderly operation. Frictional vacancy allows for move-ins and move-outs.

gross proceeds.
The gross receipts generated from lot or unit sales over the absorption period in subdivision discounted cash flow analysis. Gross proceeds can consider income from ancillary sources and are representative of the total income generated from unit or lot sales over time. Typically, gross proceeds represent the sum of the retail lot values at the start of the absorption period, plus lot value inflation over the absorption period, if any, and any ancillary income.

gross sell-out.
The aggregate of the individual retail prices of a group of lots or units as of the initial date of valuation. May also be referred to as "sum of the retail values," "gross retail value," "aggregate of retail values," "gross sell-out value," or "gross retail value." The value is as of the date of valuation and ignores future lot value inflation. The recommended terminology is "sum of the retail values."

highest and best use.
The reasonably probable use of property that results in the highest value. The four criteria that the highest and best use must meet are legal permissibility, physical possibility, financial feasibility, and maximum productivity.

holding period.
Another term for "absorption period."

holding and sales costs.
Costs associated with a holding period needed to achieve permitting, project approvals, construction, or the absorption of unit inventory over time. Holding and sales costs include items such as real estate taxes, insurance, brokers' commissions, administrative costs, marketing and promotional expenses, and other expenses depending on the individual

development and/or property. These costs do not include any direct or indirect construction costs or profit.

land analysis.
A study of factual data relating to the characteristics of undeveloped land or a site that create, enhance, or detract from the utility and marketability of that parcel.

line-item profit.
In subdivision valuation, a deduction made for profit as an expense in the discounted cash flow analysis over the period under study. Line-item profit is estimated in conjunction with the selection of the discount rate or yield rate used to calculate the present value of the net proceeds.

location.
The relative position of a property to competitive properties and other value influences in its market area; the time-distance relationships, or linkages, between a property or neighborhood and all other possible origins and destinations of people going to or coming from the property or neighborhood.

market value.
A type of value that is the major focus of most real property appraisal assignments. Both economic and legal definitions of market value have been developed and refined, such as the following.

The most widely accepted components of market value are incorporated in the following definition: The most probable price, as of a specified date, in cash, or in terms equivalent to cash, or in other precisely revealed terms, for which the specified property rights should sell after reasonable exposure in a competitive market under all conditions requisite to a fair sale, with the buyer and seller each acting prudently, knowledgeably, and for self-interest, and assuming that neither is under undue duress.[2]

net proceeds.
Gross proceeds less holding and sales costs and any line-item profit associated with a subdivision project in subdivision valuation discounted cash flow analysis.

profit.
1. *The amount by which the proceeds of a transaction exceed its cost.*
2. *In theoretical economics, the residual share of the product of an enterprise that accrues to the entrepreneur after paying interest for capital, rent for land, and wages for labor and management.* See also **entrepreneurial profit**.

---

2. See *The Dictionary of Real Estate Appraisal* for further elaboration on this term.

3. *In accounting, an increase in wealth that results from the operation of an enterprise. Gross profit usually is the selling price minus cost; items such as selling and operating expenses are deducted from gross profit to indicate net profit.*

profit motive.
The desire to earn a favorable financial return on a business venture.

project marketing period.
Another term for "absorption period."

raw land.
Land that is undeveloped; land in its natural state before grading, draining, subdivision, or the installation of utilities; land with minimal or no appurtenant constructed improvements.

sell-out.
To dispose of entirely by sale.

sell-out period.
Another term for "absorption period."

site.
Improved land or a lot in a finished state so that it is ready to be used for a specific purpose.

subdivision.
A tract of land that has been divided into lots or blocks with streets, roadways, open areas, and other facilities appropriate to its development as residential, commercial, or industrial sites.

subdivision development method.
A method of estimating land value when subdividing and developing a parcel of land is the highest and best use of that land. When all direct and indirect costs and entrepreneurial incentive are deducted from an estimate of the anticipated gross sales price of the finished lots, (or the completed improvements on those lots), the resultant net sales proceeds are then discounted to present value at a market-derived rate over the development and absorption period to indicate the value of the land.

sum of the retail values.
The aggregate of the individual retail prices of a group of lots or units to be sold over a future holding or absorption period. The values are as of the initial valuation date and do not consider the impact of future lot value inflation. Historically, the sum of the retail values has also been known as "gross retail value," "aggregate of retail values," "gross sell-out," "gross sell-out value," or "gross retail value." The recommended terminology is "sum of the retail values." The dollar amount

reflected by this calculation is *not* the market value of the subdivision or group of lots or units.

surplus land.
Land that is not currently needed to support the existing use but cannot be separated from the property and sold off for another use. Surplus land does not have an independent highest and best use and may or may not contribute value to the improved parcel. See also ***excess land***.

time value profit.
The dollar profit inherent in a subdivision discounted cash flow analysis that is reflected in the interest rate or discount rate used for the present value calculation. Throughout this book, "time value profit" is the dollar difference between the net proceeds and the present value over the absorption or holding period.